"For the first time in the English language, we are given access to some of the leading figures in China's unregistered churches. We hear of lives shaped by the tumultuous history of Christianity in China, wrestling with the church's relationship with the state and with the society, and pointed toward an eschatological vision that reorients Christians today. This window into the Chinese church is thought provoking and challenges us—' 'her in China or beyond—in our understanding of faithful Christian living."

Alexander Chow, University of Edinburgh, author of *Chinese Publ⋯*

"All Christians live as exiles in this world. For those ⌐⸍
we must ask ourselves again what it means for
that is hostile to the Christian faith. *Faithful Di⸲*   ⸴use
churches in China have paid for following Christ.   ⸴rth a clear
theological framework for why they have done sℴ   ⸴ churches are in
agreement about how to engage the political autho⸱   ⸴nmitment to Scripture
and the world to come is a witness to Chinese society   ⸴n encouragement to all global
Christians."

Timothy Keller, founding pastor of Redeemer Presbyterian Church in Manhattan

"Reverend Wang Yi is a Chinese theologian in pastoral ministry and a public intellectual in social engagement. He is sharp, eloquent, and fearless. Under his leadership, the Early Rain Church expanded the wide reach of the 'house churches,' that is the *jiating* churches, in multiple spheres of Chinese society. This collection of writings clearly shows the deepening of Chinese Christian thinking and articulation of biblical, historical, systematic, and practical theology. It is a must-read for anyone interested in Chinese Christianity, society, and culture. It is relevant for all Christians facing restriction, repression, and persecution in the contemporary world."

Fenggang Yang, founding director of the Center on Religion and the Global East at Purdue University

"This important compendium of house-church writings offers English-language readers and scholars an inside view of the house-church narrative of the arc of Chinese church history. By combining academic essays with church sermons and interviews, the volume draws attention to two key elements in Wang Yi's writings that have guided his thought and ministry: church-state relations and a theology of martyrdom within an eschatological dimension."

Chloë Starr, professor of Asian theology and Christianity at Yale Divinity School

"The things that contribute to our understanding of the relations between church and state are not only narrowly exegetical but emerge as well from our experiences as Christians. What the Bible says about such matters is likely to be configured in our minds a little differently by Christians in nineteenth-century Netherlands, tribal peoples in Papua New Guinea, and Han people in China, even though all of us want to live our lives under Christ's providential ordering of all things in this broken world. Wang Yi and his fellow contributors to this thought-provoking volume write in the full knowledge that theirs is not the only Christian voice in China, let alone elsewhere, but they argue their corner in defense of unregistered churches with exegetical skill, theological rigor, and pastoral insight. Churches in the West have much to learn from them."

D. A. Carson, emeritus professor of New Testament, Trinity Evangelical Divinity School

"Wang Yi's faithfulness under persecution highlights the gospel by shining a light on injustice and the depth of human depravity. More important is how his example as a suffering faithful servant of God archetypes the ultimate example of the suffering servant of Christ. By the grace of God, how the truthfulness of the gospel—through the suffering servant ministry of Jesus Christ—shines against the dark and hopeless world has been shown in another faithful disobedient servant of God in China."

David Ro, regional director for the Lausanne Movement East Asia and chair of the Asia 2022 Congress

"*Faithful Disobedience* is must-read for anyone who wishes to understand the vitality, scholarship, ethics, and dissident witness of the urban Chinese Christian scholar-leaders in China today. These works by Wang Yi and others carefully weave the spiritual and theological roots of the suffering and witness of early house church leaders such as Wang Mingdao to produce their own unique, informed, and trenchant public witness of truth to power in China today. One simply cannot understand the current relationship between Christianity and the state in China apart from the works represented in this timely collection of essays."

Thomas Harvey, academic dean of the Oxford Centre for Mission Studies and author of *Acquainted with Grief: Wang Mingdao's Stand for the Persecuted Church of China*

"The single, most important feature of global Christianity is the conversation that Christians from a thousand different cultures have with each other. This compelling book brings one of the world's most dynamic Christian movements into the living rooms of Christians around the world. Pastor Wang Yi's theological reflections are essential reading for global Christians who want to understand the future of their faith."

Todd M. Johnson, codirector of Center for the Study of Global Christianity at Gordon-Conwell Theological Seminary

"The dynamism of the house church movement in China in the face of difficulty is one of the most compelling and inspiring stories in contemporary history. While the movement as a whole is composed mostly of smaller, low-profile churches, Pastor Wang Yi is a major voice coming from larger, higher-profile church circles. The sobering reality of his current imprisonment calls us all the more to pray for him (and other imprisoned Christians) and to engage his ideas seriously."

Kevin S. Chen, associate professor of Old Testament at Christian Witness Theological Seminary in San Jose, California, and author of *The Messianic Vision of the Pentateuch*

"This monumentally important and unique book stands as a primary-source time capsule and also an example par excellence of not only unregistered churches in China but also global indigenous theology. Its unfiltered nature gives the reader a chance to glimpse what is really going on in God's body around the world, which helps to hone our own self-understanding of what is truly Christian versus what is simply our culture. In addition, it benefits us as learners to not just give but also receive what the Holy Spirit would have for the church."

Allen Yeh, associate professor of intercultural studies and missiology at Biola University and author of *Polycentric Missiology: Twenty-First-Century Mission from Everyone to Everywhere*

"Pastor Wang Yi's sermons carry the heart of the New Testament Epistles that still echoes down history's halls. As he covers a wide range of historical, political, cultural, and spiritual topics for his own Early Rain congregation, Pastor Yi warns, prepares, exhorts, and ultimately lives the New Testament reality of costly proclamation. Just as our prayers will strengthen Pastor Yi in his prison cell, this sermon collection will strengthen saints worldwide to endure hardship and scorn for the sake of the kingdom—even amid our own fragile freedom."

K. A. Ellis, director of the Edmiston Center for the Study of the Bible and Ethnicity

"*Faithful Disobedience* is a remarkable history of China's Christianity and the house churches in China. It contains firsthand accounts of the recent events against house churches, particularly Early Rain Covenant Church. One need not entirely agree with Wang Yi's theology, his characterization of Christians belonging to the Three-Self churches, or his way of responding to persecution to see that this book provides invaluable insights into the struggles Early Rain Covenant Church went through. This book dramatizes the questions that remain open about how China's house churches should most effectively find their voices amid persecution."

Agnes Chiu, assistant professor of systematic theology and director of research
and strategic initiatives at China Evangelical Seminary North America

FAITHFUL
DISOBEDIENCE

WRITINGS ON CHURCH AND STATE FROM A CHINESE HOUSE CHURCH MOVEMENT

WANG YI
AND OTHERS

EDITED BY
HANNAH NATION and J. D. TSENG

Foreword by Ian Johnson

IVP
Academic

An imprint of InterVarsity Press
Downers Grove, Illinois

InterVarsity Press
P.O. Box 1400 | Downers Grove, IL 60515-1426
ivpress.com | email@ivpress.com

InterVarsity Press® is the publishing division of InterVarsity Christian Fellowship/USA®. For more information, visit intervarsity.org.

Scripture quotations, unless otherwise noted, are from The Holy Bible, English Standard Version, copyright © 2001 by Crossway Bibles, a division of Good News Publishers. Used by permission. All rights reserved.

While any stories in this book are true, some names and identifying information may have been changed to protect the privacy of individuals.

The publisher cannot verify the accuracy or functionality of website URLs used in this book beyond the date of publication.

Cover design and image composite: David Fassett
Interior design: Jeanna Wiggins

ISBN 978-1-5140-0413-5 (print) | ISBN 978-1-5140-0414-2 (digital)

Printed in the United States of America ∞

Library of Congress Cataloging-in-Publication Data
Names: Wang, Yi, 1973- author. | Nation, Hannah, editor. | Tseng, J. D., editor.
Title: Faithful disobedience : writings on church and state from a Chinese house church movement / by Wang Yi, and others edited by Hannah Nation and J.D. Tseng.
Description: Downers Grove, IL : IVP Academic, [2022] | Includes bibliographical references and index.
Identifiers: LCCN 2022034695 (print) | LCCN 2022034696 (ebook) | ISBN 9781514004135 (print) | ISBN 9781514004142 (digital)
Subjects: LCSH: Christianity–China. | Church and state–China–History–21st century. | House churches–China–History–21st century.
Classification: LCC BR1285 .W365 2022 (print) | LCC BR1285 (ebook) | DDC 275.108/3--dc23/eng/20220818
LC record available at https://lccn.loc.gov/2022034695
LC ebook record available at https://lccn.loc.gov/2022034696

30 29 28 27 26 25 24 23 | 14 13 12 11 10 9 8 7 6 5 4 3

To Jiang Rong and Shu Ya.

I thank my God in all my remembrance of you,

always in every prayer of mine for you all making my prayer with joy,

because of your partnership in the gospel from the first day until now.

And I am sure of this, that he who began a good work in you

will bring it to completion at the day of Jesus Christ.

Philippians 1:3-6

Weeping may tarry for the night,

But joy comes with the morning.

Psalm 30:5

CONTENTS

FOREWORD

IAN JOHNSON

When I first met Wang Yi, he ushered me into a conference room overlooking a landscape of old and slightly run-down office buildings in central Chengdu, western China's most important metropolis. It was 2011 and his church was then called Early Rain Reformed Church, later taking the name Early Rain Covenant Church. Like many churches that weren't registered with the government, it was housed in an office building. This one was fairly old, with one functioning elevator that groaned its way up to the seventeenth floor. I had taken one look and walked up the stairs.

I explained that I was working on a book about the revival of religion in China. I had been to many rural churches in traditional Christian heartlands of China, such as the province of Henan, but felt that big, urban churches like his were becoming more important. Would he let me sit in on his services and talk to congregants?

Pastor Wang immediately agreed on two conditions: first, no photography in the church, and second, if I wanted to quote anyone, I was welcome to do so but needed their permission. His reasoning was simple: Early Rain had nothing to hide. It was a public institution. All were welcome, and no one should be restricted in what they wrote. So if I wanted to visit his church, that was my right. And if I wanted to write something, that was also my right as a free person. His restrictions were simply means to respect the privacy of those who attended and to keep the service dignified.

At that point I had worked in China off and on since the mid-1980s. I knew that for me to visit his church regularly carried inherent risks. I asked him about

Ian Johnson is a Pulitzer Prize winning journalist who has written about social change, politics, and religious life in China for the past thirty-five years. He is a senior fellow for Chinese studies at the Council on Foreign Relations and a regular contributor to the *New York Times*.

the building security guards downstairs and whether they would report to the authorities that a foreigner was regularly entering the building and trudging up to the seventeenth floor.

"Yes," he said. "But foreigners aren't banned from attending church. We are an open organization. We have nothing to hide. Come and worship with us."

We talked a bit further and I realized that compared to the many challenges that Early Rain faced, I was probably insignificant. And so I agreed to his conditions and began attending the church regularly, spending hundreds of hours in services, seminaries, prayer groups, and conversations with congregants, almost all of whom were happy to share their experiences.

That began what for me was an unusual religious experience. I was raised a Christian, in Canada, as an Anglican (Episcopal in the United States) and felt pretty comfortable going to church. But to me the beauty of the service largely resided in the music and the Shakespearean language of the King James Bible or the Book of Common Prayer. Most priests I had encountered didn't really preach convincing sermons, and church seemed little more than a worthy Sunday-morning ceremony that contained important lessons about living a good life.

Sitting in on Wang Yi's services was something else. His sermons were not homilies he squeezed into the service quickly so everyone could get to the parish hall for coffee and donuts. They were beautifully crafted, logically organized, educational experiences in Christianity. Mostly they were long. It was nothing for him to talk for half an hour and most sermons went on for forty-five minutes. And yet they didn't seem long. He didn't present Christianity as an obligation or chore but as an essential part of making sense of the society around us. At the time he was thirty-eight years old and had only converted six years earlier, in 2005, and so he was on a journey too—learning the Bible and teaching it to us.

This isn't a paean to Wang Yi. Like many leaders of unregistered churches in China, he was an autodidact, who had memorized the Bible but saw things in, at times, dogmatic ways. His views on women (they could not serve as presbyters, let alone be pastors) were also not mine. And he had knock-down-drag-out battles with people with whom he disagreed, which didn't seem like the most Christian approach to problem solving. I think other congregants had similar concerns—some would roll their eyes at his battles or joke about his fiery temperament.

But for them and me, attending Wang Yi's church was a profound experience. Part of it was that people felt that they were participating in something completely clear and open—something they could participate in and help manage.

This is a radical idea in China, where someone else, usually the Chinese Communist Party, is running one's life.

Part of it also was his personal charisma, speaking skills, and sharp mind. His sermons were electrifying, not in the sense of rhetorical histrionics but because of the clear, insightful way he explained the Bible, so that it made sense to the daily life of someone living in China. He discussed real problems and related them back to this religion, which he didn't see at all as "Western" or "foreign" but a universal faith that just happened to have been founded in the part of the world that we today call the Middle East.

My book included other faiths practiced by ethnic Chinese or "Han" people in China, and so I also spent time with Buddhists, Daoists, and folk religious practitioners. These were also idealistic people who were trying to bring a moral structure to their followers. This goal remains important to many Chinese, who feel buffeted by the essentially amoral world that the Chinese Communist Party has erected since taking power in 1949. Many of these other religious leaders also had committed followers who found meaning and value in their spiritual messages.

But Wang Yi—and other unregistered Protestant churches—connected the most directly with their followers. They offered the most help and advice and were best organized, often setting up schools, seminaries, and youth groups. This helps explain why Protestant Christianity was widely regarded as China's fastest-growing religion until a crackdown began in the 2010s.

Wang Yi was clear-eyed about these risks. He knew that he could be arrested at any time, but he refused to be drawn into the culture of secrecy that the Chinese Communist Party cultivated. This is why he rejected the term *underground church*. His was simply a church and had the same right to exist as the official churches. It was unregistered because it chose to be unregistered. I found this logic compelling, and in my writing prefer the term *unregistered* because it is more accurate than "underground" churches, which often are not underground, or "house" churches, which imply small groups of a dozen or so people. Rather, these are churches that lease office space and run kindergartens, seminaries, and even bookstores. They are what political scientists call civil society—groups that exist outside of government control.

Not all faiths around the world face these problems. Some are fortunate to exist in open societies that allow freedom of religion. Others are state-sanctioned religions that enjoy the blessings, but also the obligations, of state support. But to some degree all people of faith have to decide how to interact with authorities.

Wang Yi and the other leaders of China's unregistered churches thought deeply about this and tried to fashion answers through statements and manifestos, many of which are documented in this book.

These essays can be seen as specific to China but are also reflections of a re-markable explosion of faith that is taking place in many countries. In China, faith was long banned but is now on the upsurge, perplexing authorities. Some faiths have been co-opted, especially Buddhism and China's indigenous religion, Taoism, which enjoy state support but also tight state control. Others face out-right repression, such as Islam, against which the government has engaged in a brutal campaign of control, especially in the western region of Xinjiang. Still others, such as Catholicism, have been part of delicate negotiations over how bishops are ordained. As for Protestants, the government's aim has been to force all churches into the state-controlled organization. Those that refuse, like Wang Yi's, face destruction or at least a radical reduction in size.

Many of these battles inside China have global repercussions. China is now the world's largest Buddhist nation and tries to use it as a form of soft power in other Buddhist countries. Its suppression of Islam has met with interna-tional condemnation and caused partial boycotts of prestigious events in China, such as the 2022 Winter Olympics. And its negotiations with the Vatican are closely followed by the roughly 1.2 billion Catholics around the world. Meanwhile, the crackdown on Protestantism has attracted widespread attention, in part due to social media.

Inside China, this campaign to control religion has been implemented through new laws. These do not protect religious freedom but curtail it. This reflects a broader point in China about the legal system. Ideally, laws should be above the whims of a ruler—rule *of* law. But in China and many other countries, the law is a tool of oppression—rule *by* law. It is this kind of state-controlled legal system that for the past decade has taken aim at China's unregistered churches and re-sulted in Wang Yi's arrest in 2018. Some saw the crackdown against Wang Yi and his church as something specific, arguing that he was too outspoken. But these criticisms miss the point that the state is nervous about all religions and that all would eventually be targeted, which is what has come to pass.

All of these risks were clear to Wang Yi when I met him a decade ago. He often wrote about the potential for arrest and how to behave in the face of an oppressive state. But his conclusion was to follow a course of radical openness. He had his sermons recorded and a library of them made available to anyone who visited, worshipers or police. People at Early Rain didn't come furtively through the back door but dressed in their Sunday best and wore name tags. They were proud of attending his church and did so openly. This was their church, a small island of self-determination in a sea of state control, led by an energetic idealist.

"There is a risk of being so public," he told me that morning. "But I feel that the bigger risk is being underground. We won't have a free attitude if we don't act free. A basic attitude of being a Christian is to be free. But you can't act free if you think you're a criminal. So we try to walk the path of being open."

Wang Yi walked that path in good faith until it became impassable. Now that he is in jail, I think of something else that he once wrote in a letter to his wife, Jiang Rong, about what to do if he is arrested:

I am still a missionary, and you are still a minister's wife. The gospel was our life yesterday and it will be our life tomorrow. This is because the One who called us is the God of yesterday and the God of tomorrow.

ACKNOWLEDGMENTS

With thanks and appreciation to the many people who advised or assisted with making this book possible.

First, thank you to "Urban Farmer," who planted the seed of an idea behind this book and oversaw an early translation of *Our House Church Manifesto*. He had the foresight to see its importance long before the events of 2018 and to communicate Wang Yi's desire to share the manifesto outside of China.

Thank you to the fellows, advisors, and staff of the Center for House Church Theology for their frequent input and advice, with special thanks to Clara Kim, "Apollos Bell," "Jin Chen," and Brandon O'Brien.

Thank you to the many translators who worked faithfully on these texts over the years, particularly Ryan, whose linguistic gifts and leadership have made possible the idea of widely sharing Chinese house church theology.

Thank you to Trey Nation and Erik Lundeen for being on call to answer theological questions and for helping track down obscure references.

We are deeply grateful to Jon Boyd for taking a chance on this project and for his endless patience with us as we figured out countless details.

And last, but certainly not least, thank you to a very important group of Chinese individuals who assisted us in communicating with necessary parties within China. Their names remain anonymous, but the fruit of their faithfulness is evident.

INTRODUCTION

HANNAH NATION

On Sunday, it was Wang Yi's turn to recite. He was wearing a light blue oxford shirt, short sleeved, with a striped tie. He bounced forward on the balls of his feet, grasping the pulpit like a pogo stick. He talked about today's reading, which was the story of Jesus feeding five thousand people with just a little fish and bread—a miracle.

"China's congregations are like this today. You hear so many people say, especially intellectuals like I used to be, 'Christianity can promote economic development. Capitalism is brought by Christianity. It can help clothe and feed us. It can promote a more civilized form of commerce based on trust.'

"Christianity can bring democracy and human rights. It can make us a constitutional country based on rule of law. In other words, Christianity can allow us to feed ourselves like the manna from heaven or the loaves of bread. Christianity can bring a truly harmonious society.

"But the Gospels aren't about this. What is the relationship between the Gospels and capitalism? There is no relationship. What is the relationship between God and democracy? There is no relationship. What is the relationship between Christianity and eating your fill? There is no relationship.

"This doesn't mean we don't push freedom and democracy and people eating their fill. But this isn't what the Bible is about."

Instead, he said it was about God revealing himself through Jesus. It started with individuals taking responsibility for their own actions, he said, and it started with the Greek verb "to be." And then he began to recite.

"Ego eimi," he said in ancient Greek: "I am."

I am the bread of life.

I am the light of the world.

I am the way, the truth, and the life.

I am.[1]

---

[1] Ian Johnson, *The Souls of China: The Return of Religion After Mao* (New York: Vintage Books, 2017), 205-6.

On December 9, 2018, Pastor Wang Yi (王怡) of Early Rain Covenant Church (秋雨圣约教会) in Chengdu, China, was arrested and detained. Over the following days and weeks, all of Early Rain's leadership and hundreds of members were also detained, and the entirety of the church's substantial physical property was destroyed or confiscated. One year later, in December 2019, Wang Yi was sentenced to nine years of incarceration.

These events made the news globally. They were reported on in the US by both the *New York Times* and *Fox News*. In the United Kingdom, several outlets reported on Wang Yi and Early Rain, including the BBC. Many North American and European diplomatic agencies have commented on his sentencing and condemned the actions of the Chinese government.

In part, this global attention was drawn to Chengdu due to a statement written by Wang Yi preceding his arrest and released by Early Rain after forty-eight hours of his detention. "My Declaration of Faithful Obedience" was translated into English, as well as several other languages, shortly after Wang Yi's arrest and drew hundreds of thousands of readers as it circulated the internet. Though several other prominent house churches have also been closed and leaders arrested in the past decade, Wang Yi's written statement is one of the first widely circulated declarations by a house church pastor in the twenty-first century.

In the media coverage of Wang Yi's arrest and the closure of Early Rain, the exact nature of Wang Yi's conflict with China's governing authorities remained unclear. The easiest narrative for the media outside of China to pick up on was that of human rights violations and political persecution. Though not inaccurate, framing these events in this way had more to do with the West's perception of China and the Chinese Communist Party (CCP) than it did with Wang Yi's statements and beliefs themselves. Regardless of however the West or the CCP frames or understands Wang Yi's conflict with the state, he himself has a very specific and particular understanding of what has taken place.

For Wang Yi, the conflict between his church and the state ought to be understood primarily, and perhaps only, as a spiritual conflict within a real, eschatological dimension. For Wang Yi, the conflict between Early Rain and the CCP is a conflict between the city of God and the city of man regarding who has authority over humanity and creation. By letting Wang Yi's writings speak for themselves in English, this book seeks to introduce these theological positions to the narrative surrounding Wang Yi. No one can grasp the highly complex religious demography of China and the resulting political conflicts this landscape produces without attempting to understand the diverse theological cauldron of China's pastors. In other words, to understand the political conflicts between church and state in China from the perspective of the churches involved, one must begin to study the theology they are writing and using to inform their decisions.

WHAT IS THE HOUSE CHURCH?

Unless the reader is a Chinese national or a Sinologist, a likely first question when reading a house church manifesto will be what, exactly, the house church is. Global Christianity's understanding of the house church in China is generally murky. Our imaginations often lead us to darkened rooms where a dozen people gather and quietly whisper their prayers, unable to loudly sing, and eventually depart one by one in order to avoid attention. While this image held true for the realities of many Chinese Christians roughly thirty years ago, this is not an accurate picture of the house church today.

Let me paint another picture. I know of a house church in a prominent inland city that experienced powerful renewal roughly a decade ago through the historic Reformed gospel of grace. The pastor of this church was personally revived and spiritually freed in his understanding of the gospel, and the fruit of his personal revival was the revival of the rest of the church's leadership. In turn, these leaders began noticing many things in the apartment building where the church rented property, as well as the surrounding apartment complex, that needed to be cleaned up and repaired. They organized the congregation to publicly participate in the property's maintenance—fixing lights in hallways, collecting trash, and generally contributing to the well-being of the community. Not only did the church's immediate neighbors notice these actions, but likewise so did the neighborhood security officers and policemen, and eventually the pastor was called to meet with these low-level magistrates. These local authorities chose not to interfere, and the church grew to more than five hundred congregants spread across multiple daughter churches. Until 2018, this large church was publicly engaged and maintained a friendly relationship with the local authorities. Since 2018, its relationship with authorities has changed. Yet, the church has remained active in the community and it has continued to grow. And through all of these changes—political, theological, and numerical—it has continuously called itself a "house church." This is one of the realities of urban Chinese Christianity.

As you read Wang Yi's manifesto, do not imagine the rural house churches of the 1960s and 1970s—scattered and sheltering in place. Instead, imagine China's gleaming, rapidly growing cities, where people pursue their material and social dreams and engage the multitude of ideas and philosophies which define so many of the world's urban centers. In this light, I offer five characteristics with which we can begin to understand and define the house church.

First, the house church is unregistered. The most fundamental identity of the Chinese house church is that it refuses to comply with the government's demand to register with and submit to the official structures that exist within the People's Republic of China (PRC) for the regulation and oversight of all religious practice, including theology, preaching, and pastoral education, in short, spiritual governance. Though at times it has been severely suppressed, and even eradicated from the public eye during the 1960s and 1970s, Christianity is not illegal in China, strictly speaking. Before the Communist revolution, Chinese Protestant Christianity could arguably be understood primarily according to its relationship with the West, organized along an axis of affiliations with indigenous independent groups such as the True Jesus Church on one end and those participating in the Anglican communion on the other. However, with the removal of all Western missionaries and the severing of all denominational ties by the Communists in the 1950s this changed entirely. Since the middle of the twentieth century, the fundamental defining relationship for churches in China has not been to the West, but rather the relationship to the CCP. On one side of this new axis, a significant portion of Chinese Christianity exists within the Three-Self Patriotic Movement (TSPM), a state-sanctioned organization that submits to the authority of the CCP. On the other side, churches that refuse to register with the TSPM stand within the historical stream of the "house church." For many decades during the explosion of Christianity in China over the turn of the millennium, it seemed a middle ground might open allowing for gray semi-state-sanctioned churches. However, over the past ten years this increasingly seems to be disappearing as the government pursues compliance under the Regulations on Religious Affairs, which began to be enforceable in 2018.

Of course, this is a simple sketch of a system within which complexities abound. For example, where exactly do we place a large unregistered church in Wenzhou that worships publicly but has had its crosses demolished?[2] Or a new unregistered church that meets in a hotel ballroom in the middle of Shanghai whose pastor was converted by an American missionary in the 2000s and received his theological education overseas? Can we rightly call such churches "house churches"?

---

[2]Wenzhou in Zhejiang Province is known for both TSPM and unregistered churches that are large and visible, generally housed in their own buildings. This trend was challenged between 2014 and 2015 when local authorities removed and demolished around one thousand crosses from church buildings across the province, in a few cases demolishing entire church buildings.

As one personal friend with more than a decade of extensive on-the-ground engagement with unregistered churches has said,

> I can't think of any non-registered church that doesn't self-identify as a "house church." There is an undeniable historical legacy that non-registered churches associate themselves with. Even those that were the most public and open identified themselves as house churches, not because of where they met or even their theological background, but because of the historical legacy of non-registered churches in China.
>
> I have been in prayer meetings with Wenzhou, charismatic, urban Reformed, and completely non-affiliated house church leaders. They are all *very* different, and in some ways many of them found it miraculous that we could all come together for prayer. But when someone led worship and started a Canaan hymn, they all started to sing together as if they're from the same church. The reason is because Xiaomin's Canaan hymns are an identifying marker in which house churches share.[3] There is a common heritage among the non-registered that serves as a boundary.

Second, the house church is not secret. Simply because the house church is unregistered and therefore by some interpretations illegal does not mean it is a church in hiding. In general, house churches are cautious and seek to embody Christ's directive to be as wise as serpents and as innocent as doves. And as restrictions on unregistered religious practices have once again tightened since the beginning of 2018, most churches have taken serious precautions to cloak their activities from unwanted scrutiny and veil their members from social and government pressure. But in general, Chinese house churches are not altogether hidden. Some must be found through word of mouth, but most do not discourage local knowledge of their existence, and most Chinese living in urban centers have met at least one person who professes to be a Christian.

The house church is not secret in part because the house church is large. The new edition of the *World Christian Encyclopedia* estimates that today there are 112,030,000 Christians of all denominations in China (7.9 percent of the total population) and it projects this number will almost double by 2050.[4] Many who minister within China cast serious doubt onto these numbers and are more

---

[3] Lü Xiaomin is a popular hymn writer. Lü began composing in 1990 and has written more than 1,800 hymns, many of which are widely used within both house churches and Three-Self churches, as well as in Taiwan and across the Chinese diaspora.

[4] "China," in *World Christian Encyclopedia*, ed. Todd Johnson and Gina Zurlo, 3rd ed. (Edinburgh: Edinburgh University Press, 2019), 141.

comfortable with numbers around 70 million.[5] However, a government report from 2018 cited 38 million adherents within the Protestant TSPM, meaning that if the TSPM's numbers are accurate and if skeptics of the WCE's high numbers are correct, unregistered Christianity is still prevalent enough in Chinese society to be impossible to keep hidden.[6]

Third, the house church is theologically engaged. As the house church grows and as its demographics shift toward China's urban centers, its theologizing increases. Opportunities for theological and pastoral training both domestically and overseas have increased dramatically, and even with increased political pressure on the house churches, the amount of reflection, writing, and contextualizing taking place is impressive. Connected to this is increased global awareness and relationship. After the isolation of the latter half of the twentieth century, the house church is demonstrating increased desire to interact and converse with the global church. Much of the house church, particularly in China's multitudinous urban centers, displays a curiosity regarding church history and systematic theology and is very much seeking to locate itself within the global conversations on both topics. Yet, unlike Chinese churches of the nineteenth and early twentieth centuries, who were reliant on the oversight of Western denominations and organizations for such global interaction, the contemporary house church is better positioned to converse as an independent peer, without returning to former structures of submission to outside ecclesiastical authority. Pragmatically, this is due to the restricted contact and affiliation with outside churches it experiences under the Chinese government.

Though it is helpful to recognize the increased theological engagement taking place within the house churches, it would be false to imply that this is a new reality. In fact, by his own account the theological dispute between the liberals and the fundamentalists of the twentieth century was the diving factor for Wang Mingdao, the figurative father of the house church. Throughout this book, the reader will come across mention of an essay titled "We—For the Sake of Faith," which is widely considered a foundational document for the birth of the Chinese house church movement. Written by Wang Mingdao in 1955 as a rallying cry to Chinese Christians to not join the Three-Self Patriotic Movement, one is struck

---

[5]Joann Pittman, "How Many Christians Are in China? Preferred Estimates, Part 3," ChinaSource, March 9, 2020, www.chinasource.org/resource-library/blog-entries/how-many-christians-in-china -preferred-estimates-part-3/.

[6]Joann Pittman, "Religion in China—by the Numbers," ChinaSource, April 23, 2018, www.chinasource .org/resource-library/blog-entries/religion-in-china-by-the-numbers/.

by its distinct lack of mention of the Chinese Communist Party or even of communism or governments generally. Wang Mingdao was an independent Chinese pastor, without any ecclesiological or financial connections to Western denominations or missionaries, and as such he fulfilled many of the ideals for religious independence espoused by the CCP. He also did not speak out against the new government after the CCP came to power. His entire argument against the TSPM was a *theological* one—he could not in good conscience unite with those who do not believe in the fundamentals of the faith such as the virgin birth, individual salvation from sin, and the resurrection of the dead at Jesus' second coming. Wang Mingdao's resistance to the religious organizations of the CCP based solely on theological arguments against liberal theology demonstrates that Chinese Christianity was theologically engaged before the CCP's ascent to power and it was theology that shaped its response to the Three-Self Patriotic Movement. As Frank W. Price wrote upon the publication of "We—For the Sake of Faith" in English in 1956, "an acute theological controversy is shaking the Chinese Church. It will probably continue in various forms. New champions of the faith will arise, it may well be from among various schools of theological thought."[7] The Chinese church of the early twentieth century was not an unformed or shallow church; within it were many contemplative writers and preachers and it remains this way today.

Fourth, the house church is not uniform. To be very clear, apart from its particular refusal to submit to the authority of the CCP, there is no single house church theology or even identity. China's house churches have traditionally fallen within basic pietistic fundamentalism, and this remains a primary distinguishing theological mark of the house church. But there are charismatic, broadly evangelical, and Reformed movements to be found within the house churches, and one must not forget the Catholic house church. Out of these many streams, grace-centric theology that draws upon the historic soteriology of the Protestant Reformation is on the ascent in China's urban centers. But the house church and its theological persuasions are diverse, and this is likely to remain true as house churches engage the many various forms of Christianity to be discovered outside of China's national boundaries.

Fifth, the house church is Chinese. This sounds like stating an obvious fact. But one of the most remarkable facets of the Chinese house church is its truly

---

[7] Wang Ming-tao, "We—For the Sake of Faith," trans. Frank W. Price, *Occasional Bulletin*, March 15, 1956.

indigenous nature. Even after China reopened to the West at the end of the twentieth century and hundreds of missionaries found creative ways to enter, the church in China has never returned to what it was before the Communist revolution. With the abrupt ending of the entirety of the Western missionary endeavor in China, the Chinese church became the largest indigenously led movement in contemporary global church history.

These attributes are important to keep in mind while reading the work of Wang Yi. The first three are made plain by Wang Yi himself, but the fourth and fifth are helpful for locating Wang Yi's arguments. The audience he is primarily interested in persuading is made up of China's Christians found in the house churches, whether charismatic, fundamentalist, or Reformed. Though his writings are important outside of China, they are first and foremost for a church wrestling through cultural and political pressures, theological exploration, and numerical growth in search of its identity.

WHO IS WANG YI?

Wang Yi was born in 1973 in Santai, Sichuan, a small town eighty miles northeast of Chengdu. He graduated from the Law School of Sichuan University in 1996 and began teaching law at Chengdu University; he also became involved in human rights advocacy. Wang married his high school sweetheart Jiang Rong (蒋蓉), to whom he had written over eight hundred love letters while she attended college in another city.

Wang Yi began writing online and for various Chinese magazines at the end of the 1990s. In 2003, he became a columnist for *China News Weekly* and joined the Independence Chinese Pen Center. He also published ten books online. His writings were mostly cultural and political commentaries, and they brought Wang Yi national attention. In 2004, he was the youngest person to be selected for the *Southern People Weekly's* list of "Fifty Most Influential Public Intellectuals of China."

During the early 2000s, Wang Yi and Jiang Rong heard the gospel from Christian friends, and Wang Yi also became involved in dialogue with Chinese Christian intellectuals online. Jiang Rong believed first and was baptized in 2004. In April 2005, the couple began hosting a Bible study at their apartment in Chengdu, even though Wang Yi was not a believer. Shortly thereafter Wang Yi was converted and baptized and began to serve in a Bible study group called the Early Rain Fellowship (秋雨之福团契).

In 2006, Wang Yi was invited to meet with President George W. Bush at the White House as a representative of China's Christian intellectuals in the house church. Wang Yi returned to Washington, DC, in 2008 to attend the Conference for Global Christians in Law and was awarded the Prize for the Contribution to Promoting Religious Freedom.

After resigning from Chengdu University, Wang Yi founded and began pastoring Early Rain Reformed Church (成都秋雨之福归正教会) in 2008, which was later renamed Early Rain Covenant Church after a contentious church split in 2018. In 2011, Wang Yi was ordained as a Presbyterian minister in one of China's first indigenous house church presbyteries. Before its forced closure in 2018, Early Rain Covenant Church grew to more than six hundred members and around eight hundred attendees, planted multiple new churches, and launched a system of education from primary school through postgraduate seminary. Wang Yi's preaching, writing, and news surrounding Early Rain were followed nationally by other house churches and were often divisive among Chinese Christians.

Within China, Wang Yi has often been controversial, as many pastors and laypeople within the house churches would prefer total avoidance of the church-state question. These critics disagree with Wang Yi's outspokenness regarding the CCP and object to his publication of theological writings on political blogs and magazines. There are also those who do not agree with Early Rain's embrace of Presbyterian polity and church discipline, as well as to the introduction of historic Reformed doctrine. Additionally, Early Rain experienced a painful church split in the years leading up to Wang Yi's arrest, many details of which were publicly aired online. In many ways, Wang Yi's writings contained in this book are directed as much to critics within the Chinese house churches as they are to the Chinese government. He desires to persuade other Christians of his views regarding the state, the church, and the end destination of both.

Like all persecuted Christians, Wang Yi can be mythologized and heroicized outside of China, particularly by those unfamiliar with his cultural context. But this is not helpful either to him or to readers of this book. Wang Yi is a man like all men, and like all Christians he confesses to be a fallen and marred image of the Creator, someone who places his trust in Jesus as the Savior of humankind and the only hope for redemption. One does not have to agree with all of Wang Yi's arguments to recognize that he has a gifted mind and is an important voice from the house church that ought to be engaged. This book desires to let readers in the English-speaking world engage Wang Yi's ideas for themselves, looking deeper than the commonplace "persecuted Christian" narratives that are so prevalent and that limit our ability to actually hear from churches outside the

West. The best way to respect and encourage Wang Yi is to take what he has written seriously, whether that leads you to agree or disagree with him.

A NOTE ON SOURCES

As mentioned above, Wang Yi is a prolific writer and was a significant online presence, even before his conversion. He wrote regular public letters to his congregation; his sermons were recorded and posted publicly on his church's website before it was shut down; and he maintained a personal blog, as well as published articles in various external blogs, magazines, and journals. The sources in this book come from this wide variety of textual and verbal output. As Chloë Starr, an important scholar of Chinese theology, has noted,

> Literary form and theological content are indivisible, an integrated whole. . . . Chinese theology, like Chinese text reading, is essentially relational: this is not the virtuoso performance of a scholastic, where the reader, or student, follows along the steps to their logical conclusion, but a more open process, where the reader, conceived as a peer, is invited to make connections from within a shared intranet of allusion.[8]

Wang Yi is certainly no exception from this observation—the theology shared in this book is not an academic opus systematically answering the question of church and state. It is the theological outworking of a pastor concerned for his flock, who is writing or speaking to others as he answers questions for himself.

Shortly before his arrest and detention, Wang Yi directed Early Rain's session to make all of his writings open source online. In keeping with this direction, Early Rain collaborated with an independent group to launch the Wang Yi Resource Library, which contains all of the original Chinese documents that are translated, annotated, and in some cases excerpted in this book.[9]

This book may be read in multiple ways. Each individual chapter is able to stand alone; as such, we believe this book will serve as a helpful tool for scholars of global theology, political theology, China studies, and more. It can also be read progressively as it traces the development of Wang Yi's theology. Part one of this book, "Our House Church Manifesto," was compiled in 2010 by Wang Yi himself and distributed by Early Rain as a self-published book. It was later revised in 2015 to include the "95 Theses." This section is much denser than the rest of the book, as its content was all initially written for scholarly blogs,

---

[8]Chloë Starr, *Chinese Theology: Text and Context* (New Haven, CT: Yale University Press, 2016), 3.
[9]See Wang Yi Resource Library, www.wangyilibrary.org.

magazines, and journals, rather than adapted from spoken contexts or pastoral letters. Parts two and three, "The Eschatological Church and the City" and "Arrest and the Way of the Cross," respectively, have been chosen and selected by ourselves from among Wang Yi's many writings as representative of his theological development and of his spiritual preparation for his arrest and detention. Though there is not division in Wang Yi's thought, we see enough progression to encourage the reader not to stop with the conclusion of part one, nor to give equal weight to chapters at the beginning and the end. Several of Wang Yi's close acquaintances have noted to us that he continues to transition from thinking like a lawyer to thinking like a theologian; our desire was to demonstrate this movement in the flow of the content. It is important to note that these same acquaintances have all stated that chapter fourteen, "History Is Christ Written Large," is the single most important essay Wang Yi has produced.

In producing this book, we hope to make Wang Yi's writings accessible to the uninitiated reader. Though his writing style is accessible, he makes frequent reference to the Chinese context; therefore, we have aimed to introduce each chapter with needed contextual explanation, as well as by situating it within a loose narrative. We have also provided a glossary and ample footnoting to explain specific cultural references. Footnotes have generally been used for single-reference items. Repeated important names and events are likely to be found in the glossary with lengthier explanations. Additionally, chapters five and six contain bibliographies provided by Sun Yi (孙毅) and Wang Yi themselves, and we have chosen not to add to their references.

We find it important to note that most of the writing in this book was initially developed for either spoken contexts or as online essays, and therefore, Wang Yi did not give academic attention to the citation of his sources, many of which come from the corpus of unpublished, uncatalogued, and sometimes apocryphal stories and documents of the early Chinese house church. This, of course, made our work quite challenging at times and we ask for patience where full citations have been beyond our abilities to hunt down.

The English translations provided here have been a collaborative effort by a remarkable team of people who choose to remain anonymous. We stand on their shoulders and are deeply indebted to their commitment to make the writings of Chinese pastors available to English speakers. Their linguistic gifts open the gates between heaven's global communities.

WHY SHOULD A CHRISTIAN IN THE WEST READ
ABOUT CHINESE CHURCH-STATE THEOLOGY?

It is likely that many people will pass over a theological work from a Chinese writer on the basis of geography alone. People might be prone to think that differences in cultural context between twenty-first century democratic America and twenty-first century communist China are too great for dialogue. And yet, modern majority culture North American and European Christians readily turn to five-hundred-year-old theology from Reformation Europe, a time and place we can hardly say we have much in common with. Though we are perhaps closer to Europe geographically, are we truly any closer culturally to premodern, preindustrial, predigital, predemocratic, presecular, precapitalistic European Christendom? I do not mean to discourage readers from engaging the West's theological heritage but rather to provoke them to consider whether they might have more in common with urban China than they realize. The urban Chinese Christian certainly comes from a significantly different historical, cultural, and political context. But like the reader, the urban Chinese Christian works and lives in an age dominated by material gain, technology, and secularism. We are not so distant.

Christianity is currently making sizable inroads into perhaps the greatest single cultural identity in the history of modern civilization and it is in conflict with the ruling powers of this great civilization. One does not need to agree with Wang Yi in order to see that he and any other comparably prolific theological writer are important to hear and understand, if for no other reason than to follow the important developments within Christianity in the twenty-first century. If the twenty-first century really does prove to be the Chinese century, then now is the time to begin understanding the theological developments taking place within China, for their debates will echo throughout global Christianity. As Wang Yi himself so often implies in his writings, the Chinese house churches are the living inheritors of the Western churches' older theological debates, and they are poised to be the next frontier of church-state theology. Wang Yi himself embodies this. When was the last time a notable, publicly lauded, secular legal scholar became a Christian in Europe and then turned his full attention to the thorny issue of church-state theology? As North America and Europe race further toward the secularism modern China represents, we need the perspective of those who have considered the faith from the outside and chosen to enter in. Right now, the ideas of a former human rights lawyer who lives as a pastor theologian under an authoritarian regime are indeed relevant to churches in the throes of untangling Christianity's political allegiances.

Scholars and academics are beginning to study Wang Yi according to his particular cultural context, an important endeavor which ought to continue. However, we need to not only consider Wang Yi's writings as Chinese texts for the Chinese context, but also to place them within the conversation of global Christianity. All Christian texts are both local and global simultaneously, for the Christian faith has always been both local and global in nature.

This book highlights three important aspects of Wang Yi's writings on the house church that have the ability to reach beyond the Chinese context. First, a church's history invariably shapes its identity. Second, the eschatological destination of the church determines not only its heavenly, but also its earthly, reality. And third, the way of the cross is the road the church must walk if it is truly united with Christ, as will be seen throughout the writings this book makes available. Though Wang Yi writes specifically to the Chinese context, these are three points all churches in all times would benefit from grappling with, whatever conclusions they finally arrive at.

ABBREVIATIONS

CCC—China Christian Council
CCP—Chinese Communist Party
CCPA—Chinese Catholic Patriotic Association
ERCC—Early Rain Covenant Church
MFA—Ministry of Foreign Affairs
PRC—People's Republic of China
SARA—State Administration for Religious Affairs
TSPM—Three-Self Patriotic Movement

TIMELINE OF IMPORTANT DATES

1517—Portuguese ships arrive in Canton and seek to establish trade.

1552—First attempt by the Jesuits, under Francis Xavier, to establish a mission in China fails.

1582—Matteo Ricci, along with other Jesuit priests, is welcomed by the imperial court and establishes Catholic missions in China. Nine hundred and twenty Jesuits serve in China before the first Protestant missionaries arrive two centuries later.

1807—Robert Morrison, the first Protestant missionary to China, arrives in Canton (modern-day Guangzhou). In the following decades, Methodist, Presbyterian, Baptist, and Episcopalian missionaries establish missions in China's coastal ports opened under treaties with Western colonial powers.

1839–1842—The First Opium War ends with five treaty ports opening to foreign activity under the Treaty of Nanking, and the British gain control of Hong Kong.

1850–1864—The Taiping Rebellion is fought between the Qing Dynasty and the Taiping Heavenly Kingdom, a theocratic, syncretistic cult led by Hong Xiuquan, the self-proclaimed brother of Jesus Christ. The rebellion ultimately consumed China in complete civil war and was one of the bloodiest wars in recorded history with upward of thirty million deaths.

1854—Hudson Taylor arrives in Shanghai and begins first inland missionary activity; in the following decades, China Inland Mission (CIM) is established and methods of indigenization are practiced.

1858–1860—Foreigners, including missionaries, are given the right to travel inland under the Tientsin and Peking treaties at the end of the Second Opium War. Britain forces China to legalize the opium trade.

1894–1895—At the end of the First Sino-Japanese War, Korea gains independence from Chinese imperial rule, and Japan gains control of Taiwan.

1897–1898—Britain, France, Germany, and Russia all gain colonial power over various Chinese provinces.

1899–1900—The Boxer Rebellion breaks out against foreign colonial power in China, including the presence of missionary activity. The Boxers kill thousands of Chinese Christians and more than one hundred missionaries and their children. After the Empress Dowager Cixi threatens to kill all foreigners in Beijing, allied colonial forces overtake the capitol and demand reparations.

1911–1912—The Chinese Revolution brings an end to the Qing Dynasty and imperial rule in China. The Nationalist Party is birthed and the Republic of China (ROC) is established.

1919—Students protest colonial influence, the feudal powers, and traditional Chinese culture in the May Fourth Movement.

1921—The Chinese Communist Party (CCP) is founded.

1922–1927—The Anti-Christian Movement sparks violent protests against missionary activity across China and causes missionaries to flee the country.

1928—The Nationalist Party rises to political power under Chiang Kai-shek, who begins a military campaign to reunify China.

1934—Mao Zedong leads the CCP on the Long March after Chiang Kai-shek purges all Communists from his ranks.

1920s and 1930s—Evangelical revivals take place across China and thousands are converted and baptized.

1937—The Nationalist Party and the CCP join forces to remove Japanese imperial forces from northern China.

1941–1946—Protestant and Catholic missionaries are interned or flee during WWII; most return to China after combat with Japan ceases.

1945—The Nationalists and CCP defeat Japan.

1946—The Chinese Civil War emerges between the Nationalist Party and the CCP.

1949—The CCP defeats the Nationalists and the People's Republic of China (PRC) is established.

1950—Wu Yaozong publishes "The Christian Manifesto," declaring submission and loyalty to the CCP. Eventually, half of all Chinese Christians sign the document.

1951—The Religious Affairs Department is established under the supervision of the CCP.

1951—The PRC severs diplomatic relations with the Vatican.

1951–1952—All Catholic and Protestant missionaries are expelled from China.

1954—The Three-Self Patriotic Movement (TSPM) is founded under the leadership of Wu Yaozong and the authority of the Religious Affairs Department. All churches are required to register and submit to its authority, and all theological education comes under its supervision.

1955—Wang Mingdao publishes "We—For the Sake of Faith" in response to "The Christian Manifesto" and the establishment of the TSPM. Wang Mingdao's essay and his refusal to join the TSPM is regarded as the beginning of the house church movement.

1957—The Anti-Rightist Campaign attacks and eliminates thousands of Chinese intellectuals from leadership.

1957—The Chinese Catholic Patriotic Association (CCPA) is established to oversee Catholic churches within China.

1966–1976—The Cultural Revolution engulfs China and destroys public life. All churches and seminaries are closed and the TSPM and CCPA are ended.

1979–1980—The TSPM is officially restored after Mao Zedong's death and the end of the Cultural Revolution. The China Christian Council (CCC) is established as a sister organization to the TSPM.

1982—Document 19 is made official policy as part of Deng Xiaoping's reforms. The document allows for increased official, regulated religious activity.

1989—The June Fourth Protests at Tiananmen Square and the government's violent response impact the political ideals of a generation of students across China.

2008—The Sichuan Earthquake kills nearly ninety thousand people and leaves millions homeless in southwest China. It reveals mass corruption among government leaders and construction businesses.

2011—Shouwang Church in Beijing is prevented from occupying its purchased space for worship and begins to resort to worshiping outside in public parks.

2012—Xi Jinping rises to become president of the PRC and general secretary of the CCP.

2013—The last of the first generation of prominent house church pastors, Lin Xiangao, dies in Guangzhou.

2014–2015—A campaign to demolish more than one thousand visible church crosses takes place in Wenzhou, known as "China's Jerusalem," and across Zhejiang Province.

2016—Xi Jinping inaugurates a new campaign for the "Sinicization of Christianity."

2018—The New Religious Affairs Regulations take effect, updating Document 19 and the CCP's religious policies.

2018—Zion Church in Beijing and Early Rain Covenant Church in Chengdu are raided and closed.

2019—Wang Yi is sentenced to nine years imprisonment on charges of "inciting to subvert state power" and "illegal business operations."

PART I

OUR HOUSE CHURCH MANIFESTO

In late 2010, Pastor Wang Yi of Early Rain Covenant Church compiled a book called 我们的家庭教会立场 *(women de jiating jiaohui lichang). Translated literally, this title reads* Our House Church Standpoint, *or more literally,* Our House Church Manifesto. *The book contains writings from three of China's most prominent house churches—Early Rain Covenant Church, Shouwang Church, and Zion Church (the latter two both in Beijing), demonstrating that though these churches represent different ecclesiological commitments, they are united in their stance rejecting submission to China's state-sanctioned church agency, the Three-Self Patriotic Movement. The early 2000s were important years for house churches in China, and several events convinced the churches represented by Wang Yi's book that a particular house church identity needed to be studied, honored, and preserved.*

Two years prior, the Sichuan Earthquake of 2008 catalyzed house churches across the country into rapidly organizing a response to the humanitarian needs of western Sichuan. Throughout these relief efforts, house churches acted publicly in uncharted ways and were visible both locally in person and nationally online providing aid.[1] This level of organization and public presence did not quietly dissipate in the following years; rather, the momentum among churches in urban China continued, producing various social, educational, denominational, ecumenical, and theological movements.

Meanwhile, the global Christian community prepared for the third congress of the Lausanne Movement. The Lausanne Movement connects global church leaders in order to further the cause of evangelism and missions. The first congress took place in 1974 in Lausanne, Switzerland, and is considered a pivotal moment in modern church

---

[1]Li Ma and Jin Li, *Surviving the State, Remaking the Church: A Sociological Portrait of Christians in Mainland China* (Eugene, OR: Pickwick Publications, 2018), 106-7.

history for uniting the church for the work of the Great Commission. A second congress occurred in 1989 in Manila, the Philippines.

The Cape Town Congress in 2010 was carefully planned so that a fuller picture of the global reality of the church would be represented, with particular focus given to the voices of the Majority World. More than two hundred Chinese delegates from house churches were invited to participate in what would have been the largest delegation in attendance; however, when the delegates attempted to travel to Cape Town, Chinese authorities stopped them at various airports across the country and seized their passports. As a delegate, Wang Yi was detained for four hours and not permitted to travel. As occurred in Manila in 1989, the Chinese delegation's two hundred seats were left empty during congress proceedings and the Lausanne Movement conducted a special time of prayer for the church in China. The Chinese delegation sent a note to the congress communicating that they accepted their government's decision peacefully and with hope in Christ. The message quoted several passages from Scripture, including Philippians 1:29, "For it has been granted to you that for the sake of Christ you should not only believe in him but also suffer for his sake."

China's Ministry of International Affairs released a statement clarifying the reason for its decision to detain the delegation—congress organizers had overlooked inviting participants from the Three-Self Patriotic Movement. A statement from the government read, "This action publicly challenges the principle of independent, autonomous, domestically organized religious associations, and therefore represents a rude interference in Chinese religious affairs." Failing to invite delegates from the TSPM while including the house churches, which have no legal identity in China, was viewed as a politically subversive act.

2010 also proved to be a significant year for Beijing Shouwang Church (北京守望教会, Beijing Shouwang jiaohui), a large unregistered congregation founded in 1993 and pastored by Jin Tianming (金天明).[2] In the early 2000s, Shouwang was raided by police and told to register with the government. Jin Tianming interpreted government regulations to mean he could seek registration with the State Administration for Religious Affairs (SARA) without joining the Three-Self Patriotic Movement, which he attempted to do in 2006. Due to its size, the congregation began to have a difficult time finding large enough spaces in which to meet. In 2008, Shouwang's registration application was officially denied, and in 2009 police began raiding the congregation and harassing members' employers. The congregation was prevented from meeting in their rental property and began meeting outdoors in parks as their struggle to find

---

[2]Translated literally, shouwang means "watchmen."

a venue intensified. In 2010, Shouwang raised 27 million RMB (4.12 million USD) from among its thousand members to purchase its own property. However, according to Shouwang, after members of the church were stopped from joining the Lausanne Congress, relations with the government deteriorated further. In 2011, the government stopped Shouwang from occupying its property, which the church claims was purchased legally. In response, Shouwang declared it would begin conducting public worship services outdoors in a prominent city square. Jin Tianming and several church leaders were promptly placed under house arrest and other church members were repeatedly detained.

In addition to including chapters from Shouwang's leaders in his manifesto, Wang Yi included a chapter from Jin Mingri (金明日), the senior pastor of Zion Church (锡安教会, xi an jiaohui), one of the largest house churches in Beijing, and founder of China Christian Theological Seminary. Before leaving to join the house church, Jin Mingri was a pastor within the TSPM. He was one of the first government-approved seminary graduates after the TSPM was reinstated following the Cultural Revolution. At the time Wang Yi compiled the manifesto, Zion was a "public" urban house church, unregistered with the TSPM. It had over 1,500 attendees and six meeting places in office buildings across Beijing.

The chapters in part one are translations of Wang Yi's Our House Church Manifesto. *Whereas the chapters in parts two and three of this book were mostly adapted from spoken contexts, the chapters in part one were all originally written for various journals or books, making this section the densest and most complex. After first compiling his manifesto in 2010, Wang Yi revised it in 2015 to include Early Rain's "95 Theses." With the exception of chapter six, which has been excerpted by the editors in order to bring it closer in length to the other chapters of this book, the manifesto has been reproduced in full.*

The manifesto demonstrates Jin Tianming and Jin Mingri's influence on Wang Yi's understanding of the history of the house church, as well as the importance of this history for shaping and forming the identity of many contemporary urban house churches in China. There are several main themes to be found in Our House Church Manifesto. *First, it seeks to clarify what the tradition of the house church is and how it is different from the TSPM. Second, it seeks to explain why the churches represented by the manifesto are determined to continue promoting this tradition and refuse to submit to the TSPM. Third, the manifesto calls other house churches to join the authors, submitting to the kingship of Jesus Christ alone as the head of the church in rejection of nationalistic idolatry.*

1

WHY WE ARE A HOUSE CHURCH

WANG YI

The following document is a pastoral letter written by Wang Yi to his congregation following the detention of the Chinese delegation traveling to Cape Town, South Africa for the third Lausanne Congress. Wang Yi's pastoral letters were usually first emailed directly to his congregation, then posted online for the general public. An excerpt of this article was also published on The Kosmos, *a Chinese online journal of theology and culture.*

This chapter outlines Wang Yi's understanding of what the church is, his theological arguments for the separation of church and state, and the history of the Three-Self Patriotic Movement. At the heart of Wang Yi's theology is a question: Who has ultimate authority over the church? He believes that the various answers to this question fundamentally define the differences between China's state-run and house churches.

To my fellow communicants of Early Rain Covenant Church,

Peace. I'm thankful that on the fifteenth of this month, some brothers and sisters came very early to my home to pray, sing praises, and experience being stopped at the airport together with us. Many more brothers and sisters truly cared for us, praying for us and the other attendees. My wife, Jiang Rong, said you were like angels, embodying the Lord's comfort for our family.

This time, because the government feared the participation of Chinese house church pastors at the Third Lausanne Congress for World Evangelization, they stopped its citizens from departing on a large scale. In substance, this is a conflict between God's call to the church for "world evangelization" and the official doctrine of so-called self-governance, self-support, and self-propagation.[1] The spokesman from the Ministry of Foreign Affairs, Ma Chaoxu, said that the

---

[1]See "Three-Self Patriotic Movement" in the glossary.

Lausanne meeting's "secret communications and invitations to those outside of the legitimate Chinese church" (meaning the Three-Self church) violated the state's principle of a "self-governed church." It is a crude interference in "China's religious affairs."[2]

The Lord is using this incident to underscore again to every Chinese Christian the spiritual conflict between the house churches and the Three-Self churches. In the past, the Three-Self Patriotic Movement had also contacted the Lausanne organizing committee in hopes of participating. But the foundation of connection within the Lord's church is not based on might or power (Zechariah 4:6), but rather on a shared confession (Ephesians 4:5-6). The Lausanne Covenant upholds an evangelical perspective, believing in the authority of the Bible and the universality of gospel mission: "whole gospel, whole church, whole world."[3] This is in direct contradiction with the Communist Party's United Front Work Department and the State Administration for Religious Affairs principles. Moreover, the thirteenth point in the Lausanne Covenant says, "It is the God-appointed duty of every government to secure conditions of peace, justice and liberty in which the Church may obey God, serve the Lord Jesus Christ, and preach the gospel without interference," and it calls the church to "express our deep concern for all who have been unjustly imprisoned, and especially for those who are suffering for their testimony to the Lord Jesus. We promise to pray and work for their freedom. At the same time, we refuse to be intimidated by their fate."

Therefore, if those appointed by the Communist Party as "legitimate representatives of the Chinese church" carefully read through this statement, they could never in good faith and conscience sign it. This shows that they stand in the synagogue of Satan (Revelation 2:9), sitting in Moses' seat (Matthew 23:2). Because of their worldly "religious affairs," they dare not join together and agree with the sons and daughters of the Most High. This is why we believe that the "Three-Self" is a government monopoly within a religious industrial complex, submitting to the cause of political power, and is therefore not the Lord's church—because "the church" by nature is not a tangible organization but rather a group of spiritual

---

[2]The Ministry of Foreign Affairs (MFA) of the People's Republic of China is an executive department under the State Council of the Chinese government. This agency is responsible for crafting foreign policies, decisions, and statements in regard to the PRC. It also negotiates and signs foreign treaties and agreements, dispatches foreign affairs representatives to other countries, and represents the PRC's interests in the United Nations and other international organizations.

[3]The Lausanne Covenant is widely regarded as one of the most significant documents on evangelism and mission in modern church history. The document emerged from the First Lausanne Congress in 1974, with John Stott as its chief architect. The covenant has gained significant traction among urban house churches in China.

saints within God's invisible kingdom, chosen from every tongue, tribe, and nation (John 18:36).

At the same time, even though there are numerous church buildings (religious activity centers) within the "Three-Self" system, there is not a single independent "church" among them. The evil religious industrial complex controls all, because the schemes of Satan are to destroy the "local church." In reality, in today's China, only among the house churches can one find a true and independent "local church."

Today, why do we insist on the path of a house church, why must we warn those believers who have been abducted into the "Three-Self" to quickly break away from the sin of Jeroboam, worshiping the golden calves that were in Bethel and Dan (2 Kings 10:29), instead calling them to know the Bible and long for the truth, lest God's people are destroyed for their lack of knowledge (Hosea 4:6); why must we warn those "Three-Self" pastors who are walking in the ways of Cain, peddling God's Word (2 Corinthians 2:17), and rushing for profit into Balaam's error (Jude 1:11) to thoroughly repent; and why do we ask God to have mercy on those members and workers of the body within the "Three-Self" who are weak and suffer from pangs of conscience, to give them a faith that overcomes the world, in order that they may be right before the Lord, faithful unto death, receiving the crown of life (Revelation 2:10)?

Briefly, this is in view of the teachings of the Bible and the acknowledgment of historical facts:

1. THE FIRST OF THE TEN COMMANDMENTS: "YOU SHALL HAVE NO OTHER GODS BEFORE ME" (EXODUS 20:3)

The bride only has one husband, the church only has one head, and the soul only has one king. For believers to truly understand this commandment and take it seriously, in the face of any thing or person that craves dominion or obligation over our lives—whether it is our spouses, parents, or our country or political party—no matter if the request is accompanied with tears or guns, our response is simply this: thus says the Lord, "You will have no other gods before me." Once the church falls into the trap of being ruled by emotions, depending on power, or yielding to politics on matters of doctrine, priesthood, or sacraments, they have worshiped a false god. They will have lost the most beautiful quality of Christ's bride, purity, so that they cease to be the Lord's church.

2. THE SEPARATION OF CHURCH AND STATE: "RENDER TO CAESAR THE THINGS THAT ARE CAESAR'S, AND TO GOD THE THINGS THAT ARE GOD'S" (MATTHEW 22:21)

On the one hand, God grants the state the power to wield the sword (Romans 13:1-13), maintaining external order and peace; on the other hand, he gives the church keys to the kingdom of heaven (Matthew 16:19), to preach the gospel, administer the sacraments, and judge spiritual matters, as "stewards of the mysteries of God" (1 Corinthians 4:1). The government has no right to interfere with the faith of its citizens, or the doctrines, priestly vocations, worship, and preaching of churches. We do not accept interference in religious freedom by an atheistic political party's religious affairs bureau; we do not accept the notion of the Lord's church submitting to a "managerial department;" we do not accept "religious affairs" as a function of the government. In other words, religious matters never belong to "my country, China," nor do they belong to the United States, nor South Africa. Real religion (godliness) belongs to Christ, belongs to the world, and belongs to the conscience of every believer.

As long as the government maintains its "theocracy" model—viewing religious affairs as internal governmental matters—violates the church's keys to the kingdom, and prevents local churches from registering independently via the Civil Affairs Bureau, we are determined to follow in the footsteps of the saints before us, such as Wang Mingdao and Yuan Xiangchen, holding to the house church position unto death. On one hand we obey the government's legitimate and common governance, respecting the power of its sword; on the other hand, through nonviolent civil disobedience, we will preach the word whether in season or out of season (2 Timothy 4:2). People can be chained, but the gospel cannot be chained (2 Timothy 2:9); the servants may be killed, but our Lord has already risen.

3. ENTRUSTED WITH THE GREAT COMMISSION (MATTHEW 28:18-20; LUKE 24:46-48)

Because our sovereign God has given the church the rights and responsibility to spread the gospel to the ends of the earth, it means that the spiritual kingdom of Christ is higher than any nation state because Christ has no passport, faith knows no national boundaries, and truth knows no skin color. Without Western missionaries, where would Chinese Christians be? Therefore, we resolutely oppose the "self-propagating" principle of the Three-Self, the sham of "designated message, designated location, and designated people," and the so-called religious freedom guidelines. The half-century "Three-Self Patriotic Movement" is an antichrist movement precisely because it does not recognize a public faith and the existence of a kingdom that is above nation-states, and it attempts to set up a "nationalist church" via the regime. This is a scheme of Satan to use China to destroy the Lord's church. But God intended it for good (Genesis 50:20), using over a half century of persecution to instead raise up, fulfill, and protect the house church.

4. THE HISTORY AND REALITIES OF THE "THREE-SELF PATRIOTIC MOVEMENT"

Many in its ranks are false leaders and teachers who accuse and persecute the church and its workers; these are among the bishops, leaders, and ministers of the "Three-Self" (and its affiliates) at every level to this day. So far, they have not repented and turned from their evil ways; they continue to initiate heretical teachings based on "justification by love," advocating for religious syncretism through "theological reconstruction" throughout the Three-Self system.[4] Many local Three-Self churches continue to help their local governments persecute the house churches, following in the shameful ways of Judas—we even dare not pray for them about this sin that leads to death (1 John 5:16). They continue to receive the kind of oversight and compensation that the government gives to official ministers; they organize "political studies," receiving leadership and teaching from Gentiles; they continue to sing "red songs" in their meetings,[5] hang the national flag, and approve worshiping the state. True believers should oppose and be greatly alarmed by this following of the religion of the Canaanites, yielding to Baal's despotic power and backsliding ways.

Someone will say, but we must also love them. Yes, if you walk along this path of being a house church, suffering and paying the price for this lack of freedom, striving to spread the full gospel, working hard to observe the Lord's way, and walking in the light, then nothing is greater than this love for one's brother (1 John 2:6-10).

What is true "religious autonomy"? It is precisely holding Jesus as Lord and upholding the Bible. Any "autonomy" outside of Christ is outright rebellion against the Lord, coming from the Evil One. What is true "self-propagation, self-support"? It is believers not being unequally yoked with unbelievers. For what do righteousness and unrighteousness have in common, and what accord does Christ have with Satan? (2 Corinthians 6:14-15)

---

[4]See "China Christian Council" and "Sinicization of Christianity."
[5]"Red songs" are songs that praise the Chinese Communist Party and the People's Republic of China. They are mostly historical in nature, from the revolutionary years surrounding 1949 until the end of the Cultural Revolution.

Therefore, the fifth point of the "Early Rain Confession of Faith" that you and the elders hold to says: "We accept the legacy of the Chinese house church, holding fast to Jesus Christ as the only head of the church, and holding onto the principle of the separation of church and state."

Brothers and sisters, oh that the Lord would use our lives in this world where the darkness is passing away and the true light is shining (1 John 2:8); that we would be like Martin Luther, saying, "Here I stand, I can do no other, so help me God."

By grace, faithful to the Lord,

your fellow servant,

Wang Yi

October 15, 2010

2

THE SPIRITUAL LEGACY OF THE HOUSE CHURCH

JIN TIANMING

This essay was first published on September 20, 2009, in the Chinese theology blog The Kosmos. *Though Jin Tianming and Wang Yi do not share the same ecclesio-logical commitments, they respect each other and communicated before their various incarcerations.*

Jin Tianming has written many statements on behalf of his church. Here he identi-fies seven traits that all Chinese house churches hold in common. This is important for Jin Tianming's argument that "house church" is not simply an administrative political designation but rather is a historic Christian tradition with distinct theological and spiritual ideas and commitments.

I believe that there are seven aspects of the spiritual legacy of the house church: adherence to the essentials of the faith; holding to the separation of church and state; walking in the way of the cross; focusing on the inner life; focusing on repentance, prayer, and the work of the Holy Spirit; emphasis on the life of faith; and a special focus on evangelism.

1. ADHERENCE TO THE ESSENTIALS OF THE FAITH

House churches hold to the fundamentals of the faith. In contrast to liberal theology, these fundamentals emphasize three areas: (1) The absolute authority of the Bible. The Bible is God's complete and inerrant revelation, the absolute authority and truth for our faith and lives. This absolute authority cannot to be weakened by any means. (2) Emphasizing the full divinity of Jesus Christ. Jesus Christ is the Son of God, the manifestation of God in the flesh. For the sins of humankind, he died and rose again and will come again. And (3) Christ's death and resurrection is the heart of salvation. It is the only requirement for the salvation of the individual soul. The house churches have contributed greatly to the opposition of false teachings of liberal theology and built up the foundation of a pure faith by holding onto the above essential beliefs.[1]

However, some house churches, in order to underscore their belief in these essentials, reject and criticize all theology (thinking that theology weakens the absolute nature of the faith and of truth). They emphasize the salvation of the individual soul while neglecting the building-up of the church and caring for society (believing that the salvation of souls is most important since this world will eventually pass away). As time goes on, their faith becomes distanced from the world, and that church is slowly disconnected from the world as it isolates itself. This is a departure from the spirit of the incarnate Christ, who was "Word become flesh" (John 1:14). This is also the reason why fewer house churches are calling themselves fundamentalist and referring to themselves as evangelical instead.

2. HOLDING TO THE SEPARATION OF CHURCH AND STATE

The house church has always strongly emphasized that Jesus Christ is the head of the church and that the church cannot unite with or be held in bondage to worldly powers, lest it fall into spiritual promiscuity. Therefore, the house church has maintained the principle of the separation of church and state. Yet the author has discovered that the early house churches (and also recent ones), in the practical application of this principle, approached it from the angle of individual faith rather than directly confronting the issue of the relationship between church and state.

Why not join the Three-Self? First, Wang Mingdao put forth a reason that was later widely adopted by the house churches: "Do not be yoked together with unbelievers," meaning that we do not share the same beliefs as those in the Three-Self. However, what if Wu Yaozong and Ding Guangxun had abandoned liberal theology and held to the true faith, then how would we handle this matter? This is a key issue today. In reality, the house churches' refusal to participate in the Three-Self is not just because of its "liberal theology," but rather because behind the Three-Self is a submission to government control (leaders).

---

[1] Historically, foreign missionaries in China brought both fundamentalist and liberal theologies from the West. Additionally, many young elite intellectuals traveled overseas in early decades of the twentieth century for theological study and training, encountering the various theological traditions to be found at American and European seminaries.

Therefore, one can say that participation in the Three-Self is to acknowledge the government's power as the head, and not Christ. This kind of church is no longer a "virgin" but is rather a "prostitute" united with a worldly regime (Mathew 25:1-13; Revelation 17). Within the house church tradition, there have also been those who have raised this issue (such as Yuan Xiangchen and Lin Xiangao) from the perspective of who holds decision-making power.

If there is long-term neglect of the issue of church-state relations, thinking that it is all just politics, what will be the result? The church would completely give up its rightful place in society and in the public square. Before the Three-Self Movement, whether it was Wang Mingdao or Watchman Nee, Christian leaders were able to openly publish journals and newspapers, making their voices heard to all of society. But when the church avoided the issue of the church-state relationship, it lost its opportunity to witness to all of society and the public square. So in the past, whenever a Christian engaged with the public square, the house church would be very sensitive and nervous about it. Until recently, many house churches have been very sensitive, even purposely distancing themselves from those "activist" Christians for fear of "getting burned."[2] But today, many house churches have received help from these individuals, entering the public square and using legal measures to protect the churches' legitimate rights and interests. The Three-Self submits to the government, abandoning its mission—it dares not, it cannot, and it will not enter the public square.

But with the growth of the house church, the Lord's church will fully enter China's public square (last year's church involvement in relief efforts proves this point).[3] Sometimes we must follow the example of the apostle Paul, who often used his Roman citizenship and the laws of his time to protect and expand his right to believe and to preach, in order to adhere to the faith, and by means of the law, protect the autonomy of the church.

3. WALKING IN THE WAY OF THE CROSS

Since house churches refuse to compromise with the government, if history is a guide, they will walk in the way of the cross, giving up everything without hesitation, including their lives and families. Therefore, suffering will become

---

[2] *Weiquan* (维权律师, "rights-defending lawyers") are legal practitioners and scholars who help Chinese citizens to assert their civil rights and public interests through litigation and legal activism. It is noteworthy that among *weiquan* activists in China, a significant percentage are Christian. Before entering the ministry, Wang Yi himself was regarded as a *weiquan* activist.

[3] See "Sichuan Earthquake of 2008."

the mark of the Chinese Christian during this unique historical time. True Christians will hold onto their faith and refuse to be disciples who compromise on the truth. At that time, it will be nearly impossible to avoid suffering (unless the Lord provides supernatural care and protection). Especially those who lead the church must face the responsibility of experiencing persecution.

We believe that suffering refines the lives of pastors and believers, and it also refines the church. It is through the sufferings of spiritual elders that an un-shakable foundation is built for the Chinese church. However, extended suf-fering brings its own set of challenges as it individualizes faith, breaking down the body so that each must face his or her faith alone. Because churches of a certain size do not exist anymore, with their pastors often jailed, brothers and sisters can only pray and read Scripture (if they still have a Bible at all) and fellowship in secret (if the police have not raided their homes). Suffering indi-vidualizes faith, weakening the collective sense of the church (group identity), bringing emphasis to individual faith and witness, while ignoring the impor-tance of building up the church and its corporate witness. Therefore, house churches that experience persecution over the long haul should seek out the faith and peace of mind that accompany more peaceful times, in order to prevent the danger of seeing suffering as a source of spiritual pride. They must also learn, in actual peaceful times, to continue to lay themselves down and walk in the way of the cross.

4. FOCUSING ON THE INNER LIFE

The spiritual distinctive of the house church is the inner life of its believers, with a focus on a believer's individual relationship with the Lord. Seeking break-through and growth in their spiritual lives through devotions becomes a strong foundation as they experience suffering. Whether it is Watchman Nee, who was influenced by the pietists, or the Reformed pastor Jia Yuming, who graduated from a Presbyterian seminary, they are all in accord on this point, and this has always been the emphasis of the Chinese house church.

However, the house church often uses the phrase "spiritual" to describe the inner life, making it difficult to be objective about God's commands as an ethical standard. The result is that the spiritual life often becomes out of touch with real life. In fact, when the Bible speaks of a truly spiritual person (someone of the Spirit, filled with the Spirit), there is always a clear accordance with a biblical ethic rather than evaluations based on inner feelings or circumstances. Consis-tently, a truly spiritual husband, wife, father/mother, son/daughter, master/

servant, all have an external standard by which they are assessed (Ephesians 5:18-6:9). If we set aside the ethical standard founded on biblical truth and focus only on internal growth in life, it is easy to mistake human (or even fleshly) standards as false spiritual standards.

Moreover, an overemphasis on the inner life will inevitably create an extreme: an opposition to any church organizational effort. There are three reasons. First, as mentioned before, the emphasis is on the individual relationship with the Lord as the main medium for faith. This often leads to thinking that church governance and organization comes from humanity and is not "spiritual." Second, the church has long avoided addressing church-state relations. After leaving the public square and entering homes, the scale of churches has been small, with no need to create additional structures, disciplines, or governance. Third, in specific historical contexts (including now), organizations have been targeted; therefore, one should avoid organizing at all. Being opposed to organizing has diluted the collective nature of the church's faith and service; it only emphasized the spiritual nature of the church ("for where two or three or more are gathered in his name, there is the church").[4] This has resulted in house churches lacking a proper ecclesiology. Therefore, within this historical context, it is not hard to understand why churches entered the private sphere and became "house churches" and adopted "going into hiding" tactics (which have long been the spiritual trump card of the house church) to protect individual beliefs and growth within safe limits. This "house" nature of the house church attached great importance to intimate fellowship and relationships, so house churches typically have a tradition of fellowship.

In the past, house churches suffered for the right to individual belief; today's house church must persevere in suffering to build up the church. The church-state conflict and its essence have not changed.

5. FOCUSING ON REPENTANCE, PRAYER, AND THE WORK OF THE HOLY SPIRIT

House churches tend to emphasize confession of sin and repentance, which is also directly tied to their forbearers in the faith. Wang Mingdao emphasized the holy living of Christians as new creations, and being "emptied of sin" was the focus and climax of John Sung's evangelistic revival meetings. Currently, if anyone is willing to trust Christ, we usually lead them in a prayer of decision. However, starting at least twenty years ago, if someone was willing to trust

---

[4]Paraphrase of Mt 18:20.

Christ, typically he would be led by an elder brother or sister to a room to confess all of his sins from youth till now. Only this kind of repentance and emptying of sin was viewed as a sign of rebirth. House churches also heavily emphasized prayer and the work of the Holy Spirit due to their emphasis on the inner life. Because in specific historical contexts, other than prayer, there was not much else that could be done. In prayer they sought the Lord, and thus experienced the mighty work of the Holy Spirit. A focus on repentance, prayer, and the work of the Holy Spirit became the spiritual distinctive of house churches, which cannot be divorced from the spiritual impact of the evangelistic revivals of John Sung across all of China and even the whole Chinese-speaking world.

The Chinese house churches in the past have definitely experienced a revival by the Holy Spirit in the inner lives of believers as well as an outward flourishing of the church. Perhaps because of this, soteriology in house churches has not emphasized "justification by faith," by which faith comes from the Holy Spirit. Rather, the emphasis has been on the personal experiences of those who have been saved, born again, and emptied of sin. It lacked a biblical and theological perspective to interpret and define salvation. Today, house churches have begun to pay attention to theology and the inherited creeds.

6. EMPHASIS ON THE LIFE OF FAITH

There is an emphasis that preachers live a life of faith and that there is a pure faith and reliance on the Lord in all ministries. This kind of "not by might, nor by power, but by the Spirit" of God faith is absolutely a very precious part of the house church tradition (Zechariah 4:6). Because in matters of survival, facing an external environment that is not free, preachers need to demonstrate faith in God (if there is a lack of faith in basic areas of life, how will they teach brothers and sisters to truly lean on God?). Especially in difficult places (like in the countryside), they may need to follow Paul's example of "tentmaking" in order to protect brothers and sisters from economic burdens.

It is right for preachers to live by faith and practice self-denial in this way. However, in the past, house churches have overemphasized that preachers needed to live by faith, neglecting the fact that congregants also need to supply their pastors' needs. This should not happen. There are even cases in which a church has the means to provide financial assistance to their preachers and yet holds to the view that it is "unspiritual" for preachers to receive salaries or have the same standard of living as others (do not forget "the laborer deserves his wages," 1 Timothy 5:18). We must reflect on and correct these misconceptions before God. A Three-Self pastor may have been assigned several homes, so it is often hard for them to hold to the truth while worshiping mammon; but house churches also take it too far, often not providing enough for a preacher to have enough to eat.

In the past, we have rarely seen congregants dedicating funds to proactively support the ministries of churches. This is certainly related to the security concerns around designating an offering box. In addition, when we trust God with a pure heart, it is easy to neglect adequate planning and preparation; we typically rely on prayer alone. This approach was very appropriate given the unique circumstances, because we truly needed the Holy Spirit's clear guidance. Moreover, since the churches were so small, adjustments could be made at any time. In the past, it has been very precious to rely on the Lord alone to provide, but we cannot forget that the Holy Spirit works in other ways as well. He is a strategic, intelligent, and wise Spirit. With the growth of churches and the development of collective ministries as Christ's one body, there is a growing need to build careful planning upon the foundation of prayer.

7. A SPECIAL FOCUS ON EVANGELISM

From the late 1970s to early 1980s, rural house churches suffered widespread persecution. Preachers had no choice but to leave their hometowns, and this set off a high watermark in national evangelism and missions. Under the "Three Fixed Policy" [of the government], Three-Self congregations could not freely open new sites or cross regional boundaries to evangelize. Evangelism (here broadly defined) across the city and in rural areas became a distinctive feature of house churches. This has always been a focus of the church and has brought joy and blessing from God.

House churches have always emphasized evangelism, but they lacked a complete ecclesiology; and because of the restrictive circumstances, they have neglected the building-up and shepherding of local churches. In the early days, the harvest was plentiful and need for preachers was acute. Today, we face a situation where evangelists have established so many church sites that there is an increasing need for preachers, especially those with a solid equipping in the truth, a strong testimony of character, and enough insight and wisdom to shepherd believers full time. With the growth of churches, we are increasingly realizing the need to build up churches and form teams of staff.

With God's blessing, the urban house churches have grown significantly in recent years. The size of local congregations has also grown due to break-throughs in church-state relations—slowly evolving from the house-fellowship form of churches to a "congregational" form. Therefore, regardless of their outward manifestation and varying perspectives on ministry, house churches have now overcome some of the limitations of the house church tradition. Under this historical context, discussing and passing down the spiritual legacy of the Chinese house church has become even more precious.

3

TRADITION OF THE HOUSE CHURCH IN CHINA: NONCONFORMIST

WANG YI

Echoing the previous chapter's topic, Wang Yi argues that "house church" is not merely an administrative status but rather a spiritual and theological tradition within Chinese Christianity that connotes particular commitments and ideas regarding faith, church-state relations, spirituality, and the role of the church in the public sphere. He urges believers not to abandon the title in favor of newer terms such as unregistered church *or* independent church, *believing that it is important to maintain the "house church" identity since Christian communities who abandon their traditions and names do not know who they are, where they came from, or where they are going.*

In his writings, Wang Yi frequently declares that there is no public square in China, because all spheres of life remain under the control of the government. As such, Wang Yi maintains that the visible church is the one true public voice in China and that it ought not give up this role, and he plays with the concept of sphere sovereignty in his statement that the essence of the house church is to live out the most public faith in the most private setting.

This chapter is an excerpt from an article Wang Yi wrote on December 14, 2009, and first published on the blog Human Rights in China *under the title "On the Traditions of the House Church and the Openness of the Urban Church."*

What exactly is the "house church," and what is her tradition? Between 2003 and 2006, simultaneously from among the emerging urban churches and Chinese churches overseas, there arose a tendency to question and dilute the house church identity. Some emerging urban intellectuals, middle-class Christians, and ministers have the following view: the separation between the house church and the

church of the Three-Self Patriotic Movement (TSPM) is a conflict among believers of the previous generation and is no longer a conflict for our generation.
However, this view predominantly came from a misjudgment of the signs of
the times and from a mistaken expectation that government policy will be
more lenient toward the emerging urban churches. Some churches intentionally downplay the question of the church-state relationship as the core
concern of the present communist regime, and thus they classify emerging
urban churches as a third type of church, separate from house churches and
TSPM churches.

If we say the greatest deficiency and weakness of the house church in China
is that she has separated herself from the catholic church and the traditions of
the saints throughout all ages, we must of course recognize that the climax of this
separation happened after 1949 as a result of the persecutions by the atheistic-
autocratic government. Yet, a deeper and earlier cause was the pressure of nationalism on the Chinese Christian community. After the Boxer Rebellion and
the Anti-Christian Movement, the relationship between Western churches and
Chinese nationalism created a serious anxiety disorder for the church in China.
Indigenization and separatist tendencies were the two direct descendants of this
anxiety disorder. In light of this, the faithfulness of Wang Mingdao, the view of
sanctification of Watchman Nee, and the Reformed theology of Rev. Jia Yuming
were inescapably situated within this spell of anxiety.

At the rise of the Three-Self Anti-imperialist Patriotic Movement,[1] these
brothers kept the faith through a difficult time by God's grace. They left behind
an invaluable spiritual legacy. And, by the mercy of God, he permitted and made
use of their nationalism as well. Long before the government persecuted these
churches, a group of local churches led by Mr. Wang, Brother Nee, and Brother
Jing of the Jesus Family had already cut off ties with Western churches and their
tithes, finances, governance, and theology. In fact, they were the most "Three-
Self" group of churches, and they became the strongest opposition to and
staunchest fundamentalists against the TSPM. In fact, they were the post-1949
"Non-conformists." However, their reason for rejecting conformity to a "state
religion" has nothing to do with the state but has everything to do with their
faith. The article "We—For the Sake of Faith" by Wang Mingdao is a critique of
"unbelievists" within the church, but it is not directed against the atheist regime.[2]

---

[1]This is an earlier name for the Three-Self Patriotic Movement (TSPM).
[2]Though unusual English, the editors have chosen "unbelievists" as the best translation. It might be
understood as "the unbelieving/nonbelieving faction." See "We—For the Sake of Faith."

In other words, he avoided the topic of church-state relations. He had his own wisdom but also shortcomings in his theological position. Therefore, the position of the fundamentalists after 1949 is to uphold their soteriology but not touch on ecclesiology, views on the kingdom, or the intrinsic conflict between Christianity and communism.

The situation between the Roman Catholic Church and Chinese Catholic priests was completely different.[3] For instance, long before the founding of the TSPM, Fr. Gong Pinmei, along with other priests, pointed out with very clear biblical values and tremendous spiritual courage that the intention of the government is "to build an earthly kingdom of heaven, an anti-Christian utopia," to which he declared, "We absolutely disapprove!" In contrast, within Protestantism, almost no minister was able to provide any profound insight and accurate assessment of the sociopolitical situation of Christianity in China. The nature of the Roman Catholic Church (although we disagree with the doctrines and ecclesiology of the Roman Catholic Church) allowed Chinese Catholic church leaders to cast off the bonds of nationalism upon the Christian faith. However, within Protestantism, all were influenced by nationalism to a certain degree, from liberals to fundamentalists.

Therefore, Wang Mingdao stressed in his public statement that he would not be equally yoked with such unbelieving groups, [such as those led by] Wu Yaozong and Ding Guangxun. However, when the China Christian Council in Beijing made concessions to allow them to organize an independent political study group outside of the TSPM, the issue of church-state relations could not be avoided. At that time, eleven church leaders from Beijing who had not joined the TSPM consulted with each other. After talks, they said they could only join the study group under their identity as "Beijing residents" instead of church leaders because the church has nothing to do with the state. By the grace of God, they were permitted during that special period to assert a complete separatist position to reject the control of the government.

The formation of the fundamentalist (or evangelical) tradition of the house church is a tremendous act of grace God determined to achieve in China after 1949. In China today, this tradition is almost every single Christian's spiritual ancestor and great spiritual legacy, whether his own faith is directly tied to the tradition of the house church or not. However, we also see several defects in this tradition: (1) the latent baggage of nationalism, (2) the local church's

---

[3] See "Chinese Catholic Patriotic Association."

tendency to isolate oneself from the catholic tradition, (3) the ready affirmation of a dualistic sacred-profane view of church-state relations. These three flaws continually need to be addressed and dealt with as the house church undergoes the process of reforming according to catholic theology and the Reformed faith.

Therefore, around 2006 when the State Council was drafting and promulgating the Religious Affairs Regulations, there arose a crisis among the emerging urban churches. By creating an endless list of new terms like the "Unregistered Church," "Independent Church," "Individual Church," and so on, they attempted to separate themselves from the legacy of the house church; they attempted to reject the threat of her historical significance in order to dilute the sixty-year legacy of the house church. In terms of cultural importance, the formation of a name has historic significance; in terms of religious importance, the formation of a name is a matter of the significance of grace and the kingdom. To deny and dilute the concept of "house church" is to deny and forget the grace of God to the house church over the past sixty years. In light of this historic grace, without this Chinese Puritan-like movement of the "house church," we would not know who we are, we would not know where we came from or where we are going.[4] If we conveniently bypass China's history of salvation and say we receive things directly from God, we are being ungrateful.

I met a church coworker in Taiwan.[5] We were talking about Jonathan Chao's back problems. She said, "Many older ministers who have served among the house churches have bad backs. Year after year, they carried boxes full of Bibles, materials, and books, risking detention and deportation to visit villages." The "house church" is an incarnational tradition made up of countless details aligned together by grace. May the Lord have mercy on us so that we will not abandon such a young tradition. Moreover, if we know the defects of the house church tradition we would say, "Those Christians who deny or dilute the house church tradition are actually the 'most house church' Christians of all."

Thanks be to God, in recent years urban churches are still experiencing intermittent persecutions. "Independent registration" is impossible for the

---

[4]In using the word *Puritan*, Wang Yi is mainly pointing to the nonconformist aspect of the Puritans, in which they refused to submit to the religious authority and oversight of the Church of England.

[5]*Coworker* is a title/position within Chinese churches. It can be used for an ordained elder or deacon but can also be used for lay leaders such as small group leaders or leaders in young churches without established deacons or elders.

time being, and a new series of government religious policy adjustments be-tween 2004 and 2007 has come to an end. Particularly between 2008 and 2009, because of the Olympics, the twentieth anniversary of the June Fourth Movement, the problems of Tibet and Xinjiang, the sixtieth national anni-versary, Charter 08, the Nobel Peace Prize awarded to Liu Xiaobo, and the Lausanne Congress, the government continued to try to limit and suppress the emerging urban house churches.[6] In other words, the government has no intention of treating emerging urban churches as a new type of church apart from the house church. The topic of church-state relations has not faded over time; instead, it has become more salient. Therefore, in the past few years, as they face certain degrees of persecution, mainstream urban churches have instead identified more and more with the position of the house church. Indeed, what is the house church and what is her spiritual tradition? These have become important topics for emerging urban churches to consider, clarify, and accept.

To a large extent, what the house church is today is exactly what the church in China will be tomorrow. Understanding the concept, the tradition, and the spiritual significance of the house church directly affects our self-under-standing, our understanding of church-state relations, our understanding of church and society, our understanding of Christ's kingdom, and our under-standing of the relationship between the mission of the gospel and that of the earthly kingdom.

Let me briefly summarize four aspects of the house church tradition in China during these past sixty years:

1) The aspect of faith.

> i. Affirm Christ as the only head of the church, even under totalitarianism.
>
> ii. Affirm the inerrancy and sufficiency of the Bible, even in contem-porary culture.

---

[6]Charter 08 is a manifesto published in December 2008 by Chinese dissident intellectuals and human rights activists honoring the sixtieth anniversary of the Universal Declaration of Human Rights and demanding nineteen changes to the Chinese political system. It eventually included ten thousand signatures from inside and outside mainland China.

Liu Xiaobo (刘晓波, 1955–2017) was an academic, activist, and dissident. In the late 1980s, Liu was one of the most famous Chinese intellectuals to support the student protests at Tiananmen Square and was instrumental in negotiating their departure from the square. He became the first Chinese national to win the Nobel Peace Prize in 2010. He died in prison in July 2017.

2) The aspect of church-state relations.

    i. Affirm the separation of church and state, even under a caesaro-papist system.

    ii. Affirm submission to rulers, even amid persecution.

3) The aspect of spirituality.

    i. Affirm the way of the cross and self-sacrifice.

    ii. Affirm the tradition of fervent prayer.

    iii. Affirm our reliance on the power of the Holy Spirit.

    iv. Affirm the work of active missions in these last days.

4) The aspect of the public sphere.

    i. Affirm nation-states and nationalism as part of God's universal creation.

    ii. Affirm the most private sphere of life (the family) as the space to live out public faith.

According to the four aspects above, one's definition of fundamental truth, the exercises of practical faith, and the relationship between faith and politics, the essence of the "house church" is to live out the most public faith in the most private settings, to borrow Rev. Liu Tongsu's words.[7] Even though today the church has begun to move away from household worship to public worship in nonresidential spaces, the term "house church" still vividly portrays faith as both catholic and private, belonging both to society and the household. Even if the church is pushed against the wall, and even if it is pushed back into a secretive, private residence, the church is still the church of Christ. Today urban churches in China and rural churches are the same. They came from the same origin and received the same grace. This transition from household to society, from the most private to the most public setting, is a sign of true faith, and a premise from which we understand the opening up of the house church.

---

[7]Liu Tongsu (刘同苏, b. 1955) is a Chinese legal scholar and pastor in the United States.

4

RISE OF HOUSE CHURCHES AND URBAN CHURCHES

JIN MINGRI

Jin Mingri's essay is notable given his history with the Three-Self Patriotic Movement and his ability to criticize as a former participant. He provides an overview of what he believes to be the primary strengths of both the rural and the urban house church movements, along with some basic historical overview of their growth. He argues that the house church must answer the question, "What is the church?" The most important thing is not to fight for and establish the house church's legality, for churches should not enjoy greater rights than ordinary citizens. The most important thing is for the house church to "know itself."

This essay is excerpted from a longer article titled "The Rise and Future of China's Urban Churches." It was first published in a book called The Hope for a Whole Life, *edited by Yu Jie and Wang Yi.[1]*

I came to Christ after the June Fourth Movement.[2] After I graduated from Peking University in 1990, I felt called and entered Yan Jing Theological Seminary.[3] I was the first elite university graduate to study at a Three-Self seminary since the Cultural Revolution. Therefore, I started to teach at the seminary two years later, and then pastored TSPM churches for ten years. In 2002, I went to study theology in the United States and returned to China in 2007. On June 3, I left the TSPM and founded the Mandarin congregation of Zion Church. I started with seven

---

[1] Jin Mingri, "The Rise and Future of China's Urban Churches," in *The Hope for a Whole Life*, ed. Yu Jie and Wang Yi (Taipei: The Christian Arts Press, 2010), 49-77.
[2] See "Tiananmen Square Protests of 1989."
[3] Also known as Yanjing Seminary, affiliated with the TSPM.

people. On June 5 I founded the Korean-speaking congregation with a group of about twenty people. At the end of the year, church attendance had exceeded three hundred. In the following year, it grew to five or six hundred. When we first started our church, we sent a notice to the relevant government department in Chaoyang District. This was not a registration nor an application but a "self-introduction." That letter detailed my personal background, where I have studied, and the specific circumstances of our church. It was a clear and self-initiated report, but I wonder if they read the materials seriously or if they just trashed them.

Before 1949, the majority of the churches in China were urban churches, especially in coastal cities. After 1949, almost all the urban churches that were worshiping in the open were incorporated into the TSPM system; opponents were attacked, detained, and persecuted. During the Cultural Revolution, even the TSPM churches were shut down; therefore, urban churches were almost totally wiped out, except for a small number that continued in Shandong and Wenzhou, where the spiritual foundation was more established. After 1979, the revival of house churches started in rural areas such as Henan and Anhui Provinces. Since the 1990s, there were a growing number of urban house churches, and by 2000 it was an explicit revival.

The rural house church certainly has many problems; however, we still need to make a full assessment of its accomplishments.

First, from the perspective of church history, the gospel has never before so broadly and deeply reached the lowest, the most exploited, and the most abused people in China, namely the "least of the brothers."

Second, rural churches have formed a church tradition with Chinese characteristics. For example, a simple-hearted and pure spirituality, patience, and a strong emphasis on prayer. This somewhat resembles the Russian peasants from the Eastern Orthodox Church. These traditions should be protected.

Third, China currently is still a largely agricultural nation, with close to 60 percent of the population residing in rural areas; therefore, we cannot neglect the continued evangelization of rural areas.[4]

Fourth, the main driving force behind rural evangelization is still the rural churches, mainly with teams from rural churches (including migrant workers returning from the cities to the villages). Their strength is nationwide missionary work.

---

[4]Following the global trend, China's rural population has been rapidly declining. According to the World Bank, in 2018 China's rural population made up 41 percent of the population.

Fifth, after the 1990s, the gospel movement of urban house churches was developed with the assistance of rural churches. Urban churches would not have been able to accomplish what they did on their own.

The recent rise of the urban house church in China has important historical and contemporary significance to which we should pay particular attention. The rise of the urban house church is due to the following factors.

First, the wave of urbanization has created an important opportunity for the development of urban churches. One statistic shows that about 43.9 percent of the population in China resides in urban areas.[5] It is worth noting that government surveillance of cities is diminishing. Why did the church fail in the cities after 1949, such that the cities had no place for it? The cities were bustling during the Kuomintang era.[6] The population was highly mobile, and public space was big; therefore, urban churches developed quickly. After 1949, because of the severe and pervasive control of the Communist government and the strict household registration system, many people living in cities were afraid of losing their urban residency status.[7] They were afraid of losing their registration. This gave the church little space to grow. However, the pace of urbanization has exceeded all expectations. There was a huge influx of migrant workers who could choose their own professions; therefore, more social space emerged.

Second, after 1989, intellectuals lost their hope in institutional reform. Some intellectuals turned to religion and a large number of them became Christians.

Third, the failure of the TSPM itself. The TSPM sold its birthright for a bowl of red stew.[8] It is spineless, lifeless, and uncreative. With my ten years of ministry experience in the TSPM, I have a better understanding of the TSPM than most house church ministers. The TSPM is a state-owned monopoly like many other state-owned enterprises. In other words, it is a state-owned enterprise in the religious realm. Just like many state-owned enterprises that cannot meet the challenges of an open market, the TSPM is similarly not able to give a timely and accurate gospel response in the face of the spiritual needs of this new age; therefore, its demise is certain.

---

[5]This figure is closer to 60 percent according to the World Bank and United Nations.
[6]The Kuomintang (KMT), or Nationalist Party of China, was formed by Sun Yat-sen and Song Jiaoren and served as the ruling political party of the Republic of China 1912–1949. At the conclusion of the Chinese Civil War (1945–1949), the KMT surrendered to the Chinese Communist Party and retreated to Taiwan, where it maintained strict one-party control of the island until 1986.
[7]Within China, residency is legally determined by a household registration system called *hukou* (户口). Those who live outside of their permitted region of residency are denied access to local social services, such as retirement benefits and health care, as well as education for minors.
[8]Gen 25:29-34.

In addition, a few decades have past, but the only place where the forces of the Cultural Revolution have not been purged is the religious sphere. In other areas, the forces of the Cultural Revolution were purged after Deng Xiaoping came into power. Only in religious circles has the original cast of characters remained the same. Therefore, they are the most extreme, left-leaning group. Since 1998, the TSPM has been pushing its so-called theological reconstruction agenda, but in reality it is a hyperpoliticized liberal theology that attempts to establish its own authority.[9] At that time, the departure of Professor Ji Tai of Jinling Theological Seminary from the TSPM and the dismissal of Sun Jiaji and two other students because they opposed singing revolutionary songs at the seminary as promoted by Ding Guangxun were earth-shattering.[10] After that, many (including myself) who were advocating tolerance, unity, and compromise also left in despair.

Fourth, following the trend of globalization (including the influence of the internet), international mission teams were able to enter mainland China. Their focus has been mainly on the cities.

I think the first issue for the house church to solve is not the issue of its "legality" or registration, but the establishment and affirmation of its identity and subjective consciousness; that is, to know who it is. At the same time, urban house churches should also face society and work out their cultural mandate.

I don't have a lot of hope for the house church to get registered legally and independently in the short run. Currently, the policy of the Religious Affairs Office is not based on the religious freedom article specified in the constitution; rather, it is based upon Document No. 19 published in 1982 during the Deng Xiaoping era.[11] This Party document stipulates, "Under the leadership of the Religious Affairs Office, all venues for religious activities should be managed by

---

[9] See "Sinicization of Christianity."

[10] Jinling Theological Seminary is another name for the TSPM Nanjing Union Theological Seminary. In 1997, Ji Tai (季泰), a teacher at Nanjing Union Theological Seminary, published an article titled "Discerning the Miracles of This Time" in the *Jinling Journal of Theology*. It highlighted the eschatological significance of Mt 16:1-4 and pointed out the wickedness of the human heart, going against the official theological position of the Three-Self church. Ji was publicly criticized and eventually fired from the seminary in 2000. In protest, three Nanjing Union students and a teacher, Sun Jiaji (孙家骥), left the seminary.

[11] In 1982, the Central Committee of the CCP published "Document No. 19," with the title "The Basic Viewpoint on the Religious Question During Our Country's Socialist Period." It professed to learn from the mistakes made since 1949, acknowledged the complexity of religious issues domestically and internationally, and concluded that the CCP should protect the basic religious freedom of Chinese citizens to practice traditional religions, including Buddhism, Daoism, Christianity, and Islam.

[government] religious organizations and the professional personnel of the religious organization." The authority of a Party document has superseded the constitution; this is absurd! In fact, the TSPM does not have much religious freedom either. The Gangwashi Church where I used to serve did not have legal status; only the *liang hui* ("two organizations") in Beijing have legal status.[12] From a legal perspective, those churches that are controlled by the TSPM and our house churches are in a similar situation. They are only recognized as a "venue" but never as a "church."

Therefore, regardless of how the government defines us, we ourselves need to know what is "the church." More important than administrative registration is the religious legislation. Can legislation be done in the spirit of religious freedom? Until the government is willing to give up the desire to interfere with religion, there is no way to begin such a legislative process. I remember what actor Zhao Dan said before he passed away: "The Party and the government are micromanaging the arts." I can say the same for religion.

Lastly, I believe the house church could not and should not enjoy greater rights than ordinary citizens. In an environment where citizens do not have freedom of assembly, the house church should not expect to receive special treatment like a VIP, foregoing its witness as salt and light. Since God allows us to live in this age with no freedom, he means to let the house church continue to suffer and to be persecuted with other citizens. Today, civil rights are gradually expanding and property laws have emerged. As a part of civil society, space for the house church has also grown. This is the fruit of our hard struggle and also the sovereign guidance of God. We have to fight for religious freedom, but we also have to submit to the lack of religious freedom. If the church could be pacified like Song Jiang, it would not be the church of the Lord.[13]

The house church will need to have its legal identity affirmed eventually, but the key is that we can only accomplish this through the way of the cross. It is not possible to be registered now. And without legal status, there are of course a lot of troubles, e.g., we cannot build a church, members are harassed at their jobs,

---

[12]For many years, Gangwashi Church has served as a model TSPM church for the outside world. President George W. Bush worshiped at Gangwashi when he visited Beijing in 2005. In 1994, Gangwashi's senior pastor, Yang Yudong, was forcibly removed from his pulpit and fired from his position. See "Three-Self Patriotic Movement."

[13]Song Jiang (宋江, 12th century AD) was a legendary figure in ancient China, the rebel leader of a band of robbers. He was captured but received amnesty from the emperor and earned the position of governor of Chuzhou before dying on an expedition to combat other rebel groups.

ministers do not have a legal identity. However, the true church is not afraid of being homeless; the true church is afraid of being spineless. Christ was hung on the cross "in the air." This demonstrates that the world has no place for Christ. However, Jesus conquered the world and drew the world to God.

5

WHY DIDN'T WE JOIN THE NATIONAL TSPM?

SUN YI

Does a church's history define its corporate identity? This is the basic question asked by Sun Yi in response to arguments that the history of the Three-Self's formation no longer matters for churches considering whether or not to submit to its authority. In response, he argues that any institution that requires national loyalty above loyalty to the universal church and to the Great Commission is not fundamentally a church. Sun Yi's arguments examine all global Christian churches, asking us to reflect upon what we sacrifice for comfort and legitimacy within our own particular cultural and national contexts.

Sun Yi was an elder of Shouwang Church and an associate professor in the College of Philosophy and the Institute for the Study of Buddhism and Religious Theory at Renmin University of China. He is now the Director of the Institute of Christianity and Chinese Culture at GETS Theological Seminary in Covina, California. This essay was originally published in September 2010 in Xinghua, *a magazine published by Shouwang.*

1. THE ISSUE

During the two negotiations in March 2010, Shouwang Church in Beijing submitted a proposal to register as a religious venue or to be certified by the Beijing Municipality Religious Affairs Department. However, the church received the same response as it had previously received: according to the State Council Regulation on Religious Affairs, the application to register as a religious venue must be submitted by an existing religious organization (in this case, the Beijing Municipality Protestant Three-Self Patriotic Movement Committee, hereinafter referred to as the Three-Self church).[1] In other words, the Religious Affairs Department still demands that Shouwang join the Three-Self church or become affiliated with the Three-Self church in order to file an application to register as a religious venue.

Shouwang and other churches are often told that, at present, affiliating with the Three-Self church is just a formality, and affiliated house churches can receive benefits such as holding open assemblies and organizing activities. The Three-Self church is also a church; it is not necessary for house churches to distinguish themselves from the Three-Self church and create division. History has entered a new era. Our young generation does not need to bear the burdens of the past.

For some, such as Christians returning to China from abroad, the main reason to join the Three-Self church is that they can then have legal status and be able to carry out religious activities as they did abroad. In particular, unless they join the Three-Self church, Christians might not be allowed to bring religious personnel into China, and their gatherings may be disrupted. Therefore, affiliating with the Three-Self church seems like a good option.

When Chinese Christians travel abroad and are asked why they do not join the Three-Self church to resolve the issue of legitimacy, they should ask the following question in reply: Would you be willing to join the Three-Self church if you face the following restrictions? If a pastor is unable to fulfill his duties, the TSPM may assign another pastor to the church, even if his theological ideas are different from the church or from other pastors. The quota of people receiving baptism each year is assigned by a higher government office. Furthermore, Christians must obtain approval from a higher government office before they can promote Christianity outside of their church buildings. Many people cannot answer this question, because they do not realize how heavily the churches are restricted.

If the problem was confined to these practical issues, some would still argue that they have not heard of these restrictions. Therefore, we should look at the fundamental issue. We have to understand the nature of the Three-Self church by looking at its history. A diseased tree cannot bear good fruit.

2. THE DIFFERENCE BETWEEN THE HOUSE CHURCH AND THE THREE-SELF CHURCH

As a matter of fact, our situation today is not so different from the situation in the 1950s. In the historical context of the 1950s, many Protestant churches joined the Three-Self church because they thought that the churches would benefit and

---

[1] See "Religious Affairs Regulations."

continue to grow under a new historical environment. Only Wang Mingdao openly refused to join the Three-Self church due to "diverging beliefs." He went beyond the thinking that churches would benefit from joining the Three-Self system because then they would be able to continue with their services.

In June 1955, in the *Spiritual Food Quarterly*, Wang Mingdao published an article titled "We—For the Sake of Faith."[2] He categorized the clash between the movement to reject the Three-Self church and the movement to join the Three-Self as a clash between "fundamentalists" and "modernists." He regarded the modernists essentially as nonbelievers and regarded those who followed the modernist line as false Christians. He stated as follows:

> We will not work with these non-believers or participate in any of their organizations. Moreover, even with those who have pure belief and commitment to serve God, we can only have spiritual unity and not organizational union because we cannot find such teachings in the Bible. Our attitude towards belief is as follows: we will accept and adhere to all truth in the Bible, and refuse to accept anything that is not in the Bible. To be faithful to our God, we are willing to pay any price and make any sacrifice. We are not afraid of distortions or schemes.

Wang Mingdao focused on the essence, rather than the superficial benefits. History has shown that this view is more consistent with God's will because these so-called benefits were short-lived. As a result of the Three-Self Patriotic Movement, Chinese churches suffered unprecedented losses. For instance, during the late 1950s, more than 140 churches in Shanghai were merged into eight churches, and only four out of 66 churches in Beijing survived.[3] Dozens of theological schools in China were merged into four schools. The number of Christians and theological students fell sharply. Many faithful Christians were imprisoned for their unwillingness to join the Three-Self church.

Six decades have passed. Indeed, we live in a new era today, and the Three-Self church has also changed. During the 1980s, with the reform and opening policy, the churches in the Three-Self system resumed operations and revived to a certain degree. In 1998, the Three-Self church tried to promote the establishment of theological thought. Some local churches in various places opposed the liberal theology promoted by the movement. The phenomenon shows that

---

[2] See "We—For the Sake of Faith."
[3] The names of the churches in Shanghai and Beijing cannot be identified by the editors. The theological seminaries included Nanjing Union Theological Seminary and Yanjing Theological Seminary.

even some churches under the control of the Three-Self system tried to adhere to the position of the universal church. Although these churches are under the control of the Three-Self system, we should still consider them God's churches because of their desire to return to the universal church, and consider the believers in these churches as chosen people who were kidnapped. We should distinguish these churches and believers within the Three-Self system.

Today, we can clearly see that since house churches are required to be affiliated with certain branches, they are essentially required to submit to the Three-Self system. Similar to previous generations, when we are asked to join the Three-Self church today, we should have a clear understanding of why we refuse to join. We should focus on the fundamental issue instead of seeing only the superficial benefits. Shouwang submitted a document to the State Administration of Religious Affairs stating its position. The document explained the issue very clearly. If we review the statement, we can summarize the [church's] position into the following points.

First, the Three-Self system is a product of a unique historical period. It was created as part of a political movement of the time. Its creation violated the principle of the separation between church and state. Therefore, the Three-Self system does not have the right to represent the majority of the churches, nor to serve as a leading network representing the position of the majority of churches. Naturally, it does not have the right to validate the qualifications of house church pastors.

Second, when we examine the history of the Three-Self Movement, we find that the movement did not promote the growth of the church. Instead many churches were closed, and some pastors and believers were imprisoned for refusing to join the Three-Self church. This outcome was certainly related to the historical context of the time. Nevertheless, the Three-Self church has not expressed any repentance over this painful history.

Third, from the very beginning of its establishment, the Three-Self church has adhered to beliefs and theological positions that are different from those advocated by house churches. The position of the Three-Self church is generally known as liberal theology in church history, while the position of the house churches is called evangelical theology. This difference is one reason why some church leaders refused to join the Three-Self church during the early stages of the Three-Self Movement. Today, in the theological construction of the Three-Self church, there are still practices that challenge the inerrancy of the Bible and weaken the basic Christian doctrines such as justification by faith alone. Such teachings have deviated from basic Christian belief and cannot be accepted by the house churches, which hold fast to the evangelical position.

Fourth, holding to the Three-Self principle does not mean that churches have to join the Three-Self system. However, the Three-Self system has confused these two issues. In the process of establishing the Three-Self Movement, the Three-Self system mistakenly identified adherence to the Three-Self principle as joining the Three-Self organization. Recognizing the Three-Self principle does not mean that churches should be required to join the Three-Self system. Moreover, the Three-Self church was itself not established according to the Three-Self principles. It was established by taking advantage of the vacuum [left behind] when political movements drove missions and missionaries out of China, by seizing church properties (in most cases without proper and formal takeover), and by receiving government support for these actions. The Three-Self church enjoyed benefits from both sides and yet proclaimed that it followed the Three-Self principles of "self-propagation, self-support, and self-governance." This is inacceptable to churches who actually adhere to the Three-Self principle.

Fifth, willingness to join the Three-Self system should not be a standard for patriotism. In 1954, the name of the Three-Self Reformation Movement was changed to the Three-Self Patriotic Movement. Afterward, the Three-Self church used patriotism as a political tool to exclude other groups. Consequently, in the social environment of that time, there appeared the logic that not joining the Three-Self system meant opposing the Three-Self system, and opposition to the Three-Self system was unpatriotic, and being unpatriotic was counterrevolutionary. Today we are building a harmonious society, and this logic is considered the product of the extreme leftist.[4] If government departments continue to use this logic as their implicit rule to manage religious affairs, many Christians who refuse to join the Three-Self system but love their country will be excluded. This outcome will cause great harm to patriotic citizens, disrupt social harmony and stability, and hinder national development.

In conclusion, today we should look at the dispute from two major perspectives. We should hold fast to the principle of separation between church and state. The best way to do this is to adhere to the principle articulated by Wang Mingdao. For the sake of our beliefs, we should not unite with an official organization which is not, by nature, a church.

---

[4]"Socialist Harmonious Society" (和谐社会, *hexie shehui*) was a sociopolitical concept developed under Hu Jintao to inspire and signal reform in response to perceived economic inequities and social injustices in contemporary China.

3. NON-CHURCH NATURE OF THE THREE-SELF CHURCH

The Three-Self church is not, by nature, a church. It cannot represent churches, and it has no right to manage churches or to require house churches to join the Three-Self system. The Three-Self church is not, by nature, a church; we can explain this fact from the following three aspects. First, the Three-Self church was created during the Cold War in order to help the state reach certain political goals through various political movements. Second, in terms of its objectives and responsibilities, the Three-Self church is still an arm of the Chinese Communist Party and it holds patriotism as supreme. Third, in terms of structure and operation, the church is a quasi-governmental organ. It is not self-governing or self-supporting. It contradicts the Three-Self principle. Now we will explain these aspects in detail.

First of all, if we look at the historical background of the creation of the Three-Self church, we can see that the Three-Self church was obviously the product of a political movement during the Cold War. Moreover, from the very beginning, the church took "cutting off relations with imperialism" as its fundamental goal. From "Direction of Endeavor for Chinese Christianity in the Construction of New China," which was the founding declaration of the Three-Self Movement, we can clearly observe that the Three-Self Movement has two fundamental goals or guidelines.[5]

The declaration clearly stipulates the first fundamental goal of the Three-Self Movement as follows:

> The Chinese Protestant church and its organizations shall use maximal efforts and effective methods to make church followers clearly understand the evil that imperialism has brought to China through the use of Christianity. They shall exterminate the imperialist influence within Christianity and guard against imperialism, in particular the American imperialist scheme to foster counter-revolutionary forces through religion. Meanwhile, they shall call on the religious masses to participate in the campaign to oppose war and support peace, and shall educate the religious masses to completely understand and support the government's land reform policy.

The declaration stipulates the second fundamental goal of the Three-Self Movement as follows:

> The Chinese Protestant church and the organization shall use effective methods to foster a patriotic and democratic spirit and dignified and confident

---

[5]See "The Christian Manifesto."

mentalities among religious followers. The Three-Self ("self-governance, self-support, self-propagation") Movement that Chinese Christianity has advocated has made great progress. In the future, we should finish the task in the shortest period of time. Meanwhile, we should advocate self-criticism. In various works, we should reflect on mistakes, sort out issues, and adhere to frugality of economy, in order to reach the objective of the Protestant Reformation.

In conclusion, cutting off all the ties with imperialism and fostering the patriotic spirit among religious believers were the major principles and goal of the movement.

On September 23, 1950, the front page of the *People's Daily* published the full text of the declaration and a list of signatures. Meanwhile, the *People's Daily* published an op-ed titled "Patriotic Movement of the Protestant Christians." On the next day, major national newspapers published the declaration. Thus the declaration and signatures evolved into a patriotic movement backed by the government. The disagreement over different stances within the church became a political choice of whether believers were patriotic or not.

After the Korean War broke out, the relationship between China and Western countries became tense. China became directly involved in the war against the United States of America. During that time, the Preparation of the Chinese Protestants Resisting American Aggression and the Aiding Korea Three-Self Reformation Movement Committee was established, and Wu Yaozong was elected as the president of the committee. Afterward, this new national organization replaced the Chinese Protestant Promotion Committee and became the organization that assumed the task of completing the Chinese Protestant Three-Self Reformation in the new era. According to the summary of committee president Wu Yaozong, the committee set up tasks. First, to promote patriotic activities and patriotic education among Christian organizations and Christian masses. Second, to completely wipe out the influence of imperialism on Christianity. Third, to complete the task of the Chinese Protestant Three-Self Reformation according to the plan. The first two tasks obviously had top priority at that time. To complete these two tasks, one important measure was to carry out the campaign to force the Christian masses to denounce their evil behavior.

Using the analogy of "pulling out the root," Wu Yaozong described the denunciation of imperialism as follows:

> In the last eight months, the reformation movement, like a knife and a saw, has dealt a hard blow to the trunk of the old tree. This conference is like a huge axe

aiming directly at the trunk. The trunk is shaking. Although the tree has not fallen down, it is destined to fall. However, even if the old tree falls, we have not completely gotten rid of the problem because the tree has many roots. At a certain time in the future, we shall engage in the hard work of digging up all the roots which are still hidden beneath the earth.[a]

During a meeting that was held in Beijing from July 2 to August 6, 1954, the Protestant Three-Self Patriotic Movement Committee was formally established. At the meeting, Wu Yaozong gave "The Working Report of the Chinese Protestant Three-Self Reformation Movement in the Last Four Years." In summarizing the achievements in the past few years, he proposed the following tasks for the Three-Self Patriotic Movement in the future: first, call on Christian believers all over China to support the Chinese constitution and join the construction of a socialist society. Second, call on Christian believers all over China to oppose imperialist aggression and fight for long lasting world peace. Third, organize believers and pastors all over China to undergo patriotic education and eliminate imperialistic influences completely. Fourth, implement the principle of autonomy and promote unity within the church. Fifth, conduct research on church self-sufficiency and assist churches to reach self-sufficiency. Sixth, conduct research on the self-propagation and the spreading of Christianity in accordance to the principle of mutual respect.[6] Last, adhere to the spirit of patriotism and devotion to Christianity, promote patriotism and obedience to the law, and purify the church. Most of these tasks focus on anti-imperialism and patriotic education.

Therefore, we can see the major objectives and tasks of the Three-Self church. In summary, this religious organization is not only subjected to the leadership of the Party and the state, it also assists the Party and the state to implement the Party's policy. These are the basic tasks of the patriotic religious organization. They are clearly stipulated in Document No. 19 ("The Basic Viewpoint and Policy on the Religious Question During Our Country's Socialist Period") of the Chinese Communist Party Central Committee, promulgated in 1982, which states,

The basic task of these patriotic religious organizations is to assist the Party and the government to implement the policy of freedom of religious belief, to help the body of religious believers and personnel to raise their patriotic and socialist consciousness.[b]

---

[6]Wu Yaozong proposed abandoning calls for personal repentance as a component of evangelization and conversion.

This patriotic religious organization effectively functions as an assistant of the Party and the state. As a matter of fact, under the current political system and legal framework, the national patriotic religious organizations of various religions have effectively assumed the administrative duty of managing and controlling religions; they have become monopolistic interest groups.[c] They have oligopolistic control of the Chinese religious community.

Moreover, in terms of operational mechanisms and personnel management, on the one hand, the leadership of the patriotic religious organizations seems to be elected by such different religious organizations. On the other hand, the candidates have to be certified or approved of by the leadership departments (United Front Work Department and Religious Affairs Department). In the case of Christianity, the charters of all Three-Self churches in China stipulate that the chairman, vice chairman, general secretary, and standing committee members are to be elected by the Christian representative conference, which is the supreme power organ of the church. However, the real procedure is quite different. First, the Religious Affairs Department nominates the candidate. Second, the personnel at the Religious Affairs Department organize the election. Third, the Three-Self Patriotic Church holds a nominal election. Fourth, the Three-Self Patriotic Church submits the election outcome to the Religious Affairs Department for certification. These procedures show that the elections are held merely to implement the personnel decisions of the Religious Affairs Department. The qualifications and development of religious personnel should be based on a person's loyalty and dedication to a religion and his or her belief and command of religious doctrines. However, when religion and state are not separate, this principle is weakened or even replaced. Consequently, the certification and appointment of religious personnel is largely decided by the Religious Affairs Department.[d]

The Religious Affairs Department controls the personnel decisions of religious organizations through an undisclosed personnel system. Consequently, religious organizations have become a part of the government structure. The national and local arms of these religious organizations and national religious schools are all listed in the government structure, and the administrative budget and personnel are listed in the plan of the Party and the state. Salaries of religious personnel and administrative budgets are provided by the government.[e] In this sense, the religious organizations are extensions of the state and can be regarded as quasi-government organizations.

Therefore, in terms of the historical background behind its creation, as well as the objective, function, structure, and operation, it is clear that patriotic religious organizations are not, by nature, churches. Pastor Wang Aiming, the Vice Director of Nanjing Union Theological Seminary, has directly pointed this out:

> The existence and development of the Chinese Protestant Three-Self Patriotic Movement Committee is to carry out the ruling party's task and to safeguard the ruling party's authority and enterprises. The Three-Self movement and the China Christian Council, referred to as the "Two Organizations," are basically the civil organization in charge of religious affairs in the Chinese political structure. They are not churches.[f]

Indeed, an organization cannot be called a church if it does not make Jesus' Great Commission its primary objective but rather makes the religious policy of the ruling party and the state its primary objective.

If the Three-Self church is not, by nature, a church, yet it supervises the churches in the Three-Self system, isn't this a relationship that requires some scrutiny? Bishop Ding Guangxun reflected on the reasons and origin of this relationship from a historical perspective:

> After the Korean War broke out, foreign funds in China were frozen, and the financial support for different mission agencies suddenly stopped. Their leadership and management structures broke or even collapsed. The Three-Self organization at various levels had to assume some functions of the leadership and management structures of various agencies. Through successive waves of political movements, the government increasingly emphasized a highly centralized leadership. This emphasis affected churches. In many places, the real leadership power over churches inevitably transferred to the Three-Self organization, even though the Three-Self organization did not have the intention to take over power. However, in this way, in many places, the Three-Self organization changed from being a mass movement that advocates patriotism and the Three-Self principle to an organization that supervises churches. It is like a church but it is not a church. It is like a government department but it is not a government department.[g]

It had to be created because of the political environment during the Cold War. Does the Three-Self system then have a reason to exist today? Should we maintain this strange relationship today?

4. FUNDAMENTAL REASONS FOR NOT JOINING THE THREE-SELF CHURCH

Once we understand that the Three-Self church is not, by nature, a church, but rather is a government organization, we can understand Wang Mingdao's position from a new perspective. Wang Mingdao said that believers and non-believers cannot be yoked together. Today we can use this position as the fundamental explanation for why house churches cannot join the Three-Self church. House churches and the Three-Self church (which is essentially not a church) should not be yoked together. The Three-Self church receives funding from the state, and its primary mission is to fulfill the duty assigned by the Party and the state. What do the Chinese house churches have to do with the Three-Self church?

The Three-Self system's mission is to perform the work designated by the ruling party, or the secular government. Joining the Three-Self system would fundamentally transform the church. The system might shift the church from being part of the universal church to simply being a Nationalist church. For instance, when the primary task of the Three-Self Movement was to sever ties between Chinese Protestantism and imperialism, the movement's concern was nationalism, not its allegiance to the universal church. From the perspective of the catholic church, churches in China indeed need to develop into independent Chinese churches. However, this does not necessarily mean that Chinese churches should be isolated from churches in other countries. Chinese churches are brothers of the churches in other countries (whether they are so-called imperialist countries or socialist countries). Christian belief is above the state, and the church's universality is above nationalism. For this reason, even during the 1950s, many Chinese Christians did not agree with the conclusion that Christianity was a tool of the imperialist cultural invasion and that the pastors were at the vanguard of this invasion, because this conclusion was made from a nationalistic perspective, not from the perspective of the universal church.

The difference in the basic position tests whether the church has really adhered to the first commandment of the Ten Commandments: "You shall have no other gods before me" (Exodus 20:3). In joining the official Three-Self system, which is not a church by nature, and being subject to the leadership of the Three-Self system, churches undoubtedly have to answer a big question. Should the church wholeheartedly serve the one true God? Or should the church serve the god of the Three-Self system, which is above the church and supervises the church to treat patriotism as the primary objective? If it follows the requirements of the Three-Self system and takes "wiping out the imperialist influence" as the primary task, the church certainly loses the foundation of the universal church and adopts a nationalistic position.

Indeed, a non-church official organization can require the church to put patriotism above religion. However, for a church, to love God is always the first priority. Patriotism is not the mission and basis for the church's existence in this world. It is fundamentally wrong to put patriotism as the precondition of the church's existence in the world or in the country.

As a matter of fact, a church does not need to take the position of the state and demonstrate patriotism by speaking for the ruling party or the state. If a church sacrifices its root to express its love to the motherland, this love is basically worthless because the existence of the church is worthless, like salt that has lost its taste. "If salt has lost its taste, how shall its saltiness be restored? It is no longer good for anything except to be thrown out and trampled under people's feet" (Matthew 5:13). Only when churches stand firm in the foundation of the universal church through dependence on Christ will they be able to express their respect for secular power and their love for their neighbors. This is the proper starting point for patriotism.

Today, to continue to have significance to the Chinese churches, the Three-Self principle should be demonstrated in the following ways: first, churches should have autonomy before the government. That is, the government department would have some authority to manage social organizations, but Christian churches should have autonomy over their doctrinal teaching. Second, churches should be self-supporting and should not be supported by the government with taxpayer's money. Third, churches should have the right of self-propagation. In other words, based on their inheritance and acceptance of Christian beliefs, churches should be able to freely spread the gospel and should not be subjected to any restrictions. These measures would demonstrate the basic principle of separation between church and state. However, in reality, we see that the non-separation between church and state has caused a very ironic phenomenon. The so-called Three-Self system, which nominally promotes "self-governance, self-support, self-propagation" cannot itself have "self-governance, self-support, self-propagation." The phenomenon reveals the conflict between the non-church nature of the Three-Self church and their principles of "three-self." This conflict deserves our serious consideration.

NOTES TO THE ORIGINAL ARTICLE

[a] Wu Yaozong, *Rebirth of Chinese Protestantism*, 4.[7]

[b] "The Basic Viewpoint and Policy on the Religious Question During Our Country's Socialist Period," in *Selections of the Documents on Religious Work in the New Era*, ed. Comprehensive Research Group of the Document Research Office of the Chinese Communist Party Central Committee and Bureau of Policy and Regulation of the State Administration of Religious Affairs (Beijing: Religious Culture Press, 1995), 65.

[c] Xie Yue, *Political Communication in Contemporary China* (Shanghai: Shanghai People's Press, 2006), 32-38.

[d] Cao Zhi, "Analysis of the Archival System of the Chinese Religious Personnel," Paper at the Seventh Annual Conference of Religious Social Sciences.

[e] Xing Fuzeng, "State-Religion Relations in Contemporary China," 72. Liu Peng, "Characteristics and Development of Chinese State-Religion Relations," *Journal Ding* 88 (August 1995): 4.

[f] Wang Aiming, "On Church Belief: Thoughts on the Basic Issues of the Church Theology of Chinese Protestantism," *Nanjing Theological Journal* 4 (2008).

[g] Ding Guangxun, "Sorting Out the Relations Between the Three-Self Organization and the Churches," *Nanjing Theological Journal* 6 (1989): 2.

---

[7]Wu Yaozong, "Rebirth of Chinese Protestantism," in *The Collected Works of Y. T. Wu*, vol. 4, book 2, *From the Founding of the PRC to Wu's Late Years (1950–1979)*, ed. Ying Fuk-tsang (Hong Kong: The Chinese University of Hong Kong Press, 2020).

6

CHRISTIAN RIGHTISTS OF 1957

WANG YI

*In 1957, the Chinese Communist Party (CCP) initiated the Anti-Rightist Campaign (反右
运动, fan you yundong) to weed out intellectuals critical of the government. The CCP
first encouraged open criticism of the Party under the auspices of helping it to improve; then the CCP denounced, attacked, and punished those who spoke up. Scholars
estimate that 550,000 Chinese intellectuals, many of whom were top professionals in
their respective fields, were politically persecuted in this movement. Though less frequently discussed, thousands of Christians, mostly from Three-Self churches, were
also caught up in this movement. The CCP used the term* Rightist *for anyone deemed
lacking in revolutionary commitment, too timid, or compromising.*

*In this originally lengthy article, which we have excerpted, Wang Yi argues that the
success of the Anti-Rightist Campaign was dependent on the preceding formation of
the Three-Self Patriotic Movement and the subsequent persecution of those who refused to join, most notably Wang Mingdao. His primary thesis is that, "Before 1957, the
Communist Party used the 'Three-Self Movement' to suppress the Christian fundamentalists. After 1957, the Party used the 'Anti-Rightist Campaign' to destroy the
Three-Self Movement. The curse of universal rebellion against the Lord had such
immediate effects."*

*Wang Yi identifies liberal theology as underpinning the leaders of the TSPM and
fundamentalism as the key marker of the first generation of house church pastors.
Though Wang Yi himself does not identify as a fundamentalist theologically, he carefully names and lists the many house church pastors and leaders who suffered or
were martyred for their refusal to join the Three-Self, arguing that the blood they shed
in their steadfastness to the fundamentals was the seed of the gospel revival currently
taking place in China. A key issue Wang Yi addresses is the role of nationalism in the*

formation of the state church. He flatly rejects criticism of Western missionary activity in China and argues for the catholicity of the Christian faith.

Wang Yi first published this article on the blog Democracy in China (民主中国, minzhu zhongguo) on August 5, 2007, to mark the fiftieth anniversary of the Anti-Rightist Campaign and the two hundredth anniversary of the arrival of Robert Morrison, the first Protestant missionary in China. He later revised it in 2017 to commemorate the five hundredth anniversary of the Reformation and posted it on his personal blog. The original article is quite lengthy and has been excerpted here. The editors have used ellipses where content has been removed for the sake of brevity.

None is righteous, no, not one.

ROMANS 3:10

As a human being, to fight for my own complete, righteous, and pure right to life is eternally irreproachable. As a Christian, my life belongs to God and my faith. To continue my way, my path, the path of the servant of God! A political path for Christ! First of all, this young person has paid a heavy price mentally and physically. She earned this for you, and she paid for you.

LIN ZHAO'S LETTER FROM JAIL, WRITTEN IN BLOOD

CHRISTIAN RIGHTISTS

Christian Rightist Li Jinghang is a survivor of Jiabiangou Labor Camp.[1] A mathematics teacher in Tianshui. I know him because in the spring of 2002, author Xing Tongyi used twelve cassette tapes to interview him and wrote "The Life of a Christian Rightist."[2]

Christian Rightist Yu Yile. I know her because she was imprisoned with Lin Zhao.[3] When Beijing University student Lin Zhao was imprisoned in 1961, she was jailed with Yu Yile. They did not only become fellow inmates, they also

---

[1]Jiabiangou Labor Camp was a forced labor camp used during the Anti-Rightist Campaign from 1957 to 1961. Its prisoners suffered from overcrowding and severe starvation, leading to mass fatalities.
[2]Xing Tongyi, *Like a World: Looking Back at Jiabiangou* (Lanzhou: Lanzhou University Press, 2004).
[3]Lin Zhao (林昭; 1932–1968), was a dissident who was imprisoned and executed by the CCP during the Cultural Revolution. In 1962, while serving a twenty-year sentence, Lin used hairpins, scraps of bamboo, and her own blood to write commentaries and poems sharply criticizing Mao and the CCP. There is scholarly debate surrounding the extent to which Lin's Christian faith influenced her political activism.

became sisters in Christ. From being a follower of Chairman Mao to being an uncompromising critic of totalitarianism, Lin Zhao became a Christian and eventually a martyr who had compassion for her executioner. In recent years, she has been considered the Joan of Arc of China by liberal intellectuals.

Christian Rightist Yang Yudong. On December 26, 1957, he was labeled one of forty-five Christian Rightists during the "Beijing Christians' Socialist Symposium."[4] He was sent to a labor camp in the following year. In 1986, Yang Yudong agreed to become the senior pastor of the TSPM-affiliated Beijing Gangwashi Christian Church under three conditions: (1) the church will not study politics; (2) sermons will be based only on the Bible; (3) the Bureau of Religious Affairs will acknowledge publicly its mistake in labeling him a Rightist. During the June Fourth Movement, the young adult fellowship led by Rev. Yang was the one and only rescue team carrying the cross.[5] In 1994, Rev. Yang broke with the TSPM and has since been serving in the house church.

Christian Rightist Wu Weizun wrote in his personal reflections, "Through the study of social history, I realized that the grand narrative of ape to human, all the way to the communist society, is one big lie."[6] In 1957, he was sent to a labor camp for reform and then he was arrested at the dawn of the Cultural Revolution, during which he was sentenced to life imprisonment. Before entering jail, he laid out his principles: "Do not answer, do not explain, do not confess, do not repent." From then until his death in December 2002, he pursued these principles for the greater part of his life. Although Wu Weizun was subjected to all kinds of physical torture, he can be considered in China as "the only one who openly refused to read quotations from Chairman Mao." Up through the seventies, the exhausted prison authorities continued to give him two simple requirements: stop praying before meals and read the quotations of Chairman Mao. If he obeyed, he would be considered reformed and released from prison. However, Wu Weizun continued to resist until death. Contained within his emaciated body was the unimaginable amazing power of the Chinese intellectual.

---

[4]In 1957 and 1958, authorities gathered more than two hundred Christian leaders at Fuxue Hutong Seminary in Beijing for the "Beijing Christians' Socialist Symposium" for daily reeducation on imperialism and socialism. The meetings resulted in forty-five attendees being labeled as "Rightists."

[5]During the 1989 student protests in Tiananmen Square, a hunger strike was organized. It began on May 13 and lasted for six days, drawing global attention to the student protests. Various groups of citizens voluntarily formed teams to provide food, water, medical aid, etc., to the striking students. Wang Yi here refers to one such team organized and led by Yang Yudong.

[6]For all quotes in this chapter, see Wang Yi's bibliography at the end of the chapter.

~

On June 1, 1972, church leader Watchman Nee—imprisoned for being anti-revolutionary—passed away. Two weeks after his death, the *Hong Kong Times* printed an article using data from 156 newspapers and 57 magazines from the mainland to make an accurate but incomplete estimate:

During the Three-Self Renewal Movement between 1950 and 1953, about 60,000 Protestant Christians were imprisoned. Among them 10,690 were executed. During the TSPM-led Anti-Rightist Campaign from 1957 to 1958, innumerable Protestant Christians were classified as Rightists and about 2,230 of them were executed.

THREE-SELF MOVEMENT: THE COLLAPSE OF FAITH

Long before the Anti-Rightist Campaign, the Communist Party—with the help of the Three-Self Preparatory Committee, Wu Yaozong, and Ding Guangxun, and so on, all of whom adopted the political positions of anti-imperialism, patriotism, and affirmation of the Communist Party—attempted to unify the fragmented Christian church. In September 1949, the Communist leadership appointed five individuals, including Wu Yaozong and Liu Liangmo, as representatives of Christianity (even though they had no significant ecclesial standing) to participate in the Chinese People's Political Consultative Conference that gave birth to the new government. The government greatly promoted their status. Wu Yaozong led a delegation of religious representatives to tour the country and was welcomed by the heads of local government and Party leaders everywhere. Afterward, Zhou Enlai met with nineteen Christian leaders led by Wu Yaozong three times during May 1950 and began to show his hand to the church.[7]

During the first meeting, Zhou Enlai set the tone for Christianity in China by equating evangelism with imperialist invasion. For this, he had three recommendations: first, the church should launch an "anti-imperialism patriotic" campaign to clean up her relationship with imperialism and clean up imperialist traitors from among the believers. Second, Christianity should be restricted in the new China and should not be allowed to do street evangelism. Third, the church should be independent and cut off her relationship with imperialism to build a "self-governing, self-supporting, and self-propagating" church. Until today, the spirit of these words continues to be the guideline of the Protestant

---

[7]Zhou Enlai (1898-1976) served directly under Chairman Mao as the first Premier of the People's Republic of China from 1949-1976.

TSPM and the fundamental interpretation of recent church history by the official religious academy.

During the second meeting, Zhou Enlai began to issue threats, saying the church should fulfill her own "historic mission" and affirm the "common program," so that "religious activity would benefit the new democratic society." He proposed a specific restriction: the church should not invite foreign missionaries to do ministry in China, nor should she raise funds overseas.

During the third meeting, the focus was on the church-state relationship. Zhou Enlai turned and showed good will toward the church, saying that the united front of the government needed to expand. He asked if the church would join the United Front.[8] The key focus was not idealism or materialism but rather whether it "had severed all ties with imperialism, feudalism, and bureaucratic capitalism." But he made two vicious threats. First, to reaffirm the necessity "to clear out the black sheep and those very few bad apples from the religious community," so that the larger Christian community would not experience discrimination because of those few villains. Second, he requested the church to go through an internal self-criticism, to conduct a "review and restructuring."[9]

These three speeches of Zhou Enlai, one after another, are like the three temptations of Satan for the Chinese church in the wilderness (Matthew 4:1-11; Luke 4:1-13; Mark 1:12-13). They swiftly cornered the church leaders of the whole country. Shortly afterward, Mao Zedong addressed the plenary session of the Chinese Communist Party Central Committee on June 6, declaring that "imperialism, which has established church schools and religious reactionary forces in this country, is our enemy and we need to fight against these enemies."

What was called religious freedom under the "new democratic regime" was now ruined. Christians and church leaders in China subsequently made their choice. Most compromised and betrayed their Lord and their friends. Few were like Jesus, who rejected Satan in the wilderness, and refused the power of the Communist Party, instead taking the path of martyrdom and apologetics. The distinction between these two paths created today's Three-Self church and house church.

At that time, the faith of Wu Yaozong and others was influenced by liberalism (modernism). Including him, several key figures in the TSPM camp had studied

---

[8]See "United Front Work Department."

[9]"Self-criticism" was originally developed within Marxism-Leninism and has served as a method for public interrogation and shaming within communist societies. The National Congress added it to the CCP's constitution in 1945 and the Party has never abandoned its use.

at the stronghold of liberalism—Union Theological Seminary in New York, USA. They indeed had a sincere patriotism and anti-imperialist mentality, just like all other liberal intellectuals at that time, full of hope for the new regime and the socialist revolution. Just as liberal theologian Zhao Zichen, who was deeply influenced by the social gospel, wrote in a sad tone in 1948, "A large number of young people who have no regard for their personal safety are standing with the Communists; they will never put the hope to save the nation on the church."[10]

These Protestant liberals, who were more and more left-leaning politically, started to surround Wu Yaozong. In 1948, Wu Yaozong wrote the article "Tragic Times of Christianity," declaring that the essence of Christianity in China is "capitalism and imperialism." He said, "If our thought is the same as that of Western Christianity, we have become the unconscious tool for western imperialist aggression. In the eyes of the people who desire liberation, we are nothing but opium."

These Protestant "Christians" recognized the meaning in social services; however, because of their bondage to liberal theology, they were not able to move toward orthodox soteriology in order to properly and comprehensively understand the relationship between personal salvation and social change. Therefore, for them, "Christ's salvation and social change are the same thing." Their so-called Christian faith was not so different from secular socialism. In November 2006, Wu Zongsu, son of Wu Yaozong, defended his father before officials from the Bureau of Religious Affairs in a ceremony to move the body of his father to another cemetery and continued to insist that Wu Yaozong believed "there is no contradiction between Christianity and Communism."[11] Chinese church history expert Fr. Charbonnier from France determined in his own work that this is exactly why the TSPM developed from liberal Protestantism. The Communist Party obviously took notice of the thoughts of Wu Yaozong and others, for "they attached great importance to it and fully utilized it."

Especially after the outbreak of the Korean War, Western missionaries were expelled quickly from China. A few were arrested by the government. In the country, national sentiment was high and this touched the liberal church leaders.

---

[10]Zhao Zichen (赵紫宸, Tzu-chen Chao or T. C. Chao, 1888–1979), was a leading Protestant Chinese theologian in the early twentieth century. Zhao advised Chinese Christians to remove all Western influences from the faith and to connect Christianity to Confucianism and humanism.

[11]When Wu Yaozong died in 1979, he was buried with his wife in a Christian cemetery in Beijing. His son fought to relocate his parents' bodies from Beijing to a more prestigious cemetery in Shanghai and to reinstate their status as patriotic citizens.

Wu Yaozong wrote the essay "The Communist Party Educated Me" and the president of Chongqing Theological Seminary wrote "The Process of Change in My Political Thought." Subsequently, during the TSPM Renewal Movement, these became the representative essays for the coerced indoctrination of many Christians. The conclusions at the ends of the essays affirm that only communist theory is correct: "Only Communism can save China and the world!" They acknowledge that they have changed from reformists to revolutionaries.

After the government issued three threats, other church leaders felt that a storm was coming. They lost hope in the word in which they believed and also the sovereignty of God in history. They came to believe that if they did not compromise, the church would be thoroughly ruined. Because of their small faith, thinking that they were suffering for Christ, they accepted codependency on politics. As the president of Shanghai Devotional Seminary, Reformed theologian Jia Yuming publicly declared, "Joining the TSPM is against the will of God." However, in the spring of 1954, after several officers from the Bureau of Religious Affairs talked to him in his office for a few hours, he publicly joined the TSPM and was elected the vice president of the TSPM. Local church leader Watchman Nee opposed the TSPM in the early years; however, very soon he changed his position and even defended the TSPM saying, "The church is the cup and the government is the plate." It is certainly reasonable to place a cup on a plate. But because his influence was too great, the government decided to make an example of him. In 1952, Watchman Nee was arrested for counterrevolutionary crimes in Shenyang.

Many others just followed the trend out of fear. There were also other secret members who were sent by the Communist Party a long time prior to penetrate the church as undercover agents. They secretly organized and agitated using the same strategies as were used in the Anti-Christian Movement of the 1920s. For example, the key person and spy who organized the TSPM in Shanghai was "Reverend" Li Chuwen. In 1961, he was promoted to be the national general secretary of the TSPM. During the Cultural Revolution, when he couldn't withstand being beaten by the Red Guards, he produced his Communist Party membership card to beg for mercy. He asked the Red Guards to call Premier Zhou to verify that he was indeed a Party member. After his identity was exposed, he left the Christian community and was named the director of the Office of Foreign Affairs in Shanghai. After the Economic Reform, he was transferred to assume the position of deputy director of the Xinhua News Agency in Hong Kong.

Afterward, Wu Yaozong followed "the instructions of Premier Zhou" and quickly produced a declaration of the Christian political position, titled "The Path of Chinese Christianity in the Construction of the New China," in order to unite Christians in the country around the goal of loving the country, loving the Party, opposing imperialism, and opposing the United States.[12] According to the instructions of the government, they invited forty church leaders to join as founding members. The last draft of the declaration was personally finalized by Premier Zhou and approved by the State Council before publication in *The People's Daily* on September 23, along with the first group of 1,500 signatories. On September 26, the Central Committee of the Chinese Communist Party published "Instructions Concerning the Protestant and Catholic Response Towards the 'Christian Declaration' Movement." Afterward, with the government's support, the TSPM launched a multiyear signature movement to betray the Lord.

In China at that time, about 10,000 churches, 8,000 ministers, and 840,000 believers faced the same litmus test. They had to sign in order to protect themselves. If you signed, you were patriotic; otherwise, you were counterrevolutionary. 180,000 had signed by April 1951; 360,000 had signed by the end of the year. When the TSPM was founded in 1954, 416,000 had signed their name. That was about half of the believers in the country.

After 1949, why did the Communist Party use the carrot-and-stick method to control the church, but did not use violence to eradicate the church? A high-sounding explanation is what Chairman Mao called, "The internal contradictions among the people." However, you can consult the speech of the first director of the Bureau of Religious Affairs, He Chengxiang, when he met with the delegation of the Australian Anglican Church in November 1956.[13] He plainly said there were three reasons: first, Christians usually are skilled and could be reformed to serve the construction of socialism. Second, the good relationship between Christians and the Western countries could be used. Third, the government did not want to manufacture martyrs who would give rise to greater resistance.

In addition, the central government's Li Weihan, who was responsible for religious affairs, once directly explained this to the Party's left wing during an

---

[12] See "The Christian Manifesto."

[13] Although foreign missionaries and Christian workers were driven out of China after the 1949 revolution, the TSPM occasionally invited delegations to return for visits in order to demonstrate religious freedom in China. In 1956, Nanjing Union Theological Seminary hosted a delegation from the Australian Anglican Church.

internal meeting in 1961. Why have imperialism, landlords, and capitalists all disappeared among us and yet religion remains? Li Weihan said allowing religion to continue to exist "is more conducive to 'hindering' religious faith than 'encouraging' religious faith." He opposed radical methods, such as launching atheist education and debates among religious believers. He explained that maintaining a degree of religious freedom "takes into consideration the united front both at home and abroad, so I hope all will understand." However, this moderate position disappeared one year later and Li Weihan suffered criticism and was regarded as a revisionist. He was considered a model of capitulation. Soon afterward, the government began a season of forced religious expulsion. Li Weihan was also forced to participate in a "No-Religion Zone" experiment. He was sent to work in Wenzhou to completely "rub out" the Christian church.[14] But Wenzhou's underground church continued to grow. After the Cultural Revolution, it became an area that experienced the greatest revival, even becoming the so-called Jerusalem of China. After the reform and opening of China, Li Weihan admitted that "this policy to get rid of religion was a complete failure."

However, since the elite intellectuals in China at that time were still submerged in the romantic ideals of the New Democracy and the prejudices of the Anti-Christian Movement of the 1920s, not a single intellectual touched the topic of the relationship between communism and freedom of religion. Almost nobody took note of the political destiny of a marginalized group like the Protestants. What the Protestants encountered between 1950 and 1956 included litmus tests, coerced indoctrination, and indictment meetings. These were all repeated in 1957 and became the nightmare of the intellectual. When a society has lost its freedom of religion, it will inevitably also lose the general freedoms of thought and speech. From Premier Zhou's restriction of faith and persecution of Christians to the all-out restriction of thought and persecution personally conducted by Chairman Mao in order to "draw the snake out of its hole," these remind us of the piercing confession of Rev. Niemöller during the Nazi era:

> First, they came for the Communists; I did not speak up because I was not a unionist. Then, they came for the Jews; I did not speak up because I was an Aryan. Then, they came for the Catholics; I did not speak up because I was a Protestant. At last they came for me, but none was left to speak for me.[15]

---

[14]See "Wenzhou."

[15]This is a poetic version of the postwar confession made by Martin Niemöller (1892–1984) before the German Confessing Church in 1946.

MARTYRDOM AND APOLOGETICS: A CHAPTER IN THE HISTORY OF FREEDOM IN CHINA

The most ironic thing is this: a so-called self-governing, self-supporting, self-propagating Three-Self Movement has established a religious organization that is completely dependent on the ruling regime while it gives up on biblical truth and accepts the reality of political control. It is a phenomenon rarely seen in the two millennia of church history. Using the words of Wu Weizun, "this 'self' actually represents the absolute sovereignty of the party and government of China over the Chinese church of God." For Christians, this is no longer the church of Christ, nor is it the Christian faith. Those who openly rejected the TSPM to defend the Christian faith and the freedom of conscience were in reality the truly independent and indigenous churches in China. However, the main goal of the TSPM is to eradicate them for the regime.

Before the beast of totalitarianism, how might the dignity of human and the freedom of their conscience stand? When we observe China after 1949 and see 410,000 Christians collectively signing their names to become part of the "Three-Self Movement," it shocks the soul. It is an unprecedented spiritual battle on the land of China. When the godless totalitarians came, the Christian missionary effort that took root in China over the period of 150 years became like strands of grain in the field, turning frail and falling in the twinkling of an eye.

The value of the Communist Party is to inform all intellectuals of one thing, that is, that their knowledge and convictions are not sufficient to sustain their character before the dictator. Their backbones can be easily broken. Even for the Christians in China, their God allowed them to be weak so that they could easily fall away from their declared beliefs. This is like Israel of the Old Testament, who as a nation repeatedly betrayed and strayed away from the Lord God who saved them. Just as the Bible said, even in this kind of national betrayal, God still kept seven thousand for himself (1 Kings 19:18). In every generation, the Holy Spirit has prepared his witnesses. The promises of the Lord God to Abraham will never fail. There will be seven thousand who will not bow to the idol, whether it is a statue of wood and mud, or politics, or a nation.

In the history of the Chinese church, and in the most respectable chapter in the history of freedom in China, during the TSPM the Lord has "reserved seven thousand" among the Chinese people. From the beginning of the TSPM, approximately one hundred thousand Protestants from independent churches walked toward the house church because of their uncooperative and disobedient attitude, rejecting the coerced indoctrination of the government. Thereby they established the post-1949 house church tradition. It is also the first time in which a living tradition was born in the history of China through nonviolent means to resist tyranny for the sake of faith and conscience. This is not something humans can sustain by their ethics and strength, because many who are stronger have succumbed. This is a miracle that can only be done through the grace of the Lord and Christ's supernatural preservation of his church.

The majority of them were passively uncooperative and continued to hold underground worship. There were also other church leaders who, even under severe political pressure, held public worship, publicly expressed their views, and publicly defended their faith. In early church history, those who defended the gospel in the midst of active persecution were called "apologists." In the 1950s, the Protestants in China gave birth to this kind of apologist.

One that can be called the apologist of Protestantism in China was the leader Mr. Wang Mingdao from an independent church in Beijing. He opposed the TSPM from the start, thus becoming its eyesore. In 1954, the church in Beijing held a condemnation meeting against Mr. Wang Mingdao. At the end of the year, he published the article "Truth and Poison" against the position of Wu Yaozong and declared, "In the Bible, there does not exist the poison of imperialism, rather only the pure truth of the Lord."[16]

He warned Wu Yaozong,

You are more truthful if you directly say that these teachings are the poison of Jesus and the Apostles. I only want to ask you if the scriptures I have quoted above are the poison of imperialism?[17] If you are not willing to say yes, then please remove all these intimidating masks. If you say yes, please then remove your sheepskin, terminate your relationships with the church, and declare that you are no longer Christians or church leaders. Then perhaps you should quickly organize an anti-Christian alliance and conduct another anti-Christian campaign. Then at least you would be more honest in your work than now.

In 1955, Wang Mingdao published another lengthy article "We—For the Sake of Faith," publicly criticizing Wu Yaozong and other TSPM leaders as "unbelievists."[18] He objected to having union with unbelievers or working with

---

[16]Published in the *Spiritual Food Quarterly* in 1954.

[17]The Scriptures quoted are Ps 10:4; 14:1-3; 36:1; Prov 9:10; 13:20; 2 Cor 6:14-18; Rom 12:1-2; Eph 2:1-3; 5:6-10; Phil 2:14-16; 1 Jn 5:19; Mt 7:15-20; Rom 16:17-18; 2 Cor 11:12-15; Gal 1:6-9; 2 Tim 2:15-18; 2 Pet 2:1-3; and 2 Jn 7-11.

[18]Published in the *Spiritual Food Quarterly* in 1955.

them. He refused to cooperate because they had taken different paths. "Do not be unequally yoked with unbelievers" (2 Corinthians 6:14). Wang Mingdao's standpoint has two emphases. The first concerns the church-state relationship. The church should not lean on the government, nor should the government have any political control over the church. The second is to object to the theological liberalism of the TSPM's leaders. He affirmed the authority of the Scriptures and the fundamental doctrines of faith. His second emphasis is based on the first.

These two articles have become the classic documents for upholding freedom of religion for the Chinese house church in the twentieth century. "We—For the Sake of Faith" especially had a great impact in the church. Some who joined the TSPM were moved by the article and left. In fact, during the political persecutions after 1949, those who upheld the freedom of religion and went to worship in the house church were mostly Christians who were called "fundamentalists." Christians who did not uphold the authority of Scripture might have been believers on a regular day; however, when political authorities suddenly became harsh and brutal, they were no longer able to believe in an authority and faith that is higher than the nation. Those who believe in Christ because of the Scriptures believe in him regardless. Those who believe in themselves may not even believe in themselves when they meet the communist.

The Christian faith became the source of courage for these Christians in the face of totalitarianism. When they fell, the gospel was their motivation to repent and stand back up again. After Wang Mingdao published "We—For the Sake of Faith," the authorities decided to arrest him. On August 7, 1955, he preached his last sermon, "The Son of Man Was Sold into the Hands of Sinners." That night, he was arrested with his wife and eighteen believers. On October 29, the authorities declared that all Christian activities apart from the TSPM were illegal. Since then, refusal to join the TSPM has constituted grounds for arrest.

Afterward, the TSPM launched conventions in different regions to denounce Wang Mingdao. Believers who supported and sympathized with him were arrested as "Wang Mingdao sympathizers," and among them was the famous minister Lin Xiangao of Da Ma Zhan Church in Guangzhou. Even a sister in Shanghai was convicted as a counterrevolutionary and sentenced to house arrest for more than twenty years because she "prayed for Wang Mingdao." Another believer purchased a book by Wang Mingdao for a sister in Xiamen and was classified as part of the "Wang Mingdao Counterrevolutionary Group" and was sentenced to eighteen years of hard labor. As for Wang Mingdao himself, after being tormented in prison for fourteen months, he could stand it no longer. In September 1956, he signed a confession prepared by the police and was released from prison.

After Wang Mingdao was released, he felt that he had betrayed the Lord like Peter and had denied Christ before others. After a year of rest and recovery, one morning he held his wife's hand and walked into a police station in Beijing. He said to each astonished police officer, "That confession does not represent my faith. I come here to deny my signed confession." Wang Mingdao was imprisoned once again and was sentenced to life imprisonment, while his wife was sentenced to an eighteen-year prison term.

On that morning, that old couple, who held each other's hands, exemplified the response of true believers who trust in the Lord. When I think about the sufferings of this country after 1949, the Lord has brought me some small but definite warmth through them. There were not only one or two people like these. From 1950 to 1958, all the way until 1979, from ministers to laymen, from cities to villages, they shone like stars in the night sky. The voices of the apologists and the blood of the martyrs have been flowing from the cross to tens of millions of house church believers in China.

The political hurricane of the TSPM also blew to the Catholic church.[19] However, few priests were affected by liberalism. Their apologetics and martyrdom were more decisive than the Protestants. They were unmoved and were firmly supported by the Vatican. In a letter written by the Apostolic Nuncio Antonio Riberi of the Vatican to the bishops in China, he publicly denounced the TSPM. On September 5, 1951, he was deported by the Chinese Communist Party. In 1952 and 1954, the pope published two encyclicals, *Cupimus Imprimis* and *Ad Sinarum gentem*.[20] He criticized the TSPM for seeking "to finally establish a 'national' church, which no longer could be Catholic." This is a biblically accurate and insightful criticism. The pope encouraged the Catholics in China to remain loyal to the faith.

Like Wang Mingdao, countless priests, such as Beda Chang, Joseph Chow, Ignatius Kung Pin-Mei, and Dominic Tang, have become praiseworthy servants of the truth and defenders of the faith.[21] Under severe pressure, Beda Chang

---

[19]See "Chinese Catholic Patriotic Association."

[20]Pope Pius XII (1876–1958).

[21]These were leaders of the underground Catholic church in China. Zhang Boda (张伯达, Beda Chang, ca. 1905–1951) was a Jesuit priest who was imprisoned and tortured in Shanghai for his

publicly stated, "There is not one thing that the church has done in China that was not for the benefit of the Chinese people. Therefore, to death I will not sign this declaration."[22] He was subsequently arrested and died of torture after three months in a detention center. In Chongqing, a young priest named Dong Shizhi, gave a moving speech before a group of Catholics who were chanting patriotic slogans.[23] Although it was not widely circulated, it is comparable to that of Rev. Niemöller:

> Today, they want us to attack the representative of the pope in China—Nuncio Antonio Riberi. Tomorrow, they will want us to attack the pope—Christ's representative on earth. The day after that, will they not want us to attack our Lord, the highest God—Jesus Christ himself?

Many intellectuals struggle to understand how widespread Christianity is in China today. Or they may still have doubts; they are afraid that Christianity and communism have a similar kind of exclusivity. However, since 1949, Christians and others in China are all living in the misery of totalitarianism. But the church, although it is living in a similar kind of suffering and general fallenness, lives out a dissimilar tradition of apologetics and martyrdom. Though weak, she still lives out a firm tradition of freedom of conscience. In 1979, many intellectuals were vindicated.[24] And then it was discovered that among this crowd of social elites, you couldn't find even one clean person. You couldn't find a role model among either the living or the dead; you couldn't find a praiseworthy paragon with a majestic backbone who publicly protected a living tradition. But Christians in China had their hopes rewarded at this time. They could see among themselves saints like Wang Mingdao, Yuan Xiangchen, Lin Xiangao, Xie Moshan, and the so-called Chinese Epaphroditus, Wu Weizun. They could see

---

refusal to submit to Communist authorities. He died in prison in 1951 and he has been venerated by Shanghai's Catholics as a martyr. Archbishop Zhou Jishi (周济世, Joseph, 1892–1972) was the highest-ranking Roman Catholic priest in China when the Communists came into power in 1949. He was arrested and imprisoned for refusing to take leadership in the government-sanctioned CCPA. Archbishop Deng Yiming (邓以明,Tang Yee-ming, Dominic, 1908–1995) was a Jesuit bishop appointed by the Vatican in 1951; he later became archbishop of Canton in 1981. He spent twenty-two years in jail without trial for his loyalty to the Vatican and died in exile in the United States.

[22]Zhang made this comment in March 1951 when a leader began promoting the TSPM at an education conference.

[23]Dong Shizhi (董世祉, birth and death unknown) was a Benedictine priest who was arrested in 1951. Dong refused to denounce his bishop and criticized the CCP's demand for allegiance. After his arrest, Dong disappeared and his whereabouts became unknown.

[24]Mao Zedong died in 1976 and in 1979 Deng Xiaoping visited the United States and decided to exonerate many Rightists.

a large group of native evangelists suffering for the sake of righteousness. They were a cloud of witnesses among Chinese Christians for defending their faith and freedom of conscience. They bore witness that Chinese Christians also suffered with the Chinese people under the five-star flag.

In 1979, intellectuals were vindicated and received reparations. Some old Rightists praised Hu Yaobang and Deng Xiaoping for restoring order with the same passion they had used to praise Chairman Mao. However, ministers like Wang Mingdao and Wu Weizun surprised people once again by refusing to be released from prison. The government used all kinds of deception to coerce and threaten them out of prison, similar to the ways they were initially thrown into prison. In 1979, Deng Xiaoping visited the United States. US President Carter demanded that the Communist Party release Wang Mingdao. Deng Xiaoping promised to make it happen by the end of the year. The prison authorities told Wang Mingdao that he only needed to express a willingness to submit to reform, then he could be released. However, Wang Mingdao said, "Since I was sentenced to life imprisonment, I should comply with the government's sentence. Unless the government admits that it was wrong, I can only be released at my death." Afterward Deng Xiaoping directed that he should be released by the end of the year, whether he acknowledged his crime or not. Therefore, right before the Chinese New Year in 1980, the prison couldn't do anything but carry Wang Mingdao out of prison and shut the door behind him.

Since the 1950s, Wu Weizun wrote "Letters from Prison" one after another to be circulated among the house churches. On May 28, 1987, he was coaxed to leave the prison and wrote "An Essay Submitted on the Day of Release" to the court, saying the sentence commuted in 1981 was a lie. They had changed his "unrepentant" status to "has repented." The essay can be considered the most moving article written in Chinese after 1949. It surpasses all that has been written by millions of intellectuals combined:

> Here, risking the suspicion that I am protesting against the government and the proletariat regime, (I thought the court may understand), I want to briefly and concretely describe the unrepentant behaviors I committed for twenty some years since I was imprisoned in July 1964: On July 30, 1964, I was summoned by the Metropolitan Police Department of Tianjin. Beginning from the first pretrial, except for name and other minor details, I stopped answering the questions of the pre-trial officers, including those that had nothing to do with the subject. In fact, I refused to give account to any of the alleged crimes. . . . In these twenty some years of imprisonment until now, I have refused to speak,

write, and participate in anything that is related or possibly related to "confession" or the "reforming of criminal nature." During my sentence in these twenty some years, after innumerable big meetings, small meetings, lessons, discussions, and panel discussions, as long as they are related to reform, I have not spoken, or shown my attitude, or indicated my understanding, or responded to any inquiry from the officers or other prisoners. I would be so careful that I would not recite any documents, newspapers, or quotations; nor have I sung any revolutionary songs, etc., lest I would be implicated in the "reforming of criminal nature." Although every prisoner was required to write oaths, plans for reform, thought reports, reform reflections or summaries, sometimes even mandatory "reform diaries," I have written not a single word. In exams for political history, news, ethics, law, etc., I would submit an empty sheet of paper except for my name. From these countless facts and actions (if the court only investigates a little, it will recognize this consistent and irrefutable truth), this is to say I have not accepted any "coerced indoctrination and criminal reform." I have refused them all.

Starting today, when I step outside the prison walls, I may take further action in two respects. One, I will not use the release certificate to process any paperwork. I will not return to Tianjin or the south to reunite with my friends and relatives. I will not enjoy the freedom or right that comes with this erroneous ruling. I will not leave the prison to go anywhere to join any company, or accept any job offer (including the job of a factory worker). Even though I had to step outside the prison walls (in order to not interfere with the duties of the prison guards), I still consider myself a criminal being sentenced to life imprisonment (regarding this life sentence, although I rejected the verdict and I remained unrepentant, I still faced it with submission and I will continue to accept it with a willing attitude). On the other hand, from the day I am discharged from prison, I will fast on a limited basis (as long as I don't face any external interference or coercion, it will be maintained within limit to sustain life; however, if there is interference and pressure, it is another matter). I want to communicate two things with this fast: (1) I am not in the slightest bit repentant over any of my "crimes." (2) Accordingly, the verdict in 1981 was wrong and fictitious, and I reject this erroneous verdict.

Afterward, Wu Weizun rented a house outside the prison. He limited his movements and food. He was willing to be an inmate outside of prison. He used a sharp and yet nonviolent way to combine his absolute faith and freedom of conscience with his version of absolute submission to the state, until he left the world. At least before him no non-Christian Rightist could say, "You have not given in because you have not suffered enough." Also not one democrat or libertarian could say, "What Christian Rightist Wu Weizun left behind did not constitute a part of the grand value of freedom."

INDICTMENT MOVEMENT: DISCIPLINES DURING THE ANTI-RIGHTIST CAMPAIGN AND THE CULTURAL REVOLUTION

During the early 1950s, the TSPM brought counterinsurgency indictment meetings and condemnation meetings into the church. In the subsequent political campaigns of the Anti-Rightist Campaign and the Cultural Revolution, these evolved into exercises in coerced indoctrination of intellectuals by the state.

Although Zhou Enlai demanded the Protestants go through self-criticism and remove "imperialist minions" from the church, the influence and reputation of Wu Yaozong and others in the church were not sufficient to set off a great condemnation campaign. The TSPM definitely needed a direct push from the state. This time Guo Moruo, who was vice premier at the time, presented *The Report on the Policies of Dealing with Cultural and Educational Charities and Religious Groups Who Receive Subsidies from the U.S. (The Report)* in the State Council meeting on December 29, 1950.[25] The State Council then promulgated regulations accordingly. In *The Report*, Guo Moruo stated, "Religious groups who received subsidies from the U.S. should be transformed into groups that are completely self-governed by Chinese religious believers." He also deceptively announced that "the government should encourage religious believers' self-governance, self-support, and self-propagation movement." A few days later, led by Wu Yaozong, twenty-six Christian leaders announced that they embraced this new policy and welcomed government personnel into the churches. The government started to directly interfere with churches. In merely two months, nineteen Christian colleges, over 200 Christian middle schools, over 1,700 Christian elementary schools, hospitals, and orphanages nationwide were all put under the government's control. Since then, the Christian church, which has a history of 150 years, has been expelled from mainstream society. The *Jiefang Daily* commented that the phrase "Christian schools" had been sent to the historical museum.

---

[25] *The Report* is publicly available at www.laoziliao.net/rmrb/1950-12-30-1.

Wu Yaozong presented a report to the State Council regarding the TSPM over the previous eight months, showing that 80 percent of Christians nationwide had signed the Three-Self announcement. Patriotic and religious teachings started to appear from churches' pulpits. Chinese national flags and government leaders' portraits had been hung in churches in big cities like Shanghai, Nanjing, and Tianjing. Believers organized and led anti-imperialist, patriotic parades. And then, he also added that the movement had not been implemented deeply enough; many signers were just perfunctory.

Representing the State Council, Lu Dingyi gave the main speech, advocating for even more rigorous policies toward religion. He announced the purpose of the conference was to "completely eradicate the influence of American Imperialism's cultural invasion for over 100 years." He suggested three harsh requirements: first, Christians should fight against the American Imperialists among them who pretend to wear religious clothing. Second, Christians should be required to actively engage in the Korean War, the Land Reform Movement, and the suppression of counterrevolutionaries. Third, signatures of the Three-Self Announcement should continue to be collected.

Sadly, all 154 church leaders accepted the "Joint Statement of the Chinese Christian Churches and Groups" from the conference, which claimed to finally, radically, forever, and completely cut off all relations with the American mission boards and other mission boards, in order to achieve the goal of Three-Self Chinese Christianity. Jean Charbonnier once criticized this for completely denying the universality and transcendence of Christianity. From then on, Chinese churches started to "focus on the ideal of nationalism" instead of relating to the "sufficiency of the basic doctrines of Christianity." Furthermore, the statement proposed that the church should "aid the government in reporting any counterrevolutionaries and their followers who are hiding in the Christian religion" and should "actively promote accusations against imperialists and anti-revolutionaries" in Christian churches and groups throughout the country.

Henceforth, a large-scale movement of betrayals and accusations among Christians began in Chinese Christianity—a rare occurrence in two thousand years of church history.

In order to teach Christians to make accusations against their brothers, the council held a two-day "denunciation conference." Eighteen representatives of the conference took their place and started the process, beginning their denunciation with Morrison—the first Protestant missionary to China—then on to other Western missionaries and even down to their own brothers.

~

Additionally, Chen Chonggui published a statement titled "Accusation of the American Imperialists for Their Invasion into China Through Religion," which began with his denunciation of the English missionary Robert Morrison. The statement was deceptively concocted, and the scholarship was full of inconsistencies. For example, it said that Robert Morrison drafted the Treaty of Nanjing, but he had already died eight years prior. In reality, it was his son, John Morrison, who acted as translator in the negotiation between China and England.

The most shocking accuser was a man named Wang, the secretary of the Qingdao Christian Association. He denounced Gu Renen, a pastor who was already treated as a counterrevolutionary at the time, bellowing out this question to the 153 Christian leaders, "Should this man be executed?" Some answered from below, "Yes, he should be executed." *The People's Daily* then reported the next day, "The conference was flooded with the angry chants of 'kill, kill, kill!'"

Thus, a national denunciation movement began. After the denunciation conference, an illegitimate church leadership structure was organized under the title "Three-Self Revolutionary Movement Committee," and the chairman was Wu Yaozong. Later, he expressed in the Three-Self publication *Tian Feng* that "the unity of Christianity is not an easy matter. But now, under the guidance of the government, different denominations and groups within Christianity are united under the banner of patriotism."[26] The representatives returned to their respective origins, propagating the spirit of the conference. The Three-Self Committee opened their first meeting and passed the decision to "universally launch the denunciation movement against the imperialists and their followers, who are hiding in the church." Among others, it encouraged Christians to "organize denunciation services within the churches, then expand them to city-wide church denunciation conferences." It also commented that if a church were to hold such denunciation services, it would "receive the guidance and help of the local government." The committee recommended "conducting the denunciation services in the alternating rhythms of tension and alleviation," in order to maximize success. The accusations were then to be recorded and "submitted to the local newspaper report."

Wang Mingdao once again defended the faith and the freedom of conscience, and he opposed these denunciation conferences firmly. He believed that they went against the very teaching of "do not judge" in the Bible (Matthew 7:1-6).

---

[26]See "*Tian Feng.*"

He said to the brothers who sinned that one can only carry out discipline according to the principles of Matthew 18, not through accusations in order to attain certain political goals. In response, Wu Yaozong rebutted that "accusations perfectly fit into the teaching of Jesus." He exposited Matthew 23 as an example in which "Jesus vehemently accused the Scribes and the Pharisees." In just two short months after the committee was formed, there were 63 denunciation services throughout the country. By the end of the year, 123 churches had conducted large-scale denunciations a total of 228 times. Because of Wang Mingdao's influence, the effects of such services were less harsh in Beijing. Thus the Three-Self conducted an unprecedented denunciation service in its place of origin, Shanghai, and it was attended by around 10,000 Christians. Wu Yaozong led the accusation, saying,

> The American Imperialists sent missionaries to China, with the purpose of using Christianity as a tool of invasion into Chinese politics, in order for America to colonize China. They sent missionaries to China and they traveled across the whole country, pretending to preach the gospel to mask their spying activities.

Wu Yaozong continued, "The American Imperialists kept a bunch of so-called 'church leaders' in Christian churches and groups." He then mentioned the names of some pastors in the local region. The service ended but not without the crowd chanting, "Long live the Chinese Communist Party! Long live Chairman Mao!"

In order to eliminate some of the psychological barriers in Christians, some pastors even shared their "spiritual joy" while denouncing others. An example is Cui Xianxiang, who described that he was struggling with insomnia the night before the denunciation conference, but after a period of "painful emotional conflict," he finally received "eventual joy." Cui Xianxiang noted that he had determined to appeal to Christian leaders in two thousand other churches to hold such national denunciation conferences. Liu Liangmo, who was elected as the secretary of the Three-Self Committee, even shamelessly declared that "the joy in the heart after the denunciations is indescribable. This is what we Christians mean by being 'born again.'"

The Committee even used the results of such denunciation conferences as the criteria for setting up a Three-Self church. The requirement was that a church must denounce at least four members before they could apply for property tax exemption. However, when Satan was unleashed in the hearts of men, not even the Three-Self Committee—the devil's representative—could control the rage of such denunciation conferences. If they could betray their Lord and Savior, what could stop them from betraying their brothers? Under such hopeless, fearful, and dismal circumstances, some Christians began to deploy these satanic methods against Satan himself, and these denunciation conferences were soon directed against church leaders who supported the Three-Self Movement.

In September 1951, a believer by the name of Cui Meide published an article titled "Accusations Against the Imperialist Dog Yang Shaotang" in the *Tian Feng* publication. Yang Shaotang was a member of the standing committee, who later became the deputy secretary of the Three-Self Committee. In the same month, a denunciation conference was held in Nanjing, and Watchman Nee's supposed imperialistic spying activities were denounced. Soon after, theologian Zhao Zichen was accused of holding pro-American thoughts, and he was deposed from his position. Because these figures only passively complied with the Three-Self Movement, the Committee was still willing to let these denunciations happen. But in July of the same year, the deputy chairman of the national Three-Self Patriotic Movement, Chen Chonggui, was surprisingly accused in a denunciation conference in Chongqing, and his accusers were almost all his students. This unexpected turn of events made all Three-Self leaders extremely insecure. Some conducted public self-criticism for fear of being denounced, such as Jia Yuming, who confessed to some inadvertent ties with American imperialist ideas. Even Wei Yisa, the leader of the True Jesus Church, who had no connection whatsoever with the American missions, published a self-criticism article titled "My Reflection" in *Tian Feng*.

Meanwhile, the Three-Self Committee became the testing ground for cultural brainwashing. From November 1951 onward, they began to hold political trainings for thought reform inside the church, starting with the cohort of political trainings for Christians. This experiment was adopted nationally by political committee, and thus "The Decision to Implement Learning Exercises for Thought Reform in Every Profession" was passed in the beginning of 1952, endangering every profession in the nation. But the beginning stages of this Three-Self reformation movement was not well received. In Beijing alone, there were eleven independent representatives who publicly refused to attend these reformation classes, may the Lord remember their names.

A year later, at a national Christian conference, the director of the Religious Department of Eastern China criticized that "many were not serious in learning, and the people who attended secret meetings are increasing." In May 1953, the committee demanded that no church should invite Wang Mingdao, Wang Zhen, Yuan Xiangchen, and others to preach, in an attempt to force these eleven church leaders into submission. From August 1953 onward, other than these eleven fundamentalist groups, pastors and preachers in churches in Beijing all attended these political reformation classes.

The denunciation movement tapered down at the end of 1952. At that point, almost all the Chinese churches had capitulated to the Three-Self. Only a small minority of believers continued to hold on to the true word, transitioning themselves to underground secret gatherings. This Three-Self Movement affected everyone, from liberal Christians, to Roman Catholics and Muslims, even down to Buddhists and Taoists. The Communist Party successfully used Protestant Christianity as a launching pad to build an empire of puppet organizations in a short span of three to five years.

As a Christian, I cannot deny that the Chinese church committed many atrocities after 1949. The Lord of these Chinese Christians henceforth poured out his curse and wrath upon this race: large buildings collapsed, skies turned dark, ten plagues, the killing of firstborns. I admit that the political turmoil in China in the last fifty years was not only caused by the unprecedented totalitarianism of the Communist Party, but it was also caused by the large-scale betrayal of the Lord by Chinese Christians, which has brought curses upon their brothers.

On one hand, I am grateful for the traditions of the house church. I respect the fundamentalists who held on to the true word because they chose to be faithful until the end and to suffer together with the country. They brought blessing in a time of cruelty with their faith and freedom of conscience and thereby altered the fate of China. But on the other hand, most Christians were either assaulted by a new wave of ideas or abandoned their faith to avoid persecution. Their choices also brought the country into greater suffering. They not only crucified Jesus Christ once again, but they sold their Christian brothers, their Roman Catholic brothers, and even their whole nation to Satan.

In retrospect, believers like Wang Mingdao and Wu Weizun were the only true patriots because they also truly loved their Lord. They sacrificed themselves for their brothers and for the generation in which the Lord placed them. They knew that in order to "love your neighbor" in a dark generation and to bear beautiful witness to the gospel, there is only one pathway—to stand firm, unflinching in submission and quietness in the face of persecution, just like Christ on the cross. Today, the house churches are fighting for liberty. Although they have sympathy and support from mainstream society, the foremost agenda on their list must still be repentance. If we are the true church, then the onus is on us to confess to the sins of our unbelief before God and men which led to the apostasy of the church as a whole and her capitulation to the totalitarianism of the Communist Party after 1950.

We uphold the position of the house churches, because our predecessors lived a tradition of martyrdom and apologetics. Nevertheless, the fact remains that the Three-Self Patriotic Movement started within Protestantism. This is the shame of every Christian before the Lord and nation. Viewing the relationship of the house churches and the Three-Self Movement from this perspective, house churches ought to uphold their position while avoiding self-righteousness. They should come before the Lord and confess their sins on behalf of the Chinese churches and pray for the ignorant brothers and sisters who are still under the oppression of the Three-Self churches. May the Lord swiftly call his children away from the Babylonian exile in accordance to his will.

ANTI-RIGHTIST CHURCH: NONE IS RIGHTEOUS

The reality about the Three-Self Movement is that it is a political movement that suppresses Christianity and the freedom of religion. Some have called it the "First Cultural Revolution" after 1949. The Communist Party understood one thing better than the intellectuals of 1957—in order to destroy freedom of speech, they first had to destroy freedom of religion. Thus the nationalization of the Communist Party after 1950 followed this order: first, they "confiscated" the religion of the church; then they "confiscated" the assets of the capitalists; finally, they "confiscated" the speech of the intellectuals.

Intellectuals were the last to be plundered because their applause and support were needed during the first two rounds of confiscations. Decades later, the last two rounds of confiscation were denied, on paper at least, but regretfully the results of the First Cultural Revolution are still part and parcel of contemporary Chinese society and politics. So much so that the majority of intellectuals and the general public are still living in a religion-specific "cultural revolution" today.

In 1954, the intellectuals were still ignorant of the tempest that was only a few years away; they were still full of passion for the early stages of a utopian nation; they were still indifferent to the religious groups who seemed to be so foolish. That year, the Party arrested almost all the Roman Catholic priests who opposed the Three-Self on the basis of alleged spying. Gong Pinmei, a Roman Catholic priest in Shanghai, not only protested publicly against the Three-Self Movement under such circumstances, but he firmly asserted his opposition toward the entire "New China." In *Opposing the Grand Strategy*, he declared that "the government appealed to a grand strategy to build a socialist New China—that is to build a heaven on earth. This is impossible and temporal, socialism cannot be realized, and we cannot defend this grand strategy." In reality, in 1954 none of the intellectuals were clearer in their thoughts than him. Gong Pinmei was a parallel of Wang Mingdao in the Roman Catholic camp. In a few months, he was arrested as a counterrevolutionary, and a movement to expose and defame Gong Pinmei started throughout the country in the Roman Catholic Church.

Hence, before the tempest of the Anti-Rightist Campaign in 1957, the political persecution to eliminate outsiders from within Christianity was almost complete. Huge swathes of fundamentalist Christians who held on to the truth and opposed the Three-Self Movement were arrested, condemned, exiled, or executed as counterrevolutionaries, spies, or thugs. Watchman Nee, who had already been imprisoned for four years, was sentenced to fifteen years imprisonment before the Anti-Rightist Campaign. Together with Wang Mingdao, their imprisonment marked the end of the First Cultural Revolution. Thus, the Anti-Rightist Campaign in Christianity was not directed toward Christians outside of the Three-Self but toward the newly established Three-Self Patriotic Movement. The arrest of Watchman Nee caused many congregations in the Three-Self to leave; the arrest of Wang Mingdao encouraged many believers to continue on this path of the cross. Thus, many Christians who opposed the Three-Self were arrested or imprisoned during the Anti-Rightist Campaign. For example, Lin Xiangao of Guangzhou was sentenced to twenty years of imprisonment on November 24, 1958. Song Tianying, the daughter of evangelist John Sung was also arrested in 1958 and was sentenced to eighteen years of imprisonment as a counterrevolutionary. But this is merely an extension of the First Cultural Revolution, and it basically has nothing to do with the Anti-Rightist Campaign.

Of course, there were still some independent leaders who were not labeled as "counterrevolutionaries." These were labeled as "Rightists" during the Anti-Rightist Campaign. One of the more famous individuals was Mr. Yuan Xiangchen. Just after Christmas in 1957, the Religious Department of Beijing organized a church leadership reformation class, and Yuan Xiangchen attended the class without saying a word for several days. Eventually, the director by the surname Li requested that he speak. After a period of silence, Yuan Xiangchen noted two points. On the first point:

> The current religious policy is not reasonable, and it is unfair to different religious groups. For example, it is very relaxed toward Islam, but strict toward Christianity, so much so that there is no freedom in Christianity.

On the second point:

> There are some in the Three-Self Movement who have been through three dynasties—when the Japanese came, they relied on the Japanese; when the Americans came, they received their paycheck from them; and now that the Communist Party is in charge, they sided with the Three-Self. In reality, they are the furthest away from "Three-Self." They are merely earning a living within Christianity, and they devour the religion.

According to reporters, the crowd was silent after his speech, and the director of the Religious Department dared not speak hastily. He returned home to his wife Liang Huizhen and told her, "From today onward, I am a Rightist."

After half a year or so of being a Rightist, Yuan Xiangchen was arrested on the charge of being a counterrevolutionary on April 20, 1958, and he was sentenced to life imprisonment after half a year. Before the Anti-Rightist Campaign, nobody in the Three-Self imagined that after the Party put the last fundamentalists behind bars, their target would become the Three-Self. Generally speaking, before 1957, the Communist Party used the Three-Self Movement to suppress the Christian fundamentalists. After 1957, the Party used the Anti-Rightist Campaign to destroy the Three-Self Movement. The curse of universal rebellion against the Lord had such immediate effects. The Christians who abandoned the Lord and sold their brothers in 1952 were all labeled Rightists in 1957. The Three-Self leaders who sided with evil to escape persecution in 1957 were then condemned in the Cultural Revolution. Regardless how the Three-Self Movement followed the trend, they could not escape the fate of being disposed of after their purpose was served.

In 1961, Sunday school and fellowship groups were forbidden. The Three-Self Movement labeled children's Sunday school as a tool of imperialist intrusion.

In 1964, the Socialist Education Movement and the Four Cleanups Movement took place nationally.[27] One of their main points was atheistic education against religion. *Tian Feng* began to be criticized, and a "Church-Exit Movement" began in various places. A group of pastors declared that they had given up their faith and severed their ties with Christianity.

In 1966, Wu Yaozong, the originator of the Three-Self Movement was condemned and sentenced to hard labor. The Three-Self Movement was also dissolved. After that, the history of the Chinese church was at its darkest. In the subsequent persecutions, the experiences of the true Christian martyrs and of those who betrayed their brothers were equally shocking and ghastly. Before long, there would be no churches left in China except the underground house church.

The ironic thing is that the Three-Self was criticized as "the scheme of Liu Shaoqi and Wu Yaozong." A long document later criticized this so-called Three-Self Patriotic Movement Chairman, who had denied the deity of Christ and the authority of the Bible, by saying Christian leader Wu Yaozong is a conservative, and he has always wanted to reclaim the lost territories of religion by heckling and poisoning everywhere, babbling that there is still truth in religion, and that God does not contradict Marxism.

As mentioned previously, there was a group of leaders within the Three-Self who had lost a clear doctrine of soteriology during this period because they strayed from the truth theologically. In their weaknesses, there was also a "sincere concern" for religion and a romantic longing for the revolutions of the Communist Party and its socialist ideas. There was also another group who self-righteously endured humiliation as part of an important mission of the church. They thought that after such a pitiful sacrifice, the Party would at least give the Three-Self some form of religious liberty. After 1954, these two groups of people were deeply disappointed by the increasing persecutions of religious policy and government departments. Perhaps this disappointment also brought forth their guilt concerning the church. Thus during the open period of 1957, various leaders of the Three-Self (who were also simultaneously representatives or

---

[27]The Socialist Education Movement, also known as the Four Cleanups Campaign, was launched by Mao Zedong in 1963 to reeducate students and intellectuals within the CCP in order to purge reactionary thought from politics, economics, management, and ideology (i.e., the "four cleanups").

standing committee members of their respective people's congresses) started to heavily criticize the religious policies of the Party.

At the same time, the Three-Self once again responded to the call of Chairman Mao in their fight against the Rightists, and they suggested that the church needed to carry out a "socialistic education movement." They also emphasized that this "must be under the direct guidance of the government." At the end of October 1957, the Three-Self conference at large decided to carry out "socialistic education among all Christian workers throughout the country." From January 1958 onward, political classes were held in various provinces. Other than "commitment to the Party" and other self-reflections, they encouraged the exposure of "anti-socialistic" ideas.

Another aim of these political classes was to reform teaching to be "aligned with socialism." The general changes are listed below:

- Revoke each church's board of elders, diaconate, and other governing bodies.
- Centralize leadership under the Three-Self.
- Inspect Bible commentaries, discarding all that are "poisonous."
- Standardize hymns on a national scale, and eliminate all works by anti-revolutionary preachers (such as Watchman Nee).
- Prohibit the teaching of eschatology and other "pessimistic" doctrines.
- Prohibit any emphasis on the difference between believers and unbelievers (for example with regards to marriage).
- Prohibit the practices of exorcism, healing, and praying for the sick.
- All tithes made to the Three-Self under a unified financial plan.
- Prohibit any religious activities outside of church buildings.
- Support "socialist progress" by canceling Sunday services on harvest day or other busy seasons.

After the political classes, a certain portion of people would be labeled as Rightists and sent to prison camps. At the end of the year, Wu Yaozong reported to the Shanghai CNPC his work to "emphasize the patriotic work of anti-imperialism, eradicate the remnants of anti-revolutionary." He noted that after socialist education, they now understood that the pastoral staff belongs to the "exploiting class" and thus must be sent to prison camps for reform. Henceforth, many preachers left the church and entered prison camps. With the lack of pastors in the church, the Three-Self once again helped Satan launch a radical movement of merger and joint church worship, reducing the number of churches in the nation from two million to less than one hundred.

A TIME TO DEMOLISH, A TIME TO BUILD

The Rightist Christians of 1957—whether they were important figures within the Three-Self or independent martyrs—were all part of a grand tragedy that was far worse than any of their individual experiences. The grand tragedy was that the Christian church in China was being deserted and demolished. Nevertheless, the fundamentalists bore a great witness for their faith with their blood, and they turned the curse of God on this civilization into a blessing. On the other hand, the true tragedy of the church under the Communist Party was a generational, ethnic, and national concept that lifted sinners above the tower of Babel. In reality, this controlled both the liberals and the fundamentalists in different ways. To the liberals, it meant utterly abandoning the faith and worshiping the nation and Chinese civilization. In 1984, Ding Guangxun, the successor of Wu Yaozong, famously said in explanation of the Three-Self's faith, "My religion is not a circle with only one center. My religion is an ellipse with two foci—Christ and the nation." This saying could be considered the true "doctrinal creed" of Wu Yaozong and many other Three-Self leaders.

Wang Mingdao was not wrong to call them the "unbelieving party." Real believers will oppose this double-minded "ellipse-ism," which compromises both the gospel and the world. But for Wu Yaozong and his followers, Wang Mingdao's pietism and Watchman Nee's spiritualism was also unpersuasive. This was because the nation's situation in that particular generation also controlled the fundamentalists in a negative way—forcing them into a dualism that separated the sacred from the secular. They sought to completely leave the world of Satan, drawing a clear and distinct line between their faith and the world. They only wanted to preach the gospel and wait for the second coming of Christ. Thus in 1950, Wang Mingdao's church was actually the most contextualized and the most "Three-Self-ish." It does not matter whether the Western church was "imperialistic," because the line had already been drawn clearly. Under the pressure of nationalism as early as before 1949, the Chinese churches had already started a movement of contextualization and separatism that was divisive to the traditions of the universal church in its two-thousand-year history. Almost all denominations are subject to this tendency in varying degrees.

The most heroic part of the fundamentalists' faith is that the darker things got, the firmer they stood. But their weakness was that when the darkness began to fade, they were unable to respond effectively to their times. They could not utilize the entire gospel of the Bible to address the relationships between church and society, gospel and culture, faith and politics. When the Communist Party entered the cities and villages, how should a Christian make sense of the world that was changing before him? The unbelieving party would of course abandon their faith, but the fundamentalists were equally helpless in answering these questions. It was due to this shortcoming in the fundamentalists' camp that many Christians in the Three-Self Movement started to doubt their faith when they were tempted by new knowledge and glorious revolutions. So much so that Wang Mingdao's son also doubted his faith and abandoned the church, becoming the most painful heartache for Mr. Wang in his later years.

The internal essence of the Three-Self was idol worship. To outsiders, they were shut tight. The fundamentalists internally preserved the faith, but to outsiders they were also separated from the catholicity of the church to different degrees, thus setting themselves apart from the church catholic and church traditions. On a cultural level, "imperialism" and "socialism" became the most celebrated worldviews of that time. Facing these worldviews, be it rebuffing or compromising, the faith of the church never provided a comprehensive response.

In the contemporary West, the "evangelicals" were also breaking away from the traditional fundamentalists. The evangelicals rejected liberalism and held on to the fundamentals of the faith, but they were not satisfied with the fundamentalists' escapism that gave up on the world. This was especially true of conservative evangelicals like the Presbyterians—they held on to the traditional Reformed faith; they emphasized the Christian posture of "in and not of the world" for social engagement; they preserved a comprehensive faith in the relationship between the gospel and culture. The faith of the evangelicals was not a double-centered ellipse but a series of concentric circles around a common center. The evangelicals responded to their times with a thoroughly Christian worldview, enabling the church to bear a wholesome witness. This was especially true after the moral crisis and pluralism of the 1960s. Their witness gradually became a strong conservative force in the moral, cultural, and political spheres of North America.

But in the 1950s there was no such lasting tradition in the Chinese churches. Both the liberals and the fundamentalists were influenced by their times to approach faith in an individualistic way, embracing a privatization of religion that is separated from the kingdom. When they were faced with the cruelty of the

Communist Party, the fundamentalists in the house churches continued in the heroic Christian faith of that time. The Three-Self abandoned the way and sold the Lord. The fundamentalists retreated underground. Suffering made China into a giant monastery; and the blood of the martyrs thus became the seed of revival in the house churches.

At the end of 1958, the total number of Christians in China declined rapidly. Most Christians did not attend church, and those who did were of the elderly generation. Chinese church historian Jonathan Chao commented, "In 1954, the Communist Party controlled most of the churches through the Three-Self." However, in 1958 "the Communist Party entirely destroyed any organizational churches in China through the Three-Self." Many Western church historians stopped at this point and penned similar words, "Henceforth, the world lost any connection with Chinese Christians, and they wait in pain and agony for any revivals to come."

For the Christian, the essence of totalitarianism is worshiping a political nation as an idol. From 1950 to 1958 Chinese Christians resisted the violence of Caesar with a peaceful faith under the reign of the Communist Party. Among them, there were shameful failures but also spiritual victories. The saints and martyrs among them were like the elites of society, bearing the labels of "counterrevolutionary" or "Rightist" as part of the struggle for liberty in China. Their suffering was also part of the sufferings of the Chinese people. So much so that their faith in Christ has become part of the contemporary spirit of China.

As a Christian, I note two things when observing the history of Christianity under totalitarianism. The first is the total depravity of humanity. "As it is written, none is righteous, no not one" (Romans 3:10). The second is the perseverance of true saints. In this perseverance, we do not see several outstanding holy men but the grace and providence of God. No matter how many have fallen, there were always some who by grace abided in Christ's victory over the world. In other words, I see two infinities of humankind in this episode of 1957. The first is the infinite nature of the fallenness of men. Though a dog will never fall to the nature of a pig, people can and will fall infinitely beyond their own nature. The second is the infinite nature of the salvation of people. Even if people have fallen beyond their nature, Paul's words still resonate, "But where sin increased, grace abounded all the more" (Romans 5:20).

For the repentance of the church and the advancement of the gospel, I commemorate the fiftieth anniversary of the Anti-Rightist Campaign and the two hundredth anniversary of Morrison's arrival in China with this article.

Written on August 5, 2007, giving thanks to God for the martyrs, mourning the sins of the church, praising God for his tearing down and building up.

BIBLIOGRAPHY

Charbonnier, Jean. *Histoire des Chrétiens de Chine.* Translated by Geng Sheng and Zheng Dedi. Taipei: Taiwan: Kuangchi Cultural Group, 2005.

Li Diya. *Living Sacrifice: A Biography of "Allen" Xiangcheng Yuan.* China Soul for Christ Foundation. chinasoul.org/-/living-sacrifice.

Lueng Ka-lun. *Blessing upon China—Ten Talks on the Contemporary Church History of China.* Hong Kong: Tien Dao, 1999.

Su, Edwin. "History of the Church in China." ocochome.info/主日课堂/中国教会史1/.

Wang Mingdao. *Another 40 Years.* Scarborough, Ontario: Canada Gospel, 2010.

Jonathan Chao and Zhuang Wanfang. *The History of Development of Christianity in Modern China: 1949–1997.* Taiwan: China Ministries International, 1997.

7

RAISING OUR VOICES TO END SIXTY YEARS OF RELIGIOUS PERSECUTION

WANG YI

Wang Yi argues that despite their "nonviolent noncooperation" with government regulations, the house churches are the ones truly obeying the Constitution of the People's Republic of China, making them more obedient citizens than the Chinese Communist Party itself. The churches practice and promote true constitutional freedom, whereas the government violates the law by diminishing constitutional freedoms; therefore, it is ultimately illegal. It is perhaps in these arguments that Wang Yi's legal background is most apparent; his thoughts are clearly influenced by and rooted in Samuel Rutherford's and John Locke's seventeenth-century political theory that the law exists above the king.

Despite drawing upon seventeenth-century Western political philosophy, Wang Yi's argument retains many dissimilarities to Rutherford and Locke, most notably in his commitment to nonviolence. Wang Yi even goes as far as claiming the house church's suffering is a sign of God's blessing upon his people. He gives three reasons to call for the end of persecution, none of which are centered in individual rights. They are (1) to seek mercy for those who persecute the church; (2) out of pity for those unable to hear the gospel due to restrictions on Christianity and evangelism; and (3) to protect Christians from the temptations they face in times of duress.

Wang Yi's arguments are complex and difficult to unpack from their layers of nuance, particularly for those from theological traditions which have been influenced by rights-based political theory. On the one hand, Wang Yi desires to see contemporary evangelicals in China more active in the public square and in societal transformation. He believes the church is salt for a decaying society and rebukes the cultural withdrawal of the fundamentalists. On the other hand, Wang Yi's vision for the church is razor sharp—the mission of the church is the corporate worship of God and the Great Commission. Called to submit to God's ordained authorities on earth, so long as it is not inhibited in its worship, the church has no right to agitate for its own benefit and safety, even if this means it is reduced to persecution, slavery, or death.

This essay was first written as a pastoral letter to Early Rain Covenant Church on April 29, 2011. Wang Yi's pastoral letters were first emailed to his congregation and then posted publicly online. This essay was also published on the blog Human Rights in China *in 2017.*

1. HOUSE CHURCHES ARE LAW-ABIDING ROLE MODELS

In 1955, Mr. Wang Mingdao wrote, "We—For the Sake of Faith," which became the Chinese church's statement of defense before kings and society.[1] For decades, house churches in China have defended and sought religious freedom and freedom of conscience for the sake of the gospel. Although it continues to suffer government persecution, the church strives to preach the gospel of Christ, and it does not stop worshiping and gathering together. Although it lacks legitimate legal status, the church still forms community life for tens of millions of citizens in contemporary China.

People ask, "Aren't house churches illegal?" I want to answer honestly: yes. For sixty years, house churches have been illegal in terms of church worship, assembly, doctrine, religious property, the sacraments, evangelism, missions, theological training, pastor ordination, publishing, children's Sunday school ministry, and charity work. For sixty years, house churches have taken a posture of "nonviolent noncooperation" to violate all aspects of China's religious management and related legal enforcement. To deny this is to deny the road house churches have been traveling on and to deny the reality of church-state conflict in China for the last half century.

But, here is the more important question: Is the Chinese government illegal? We should honestly and courageously respond: yes. For sixty years, this country has continuously trampled upon its own constitution and laws regarding religious freedom.[2] Whether it is church worship, freedom of assembly, doctrine,

---

[1] See "We—For the Sake of Faith."

[2] Article 36 of the Constitution of the People's Republic of China states, "(1) Citizens of the People's Republic of China enjoy freedom of religious belief. (2) No state organ, public organization, or individual may compel citizens to believe in, or not to believe in, any religion; nor may they discriminate against citizens who believe in, or do not believe in, any religion. (3) The state protects normal religious activities. No one may make use of religion to engage in activities that disrupt

religious property, the sacraments, missions, seminary training, pastor ordination, publishing, children's Sunday school, charity work, and so on, the government uses illegal, autocratic, and barbarous methods to oppress the church and the children of Christ in China.

So, again we ask, "Aren't house churches illegal?" If the Bible is the "constitution" for Christians and the church, then in the areas of worship and preaching over the past sixty years, the house churches have been the paragon of following God's law and freedom of conscience in Chinese society. I must say that we have not violated the higher, most supreme law (James 2:8). Moreover, precisely because we must observe that law within our hearts, we have not dared not to violate the system of religious regulations over the last fifty years because this system deprives and controls the Christians' mission to worship God and preach the gospel.

So, we ask again, "Aren't house churches illegal?" If the constitution is "the king" of the modern state, if the Chinese government claims that its power comes from the Chinese constitution and that it must comply with the constitution, then I must honestly answer that for sixty years the house churches are the perfect model for submitting to the king and following the constitution. The church follows the constitution up to a point, even though all government officials have chosen to defy the constitution and imprison those who do not violate the constitution with them. Still, the church continues to act "according to law" by upholding their constitutional right to worship God and preach the gospel just as before. And because we must abide by a higher "constitutional power," we dare not to comply with the unconstitutional actions of the religious administrative system and their law enforcement actions.

The demands of the house churches are, in essence, the demands of the gospel. This demand is in direct conflict with the state. The focus is on Article 35 of the Constitution, which guarantees "freedom of religious belief." In other words, social transformation, political progress, freedom, democracy, the rule of law, human rights—these are all good things in the eyes of Christians. But, they are never the true pursuit of the church. Whether it is slavery or democracy, monarchy or rule of law, the Bible teaches that the church must obey the government's authority. In short, the church of Christ is not at all interested in any political and legal system. However, what the church is interested in under any political and legal system is the freedom to worship God and proclaim the gospel.

---

public order, impair the health of citizens or interfere with the educational system of the state. (4) Religious bodies and religious affairs are not subject to any foreign domination."

Therefore, during sixty years of religious persecution, the house churches have continuously adopted peaceful, patient means to become law-abiding representatives of Chinese society. Lord permitting, the church is also willing to suffer under any system in order to comply with any unfair and unjust law. In fact, over the past sixty years the house churches have done just that. However, the one law that the church cannot obey is the law that attempts to deprive and control our worship of God and proclamation of the gospel. In the public sphere, the church must regard these laws as "unconstitutional." In terms of our faith, the church must also regard these laws as evil and antichrist.

Whether confronting the Roman emperor or the Chinese Communist Party, ancient society or modern society, the shocking fact is that this position has never changed. And practically, it is because the Christian church has insisted on and invested in this position for almost two thousand years that the concept of religious freedom has taken shape in modern states and constitutional systems.

The demands of the house churches have all along been written in black and white on the Constitution of the People's Republic of China. Apart from ending religious persecution and ensuring religious freedom, the gospel mission of the church and the authority of the state have nothing to do with each other; the church seeks nothing else from the state.

2. THIS IS NOT "POLITICIZING," BUT POLITICAL PERSECUTION

The newspaper *Global Times*, which is run by the *People's Daily*, published an article on April 25 in which the author refers to the outdoor worship activities of Shouwang Church in Beijing, as well as the house churches' quest for public worship, open evangelism, local church communities, and legalization as "politicization."[3]

Even among believers, we often puzzle over this issue. I believe that to understand the history and reality of the church-state relationship post-1950, we must clarify the following facts:

First, the past sixty years of religious persecution has never just been about legal persecution but about political persecution. Just as when the Lord Jesus was on trial, it was not a trial in the legal sense (Pilate said Jesus was innocent by Roman law). Rather, it was a religious and political trial. Jesus said, "'A servant is not greater than his master.' If they persecuted me, they will also

---

[3]"Individual Churches Should Avoid Politicizing Themselves," *Global Times*, April 26, 2011, news. sina.com.cn/pl/2011-04-26/082922358619.shtml.

persecute you" (John 15:20). Brothers and sisters, I want to tell you that if the Jesus Christ we profess was nailed to the cross for the crime of inciting subversion, then is not our "politicizing" label under persecution a glory itself because we consider ourselves disciples of Christ? On the cross our Lord bore the sign "king of the Jews" because he is in actuality the king of glory. Similarly, the Chinese house churches bear the sign "politicization" because we ourselves are a royal priesthood.

Second, the church-state conflict has never been a legal problem but a political problem. Both the government and the church have to face this fact. The house church problem has never technically or administratively been a problem of law enforcement or legality. "The house church problem" is that millions of Christian citizens have upheld the freedom of religion and freedom of conscience for sixty years, thereby forming one of the most serious public and political issues in contemporary China.

Third, it is the government's persecution of the church for sixty years, not the church's noncompliance at the administrative level for sixty years, that has led to the house church issue becoming a political problem.

Fourth, it is the faith of the church that has become a part of politics, not politics that has become a part of the church's faith. For the church, all are matters of faith regardless of whether it is church worship, assembly, doctrine, church property, the sacraments, evangelism, missions, theological training, pastor ordination, publishing, children's Sunday school, or charity work. They are never political problems. But for the state, as long as the government decides not to recognize the church's sovereign right to worship God and proclaim the gospel, then these issues will forever remain political rather than religious.

Fifth, the position and request of the house churches is simply to ask those in power not to make us out to be a political problem anymore. This is exactly why the house churches insist on not joining the Three-Self Patriotic Movement. As a result, the house churches have already borne the weight of political persecution, isolation, and discrimination for sixty years. We are sick of sneaking around to gather for worship; we are fed up with having to deal with the secret police; and we have had enough of this country's fear of the gospel. Whoever has fear in his or her heart will continue to "politicize" matters of faith.

Sixth, the politicization of "the house church problem" and "the politicization of the church" are two entirely different things. In addition to the church's use of nonviolence and civil disobedience as methods to advance religious freedom, doesn't the idea of intervention and drawing support from special "political" power and methods lead to the church "politicizing" itself? According to my understanding of the contemporary house church, I must decisively respond: I do not believe the house churches or their preachers have the tendency to post any danger of "politicization," just as I do not believe the Three-Self churches and their preacher do not have the tendency to post any danger of "politicization." Those who politicize the church are those who simply follow the official teaching of the Three-Self Movement, not the house churches who resist the Three-Self Movement.

Seven, the only way to "unpoliticize" the house church issue is to end religious persecution and guarantee religious freedom. Today's house churches, especially the pastors and preachers in the urban churches, have a responsibility to raise their voices on this issue. The previous generation of preachers suffered greatly for the Lord under religious persecution. This generation of preachers is preparing to suffer greatly for the Lord in order to end religious persecution.

3. RAISE YOUR VOICES TO END RELIGIOUS PERSECUTION

In the history of "being politicized"—from the church father Justin's *Apology* and early church fathers' apologetic writings, to Martin Luther, John Calvin, and other Reformers who wrote essays and books to kings and feudal lords in defense of their faith, to Wang Mingdao's "We—For the Sake of Faith" in the previous generation of the Chinese house church—the Lord Christ has guided and opened up for his church a path of public apologetics and proclamation of the gospel.

Today, God has provided house church leaders and believers with much more expansive protection, permission, and technological conditions for information dissemination, public discussion, internet forums, civil society, and access to modern legal protection. If we cannot give a more open and undisturbed defense of the Christian faith in the face of China's rulers and the Chinese people, and raise our voices against sixty years of political persecution, moreover, if we do not advocate for our freedom to proclaim the gospel and the church's right to doctrine, church property, and ordination, then woe to us pastors.

I urge pastors to raise their voices together and ask all members of the church body in China, as well as government officials and additional citizens, to honestly confront the following facts:

- First, 1950 marked the beginning of the People's Republic of China's religious persecution against the Christian church, and to this day it has not ceased.
- Second, the freedom to worship, to assemble, to evangelize, and to conduct missions is still not recognized by the Chinese government.

- Third, the Chinese constitution's religious freedom clause to this day exists in name only.

- Fourth, Christians who hold public office, receive education, serve in the academy, and work in publishing are publicly and severely discriminated against.

I also ask China's rulers and every government official, who has or has not participated in religious persecution, to acknowledge and face the following facts, based on the conscience inscribed on your soul (Romans 2:15):

- First, on September 26, 1950, the CCP Central Committee released *Directives to Expand the Response to the "Christian Manifesto" Movement in Christianity and Catholicism,* in which they regarded the church as a "tool of imperialism."[4] Soon after, through successive political campaigns and persecutions, countless pastors and preachers were imprisoned and executed as "counterrevolutionaries." They persecuted those who did not join the official "Three-Self Patriotic Church," including our most respected preachers Wang Mingdao, Watchman Nee, and Allen Yuan. So far this political damage has not been restituted, reinvestigated, and resolved.

- Second, on December 29, 1950, the Administrative Council released *The Report on Guidelines to Manage Cultural, Educational, and Relief Organizations and Religious Groups Receiving Funds from the United States.* Soon after, nineteen Christian high schools, over 200 Christian middle schools, over 1,700 Christian elementary schools, as well as Christian organizations such as hospitals and orphanages around the country were all seized by the government. This act of stripping and violating the freedom of religion and church property has never been fully and positively made right in the past sixty years.

- Third, on March 31, 1982, the CCP Central Committee's *Document 19* corrected the extreme leftist religious policy at the time to some extent. But, it still restricted and suppressed Christian worship, assembly, and missions. Since then, for the past thirty years, it has directed all levels of government to heap wrongful legal action upon Christians and the church, including fines, detentions, reeducation through hard labor, imprisonment, prohibition, torture, and other illegal measures. The impact of this wrongful policy has still not been extinguished.

---

[4]See "Three-Self Patriotic Movement."

- Fourth, the State Council violated China's Legislation Law pertaining to the clause to "legally restrict any control over a citizen's political right" by illegally formulating the *Regulations on Religious Affairs* in 2004. These regulations led to many restrictions and violations of Christians' constitutional rights to worship, assemble, and do missions. And the regulations continued to regard large-scale Christian worship, assembly, and missions outside of the Communist controlled Three-Self church as illegal.

As a house church pastor, I thank and praise God Almighty for all persecution and restrictions suffered by the church. God foreordains everything according to his good and blameless will. He trains and purifies his church and his children in China. Moreover, he gives us the most unmerited blessing of suffering for righteousness' sake (1 Peter 3:14). In a larger sense, and even on a personal level, I actually prefer for persecution to continue existing. I am also willing to submit to God's will and am prepared to endure a more protracted church-state conflict, because this would be incomparably better for our spiritual life and for our final hope.

But, the reason we raise our voice is to seek mercy for all of our persecutors. They do not believe in the gospel of Christ and they do not believe in God's righteous anger and curse—but, don't we believe the gospel?

The reason we raise our voice is because we take pity on those compatriots who cannot have more freedom and more opportunity to hear the gospel. They cannot attend churches because of religious persecution. They do not believe the gospel of Christ and they do not care about what they have lost—but, don't we care?

The reason we raise our voice is also due to our frequent weakness under persecution. "If it be possible, let this cup pass from me; nevertheless, not as I will, but as you will" (Matthew 26:39). With year after year of persecution and restrictions, we recognize that Christians often feel cowardly and afraid. They carry anger and bitterness, and even in the midst of suffering it is hard to avoid feeling self-righteous and prideful. Therefore, we are not chasing after the hero of religious freedom. We are petitioning the Lord Jesus Christ to keep our generation from temptation and deliver us from evil, lest we are "so utterly burdened beyond our strength" (2 Corinthians 1:8) that we dishonor the name of the Lord.

Sixty years ago, the Chinese government terrorized Christians into handing over their names and identities to Caesar. From 1950 to 1954, some 410,000 Christians (approximately 50 percent of Christians at the time) voluntarily or under duress signed the Three-Self Patriotic Manifesto. They openly betrayed the Lord Jesus Christ and his church and were forced to withdraw from public society.

Sixty years later, the Lord's church needs to call every Christian once again, for the sake of the gospel, to hand over their names and identities. We have a responsibility to use some similar methods (a different type of appeal, voice, petition, apologetics, and signature campaign) to make our own public confession to defend the gospel and the church in the face of those in power. By the blood of Christ, we will wash the Chinese church clean of the Lord's shame.

What we need is not a religious "civil rights movement." What we need is a genuine gospel movement. Our support, petitions, and voices are closely related to this currently unprecedented period of urbanization and social transformation, in which house churches can conduct evangelism trainings, church planting, church transformation, missions work, and obey the gospel's cultural mandate. In this process, the house churches can more firmly establish church membership, build local churches, and form a visible Christian community for the world. And, through this process, the house churches can use the issue of religious freedom to challenge other citizens' consciences, embolden the courage of church members, and call those believers who have drifted away to renew their commitment.

The church does not need to proudly fight the state for our nonexistent rights. The church is to be humble so that this country can be blessed by the benefits of the gospel. We need to request the state to recognize and respect the freedom we already have.

The church also does not at all need or rely on any external "religious freedom" in order to maintain and live out the Christian faith. On the contrary, over the past sixty years the church has lived out a true "freedom" because of the Christian faith. Therefore, the church's petitions, appeals, apologetics, signature campaign, and calls to end religious persecution are not for the sake of external benefits for the visible church; rather, they are for the expansion of Christ's kingdom and the blessing of other communities. "Not only to avoid God's wrath but also for the sake of conscience" (Romans 13:5).

Grace and peace from God our Father and the Lord Jesus Christ to all who are sanctified in Christ Jesus, called to be saints, together with all those who in every place in China call upon the name of our Lord Jesus Christ. Because Jesus is both their Lord and ours (1 Corinthians 1:2-3).

8

NINETY-FIVE THESES

THE REAFFIRMATION OF OUR STANCE ON THE HOUSE CHURCH

WANG YI AND EARLY RAIN COVENANT CHURCH

On August 8, 1955, Wang Mingdao, one of China's most influential house church leaders, was arrested after publishing "We—For the Sake of Faith," an article publicly declaring why his church refused to join the Three-Self Patriotic Movement. On August 30, 2015, Early Rain Covenant Church published 95 theses to commemorate the sixtieth anniversary of Wang Mingdao's arrest and to reaffirm the house church's position before society at large. Wang Yi drafted the theses during a three-month sabbatical at the Center on Religion and the Global East at Purdue University. They were first published publicly on Weibo, one of China's largest social media platforms.

This document demonstrates the deepening theological engagement of the house church in China, as well as its desire to locate itself within global church history. Early Rain's theses start with the doctrine of creation and place God's eschatological plan of salvation at the center of the church's call. They then move toward a foundational doctrine of the kingdom of God to form the church's understanding of its engagement with the world at large. Early Rain's language is at times strong and divisive; it is now rare to use the language of the "antichrist" in some theological traditions. It is important here to understand the spiritual reality in which Wang Yi and the leaders of Early Rain believe. Early Rain's 95 theses reflect Luther's work in more ways than numerical delineation. Wang Yi and Early Rain's frequent discussion of the church's battle with the spiritual powers of the world are strongly reminiscent of the Reformer's writings.

Out of our obedience to Christ, in our hope to be loyal to the whole family of God, and in firm commitment to his leadership, the pastors and elders of our church have resolved to publish "The Reaffirmation of Our Stance on the House Church" and the following 95 theses based on our confessional faith in the truths of the Bible and our never-ending endeavor to seek the guidance of the Holy Spirit. We welcome any believers who have openly confessed their faith in Jesus Christ as their personal and as humanity's Savior to offer their written critical opinions. Using this official publication as a foundation, our church is also willing, independently or jointly with other churches in our Lord Christ Jesus who accept our public theses, to have open and peaceful dialogue with any level of the Chinese government and its agencies, at any time, place, and method that they deem appropriate.

OUTLINE

Theses 1–17: God's Sovereignty and Biblical Authority

Theses 18–31: God's Law and Christ's Redemption

Theses 32–39: Against the "Sinicization of Christianity"

Theses 40–44: The Church as the Body of Christ and His Kingdom

Theses 45–72: The Relationship Between the Two Kingdoms and the Separation of Church and State

Theses 73–95: Against the "Three-Self Movement" and Affirmation of the Great Commission

GOD'S SOVEREIGNTY AND BIBLICAL AUTHORITY

1. The Bible says, "Yet for us there is one God, the Father, from whom are all things and for whom we exist" (1 Corinthians 8:6). This means even for the Chinese, this God is the only God. The domain of, history of, culture of, and everything in China are all created, granted, administered, and superintended by this one true God of the universe.

2. The Bible again says, "For there is one God, and there is one mediator between God and men, the man Christ Jesus" (1 Timothy 2:5). In other words, the only Son of God, begotten from all eternity past, born into this world, taking on the body of a fallen man in the form of Jesus Christ, is the only Savior and Lord of all Chinese people.

3. When the Bible says, "So God created man in his own image, in the image of God he created him; male and female he created them" (Genesis 1:27), this means every Chinese individual is created in the image of God. All the

people groups of China are descendants of Adam, who is our first ancestor, along with all people groups of the world.

4. In the depths of our souls is the image of God. Thus all Chinese people, like all the peoples of the world, are all equal in the divine values of personhood, dignity, justice, and love.

5. Therefore, in essence, all humans are personally governed by God. Individuals cannot enslave and humiliate each other. Also, without God's authorization and approval, an individual cannot be governed by another person.

6. When the Bible says, "Let every person be subject to the governing authorities. For there is no authority except from God, and those that exist have been instituted by God" (Romans 13:1), this means that all authority in Chinese society ultimately originates from God, regardless of whether it is within a family, social institution, or the state. All government officials, including the ones on the lowest levels, are all in essence God's "appointees."

7. Therefore, the only legitimate reason why any person should respect and obey the law, or why any low-level official, member of an institution, or family should respect and obey a higher authority is because God has established these institutions according to his order and delight.

8. Therefore, in ultimate meaning and personal conscience, every individual, especially if he or she holds any kind of authority, must be held responsible for his or her actions toward the "the Living God" (Hebrews 10:31), and in the end submit to his righteous judgment.

9. Only God (and his Word) is Lord over a person's conscience. Any manmade and worldly law, mandate, or opinion cannot negate the moral responsibilities of a person's conscience before the "God Most High" (Genesis 14:19).

10. Because of this, every individual enjoys the freedoms and responsibilities of his conscience. Based on God and his words, every person should use his conscience to examine and judge all authorities, ideas, and mandates from the state, social institutions, or families.

11. When a person's conscience is aligned with God and his words, "doing the will of God from the heart" (Ephesians 6:6), only then can this person's obedience of others and respect for the law be viewed as equivalent to

obedience of and respect for God, and not a capitulation to human authorities, because they are "rendering service with a good will as to the Lord and not to man" (Ephesians 6:7).

12. When the Bible says, "All scripture is breathed out by God and profitable for teaching, for reproof, for correction, and for training in righteousness" (2 Timothy 3:16), this means that only the Bible is God's inerrant Word. It is the only standard for teaching through which all Chinese people may come to know God's will and mandate.

13. This means that once we stray from the Bible, ultimately, we cannot judge anything to be right or wrong, good or evil. Outside of the Bible, we cannot make a rightful, conscious judgment on any worldly authorities and standards. Also, we will not be able to determine whether our obedience to those in worldly authority is done in obedience to God and thus receives his delight or whether we have given up our personhood and dignity by being enslaved by men.

14. Once we stray from the Bible and act according to the extrabiblical standards and authorities, then it is as God's servant, Martin Luther, once said: our conscience will neither be moral nor secured.[1]

15. All Chinese people, regardless of whether they believe in God, have an ultimate standard of morality and values in their hearts, even though these values may be blurred, erroneous, and fickle. We are always using these highest standards to evaluate whether things are right or wrong, good or evil, and to teach and evaluate the actions of ourselves and others.

16. If any Chinese individuals or any worldly Chinese authorities and powers should force extrabiblical standards, ideals, or mandates on others, or forbid anybody's conscience from using the Bible as the highest standard to judge other worldly standards, ideals, and mandates, or force people to unreservedly and blindly believe and obey them, then these lead to the destruction of a person's reason and conscience and constitute an attack on God's sovereignty over a person's conscience.

17. Anybody who willingly believes and submits to antibiblical standards, ideals, or mandates has in reality betrayed the true freedom of his conscience and is living a life of slavery and hostility toward God. He may

---

[1] Likely intended as a loose paraphrase of Luther's famous "Here I Stand" speech, delivered at the Diet of Worms.

not recognize this, or even if he may have some suspicion of this reality, he has become accustomed to using all kinds of methods to suppress his own soul's distress.

GOD'S LAW AND CHRIST'S REDEMPTION

18. To spare us from these distresses, God personally intervened in the history of ancient Israel, saving the Israelites from slavery under the Egyptians, and through his chosen leader Moses, made a covenant with his people, giving them his law, which is now known as the Ten Commandments, so that the Israelites may know God's justice and holy will and recognize the sins that disturb their conscience.

19. The First Commandment says, "You shall have no other gods before me" (Exodus 20:3). Just like a bride can only have one husband, the soul can only have one king, and the church can only have one head.

20. Therefore, whoever wishes to be king of our lives replaces God's will with their own will or asks for unconditional obedience, worship, and praise—regardless of whether it is our spouse, parents, children, or a nation's government or political party, regardless of whether it is done with tears or swords. These kinds of impositions and demands are in essence all religious. They are really seeking to be the "god" of a family, an institution, or a nation. They are seeking the highest allegiance and obedience of a people's conscience.

21. These kinds of demands and impositions on the will are morally evil. It is antagonistic to God and to humanity. Those who are in submission to them are also committing evil and acts of idolatry.

22. The rest of the Ten Commandments are all based on the principle of the First Commandment. Just as Jesus once said, "And he said to him, 'You shall love the Lord your God with all your heart and with all your soul and with all your mind. This is the great and first commandment. And a second is like it: You shall love your neighbor as yourself. On these two commandments depend all the Law and the Prophets'" (Matthew 22:37-40).

23. Just as another passage of the Bible says, "The aim of our charge is love that issues from a pure heart and a good conscience and a sincere faith" (1 Timothy 1:5). However, nobody, including the Chinese, can rely on themselves to have "a pure heart and a good conscience," and cannot birth

within themselves "a sincere faith." Nobody can rely on himself to be in full compliance to God's command for love, regardless of the kind of painstaking and godly religious life he may live. It is not possible.

24. Ever since humanity's first ancestor, Adam (and Eve), disobeyed the covenant (Hosea 6:7), "all have sinned and fall short of the glory of God" (Romans 3:23). This means that from ancient China until today's China we have not one righteous person, because no one has not been totally depraved in his nature; therefore no one can save himself.

25. The hope for the Chinese is the same as for people of all nations—it is in God alone. Not only through the covenant of law, "since through the law comes knowledge of sin" (Romans 3:20), but God personally prepared the covenant of redemption for his chosen people, through the suffering of the Messiah (Isaiah 53), forgiving the sins of all people that believe in him (John 3:15). Also, God will pour out his grace, so those who have been chosen to be born again in the Spirit (John 3:3) may believe in the Messiah and his work of salvation.

26. Around two thousand years ago in the land of Judah and the city of Bethlehem, Jesus, born of the virgin Mary, was the Christ (Messiah). The Bible declares that this Jesus "and the Father are one" (John 10:30), that he is with God, and that he is God (John 1:1).

27. The Bible has prophesied that all the nations have been waiting for this savior to come, "that your way may be known on earth, your saving power among all nations" (Psalm 67:2). It has also prophesied that Christ will be the king that rules the nations (Psalm 47:8), for "he rules over the nations" (Psalm 22:28). Since it says "the nations," it clearly includes both ancient and modern China.

28. The prophets of the Old Testament prophesied that this Christ will use a shocking way, which means a way that is completely contrary to the ways of the authorities of this world, to save sinners from the powers of the world, flesh, and death. "He was pierced for our transgressions; he was crushed for our iniquities; upon him was the chastisement that brought us peace, and with his wounds we are healed" (Isaiah 53:5).

29. The series of prophecies regarding the Messiah are all fulfilled in Jesus Christ. He is the holy and sinless God, and also the mediator of God's chosen people and a representative of sinners. He was judged by the

worldly authorities, suffered, and nailed to a cross under the Roman Empire, was buried, and descended to hell. On the third day, by the power of God, he resurrected from the dead.

30. This core message of the Christian faith is called the gospel. The gospel is not just about repairing an individual's relationship with God through Christ's sacrifice. It is also about the coming of God's kingdom, so all the kings of the land, all the nations and their peoples have been ordered to submit to this gospel, and this includes China.

31. Just as the apostle Paul said, "In past generations he allowed all the nations to walk in their own ways" (Acts 14:16), and also said, "The times of ignorance God overlooked, but now he commands all people everywhere to repent, because he has fixed a day on which he will judge the world in righteousness by a man whom he has appointed; and of this he has given assurance to all by raising him from the dead" (Acts 17:30-31). The terms "nations" and "peoples" include China and the Chinese.

AGAINST THE "SINICIZATION OF CHRISTIANITY"

32. God has used the Chinese culture and the wisdom of ancient Chinese people in the past to reveal his existence to us, because through creation we can see his eternal power and divine nature (Romans 1:20). As the Bible says, because of God's merciful love and for our benefit, "he did not leave himself without witness, for he did good by giving you rains from heaven and fruitful seasons, satisfying your hearts with food and gladness" (Acts 14:17). Through the Chinese culture's quest for charity, justice, truth, and morality, God has also revealed to us what was written in, or whatever is left of, the use of the law in our conscience (Romans 2:15).

33. However, God does not discriminate (Romans 2:14). He did not offer a path of salvation outside of Christ within Chinese history and culture. For all Chinese are like the lawless Gentiles, "for although they knew God, they did not honor him as God or give thanks to him, but they became futile in their thinking, and their foolish hearts were darkened" (Romans 1:21).

34. Not only so, but for a very long time, rather than living a life of worship for the one true God, the Chinese people have been living in an evil culture of idolatry, which worships autocracy and prostrates before the emperor. The philosophical teaching of "no ultimate truths, only virtues"

resulted in moral self-righteousness.[2] These cultural norms have been binding the hearts of the Chinese people and our institutions until today.

35. Therefore, like all peoples of the world, we are mercilessly indicted by the Bible: "And since they did not see fit to acknowledge God, God gave them up to a debased mind to do what ought not to be done. They were filled with all manner of unrighteousness, evil, covetousness, malice. They are full of envy, murder, strife, deceit, maliciousness. They are gossips, slanderers, haters of God, insolent, haughty, boastful, inventors of evil, disobedient to parents, foolish, faithless, heartless, ruthless. Though they know God's righteous decree that those who practice such things deserve to die, they not only do them but give approval to those who practice them" (Rom 1:28-32).

36. Therefore, if anyone advocates or requires any type of "Sinicization of Christianity" with regards to the fundamentals of our faith, biblical theology, and the doctrines of the church, they reject Jesus Christ and are antagonistic toward Christianity. It is an act of anti-Christianity and will fall under the righteous curse and judgment of God.

37. These campaigns or requirements for the "Sinicization of Christianity" include: believing that traditional Chinese culture or religion contain ways to worship the unique, one true God revealed in the Bible, or ways of redemption similar or even equivalent to that of the redemption of Jesus Christ; proclaiming that traditional Chinese culture and religions include unique revelation about redemption outside of God and the Bible; proclaiming that the fundamental teachings of the catholic church must and need to be assimilated with traditional Chinese culture or modern Chinese society and political structures; teaching a type of "universal doctrine of Christ" that denies the historical Jesus and affirms that the Chinese traditions have implicit teachings about the redemptive saving ways of Christ; and teaching a "justification by love" or any such teaching that seeks assimilation with traditional Chinese moralistic teachings, and thereby weakens or even denies the necessity of Christ's atonement on the cross.[3]

38. The church needs to oppose the "Sinicization of Christianity." That means opposing the use of culture to alter the gospel, the use of politics to bind

---

[2]This is an interpretive paraphrase of the 38th chapter of the *Tao Te Ching* by Lao Tzu (老子).
[3]See "Wu Yaozong."

the faith, the use of Chinese tradition that is antagonistic toward God to destroy the faithful traditions of God's catholic church.

39. This does not include actions taken by the church to respect the Chinese culture and traditions or to willingly accept the limitations of existing culture for the sake of proclaiming the gospel in accordance to the truths of God. As the apostle Paul says, all these for the sake of the gospel, "I have become all things to all people, that by all means I might save some" (1 Corinthians 9:22).

CHURCH AS THE BODY OF CHRIST AND HIS KINGDOM

40. The Christ who was resurrected from the cross personally chose the apostles, poured out the Holy Spirit with God the Father (John 14:26), and established the church (Matthew 16:18). Christ, using his own precious blood, established a new covenant with the church. This church is not limited to the biological race of Israelites but consists of all peoples who have publicly confessed their faith and are baptized, including Chinese believers. As the Bible says, "Worthy are you to take the scroll and to open its seals, for you were slain, and by your blood you ransomed people for God from every tribe and language and people and nation" (Revelation 5:9).

41. The Bible proclaims that the resurrected Christ has been given all authority in God's created world and the entire universe, "far above all rule and authority and power and dominion, and above every name that is named, not only in this age but also in the one to come. And he put all things under his feet and gave him as head over all things to the church" (Ephesians 1:21-22). The Lord says, "All authority in heaven and on earth has been given to me" (Matthew 28:18).

42. Since it says, "all things are under his feet," therefore China is also under Christ's feet. Since it says, "all rule and authority and power and dominion," therefore the authority given to the Lord Jesus includes the authorities of the Chinese government and its society.

43. This means, regardless of how many Christians are in China, regardless of what kind of political platform China adopts, regardless of the attitudes of the Chinese government (or any other government) toward the gospel, Chinese society is under the sovereignty of Christ. Spiritual reality is that the resurrected Christ, not any rulers, political parties, cultures, or wealth,

is the one ruling and administering this nation's history and the hearts of its citizens.

44. Also, the Bible calls the church "his body, the fullness of him who fills all in all" (Ephesians 1:23). Therefore, although the church of Christ is spread out among the nations, it does not belong to any nation. The church is a kingdom that eyes cannot see, whose citizens are loyal to the sovereignty of Christ. Even though the nations see the church as a religious institution, the relationship between the church and state is in essence a two-kingdom relationship.

THE RELATIONSHIP BETWEEN THE TWO KINGDOMS AND THE SEPARATION OF CHURCH AND STATE

45. In church history, the relationship between these two kingdoms is the relationship between the "city of God" and the "city of man," or sometimes referred to as the relationship between the spiritual kingdom and earthly kingdom, or the relationship between an eschatological kingdom of the "already-but-not-yet" of the coming age and the kingdom of this age known as "today's world that will ultimately be destroyed."

46. Before our Lord Jesus was crucified on the cross, he proclaimed to the Roman governor who was judging him, "My kingdom is not of this world. If my kingdom were of this world, my servants would have been fighting, that I might not be delivered over to the Jews. But my kingdom is not from the world" (John 18:36). This shows that the kingdom of Christ is higher than any nations on earth. It also shows that before the judgment day arrives, the kingdom of Christ will refrain from the use of coercion or forceful action to enforce its rule on this world. Rather, through great love and mercy, it allows the political powers of this world to exercise the power of the sword.

47. Christ, as the sovereign king of all the earth, demonstrates the reality and power of his rule through the spreading of the gospel by the church and the actions of believers in accordance to their renewed faith and conscience. When the Roman governor asked Jesus, "Are you the king?" our Lord Jesus in his answer once again talked about the authority of his spiritual kingdom: "You say that I am a king. For this purpose I was born and for this purpose I have come into the world—to bear witness to the truth. Everyone who is of the truth listens to my voice" (John 18:37).

48. Because of this, when the Chinese political authorities ask the church: Is Christ your king? Is your faith antagonistic to the government? Do you seek to influence the political landscape? We give three answers.

49. First, we answer: God's kingdom is already here in China, it cannot be denied by the power of the sword because his kingdom is brought forth by the only begotten Son of God, our Savior Lord Jesus Christ, who brought forth this kingdom on the cross through his own death under the power of the sword. Genocides and persecutions can only cause this kingdom to gain more ground in China because the cross is the mystery of the church and the gospel. Since the church is the body of Christ, every time the true church is persecuted, it will bring forth the power of resurrection.

50. Second, we will answer: the church in China does not belong to the Republic of China of the past, nor does it belong to the People's Republic of China of the present, and it will not belong to any other political power in the future. The church in its nature will be obedient to any authority of the sword granted to the state. We do not seek to rebel against any existing government, nor do we seek special executive privileges or any other governmental coercion to help us influence society. For God has given this authority of the "sword" to the state (Romans 13:4), and not to the church. "Therefore whoever resists the authorities resists what God has appointed" (Romans 13:2).

51. But this does not mean that individual believers, when confronted with violence or illegal infringements from the government or other individuals, are stripped of what God and the laws have granted them, including the rights of regular citizens to use any and all legal means to lodge their protest, opposition, and to exercise proper self-defense. The church does not require its members, under any circumstances, to give up their right to protest or self-defense against any illegal infringements.

52. Although by faith one may give up physical resistance and protest, which delights God and is consistent with what the Lord has done, this kind of choice can only be said to have the virtue of godliness when it comes out of an individual's own faith and conscience.

53. Third, we will answer: just as the government has been granted the authority of the "sword" to help humanity maintain order in society, the church has also been granted the Great Commission, especially to be a

witness for the truth, calling out those who belong to the truth to leave their idols, listen to the teaching of the Lord Jesus, and worship only the one true God.

54. As we have said earlier, if the church resists the authority of the "sword" from the government and usurps the authority and power of enforcement, it is disobeying God. In the same way, if the government or any social institution or individual use political power to deny the church's spiritual authority to spread the gospel in accordance to the Great Commission and to worship God, they are also disobeying God. The church has a duty to either privately or publicly rebuke, criticize, and speak up against the fearful consequences of these sins, and also to use the passionate love of Christ to call them to repentance.

55. The Bible teaches that Christ gave the church this spiritual authority called, "the keys of the kingdom of heaven." Christ said to his church, "I will give you the keys of the kingdom of heaven, and whatever you bind on earth shall be bound in heaven, and whatever you loose on earth shall be loosed in heaven" (Matthew 16:19).

56. Not only so, but Christ also commands his church to go and proclaim his gospel, saying, "You will be my witnesses . . . to the end of the earth" (Acts 1:8). After Jesus rose from the dead, but before his ascension to heaven, he came to the apostles and said, "All authority in heaven and on earth has been given to me. Go therefore and make disciples of all nations, baptizing them in the name of the Father and of the Son and of the Holy Spirit, teaching them to observe all that I have commanded you. And behold, I am with you always, to the end of the age" (Matthew 28:18-20).

57. This indicates that, on this earth, there is no nation who has the proper authority to stop the church from legitimately using biblical methods to spread the gospel or stop the church from sending evangelists into different regions to conduct worship or missional gatherings. Other than for the benefit of social order or administration of public good, or the equal treatment of all citizens, the church should not be discriminated against, monitored, or limited solely for religious reasons. For the church's religious freedom to proclaim the gospel and worship our God is given to us by Christ himself. Any infringement or stripping of such freedom is the evil act of the antichrist and will not be spared from the fury of hell fire and God's righteous anger.

58. This indicates that the church also does not have any power, nor can she use submission to extrabiblical and worldly laws, ideas, or orders, as an excuse to give up or weaken the Great Commission, or to hand over this ministry that concerns the souls of humanity and the glory of eternal consummation to the control or management of the government, institutions, or individuals.

59. Saying the Great Commission cannot be weakened means all peoples, places, social groups, genders, classes, and cultures should have the gospel of Christ proclaimed to them to establish the church of Christ and to worship the only true God. The church cannot accept any individual or institutional discrimination or prohibition against the Great Commission to evangelize all people, ages, and political domains.

60. This does not deny that the church, in specific societies or cultures, must accept the reality of environmental limitations such as transportation, safety, or other structural or technological limits on the ministry of missions. When such historical conditions cannot support the church's expansion on a greater scope or provide avenues to achieve better results for the Great Commission, the church should exercise great restraint but at the same time earnestly pray, wait, and work toward the betterment of these environmental limitations.

61. Under all circumstances, if the church actively and publicly weakens the Great Commission by cooperating with the local government or social culture, by stripping itself of the divine ministries of gospel evangelism and public worship, or due to the pressures of secular authorities limits or discriminates or self-censures the works of the Great Commission, then the church openly betrays our Lord, betrays what Christ has commissioned the church, and blasphemes its glorious role as "stewards of the mysteries of God" (1 Corinthians 4:1).

62. In roughly two thousand years of church and world history, the relationship between the two kingdoms, in which the church holds the power of "the keys of the kingdom of heaven" and the government holds the "sword," is commonly called the principle of "separation of church and state," or the dichotomy of the church and state.

63. The Bible has recorded that while answering the Jew's question whether to pay taxes to the Roman government or not, our Lord Jesus said,

"Therefore render to Caesar the things that are Caesar's, and to God the things that are God's" (Matthew 22:21). This means that first, even in this fallen world, there are still certain things that Christ claims to be "things that are God's." So in China today, there exists "things that are God's." This is the hope of humanity, and this is the hope of China.

64. Second, Christ has proclaimed that "the things that are God's" are not the same as "Caesar's things." Also, God's things are above Caesar's things. For God's things do not belong in the sphere of Caesar's rule and power. This question and answer happened before Christ was crucified on the cross. Christ had not yet resurrected from the dead, had not yet been given glory and powers, but he still commanded giving "things of God" directly and only to God, and not to Caesar.

65. Third, when Christ pointed to a silver coin and made this statement, he also proclaimed that "God's things" and "Caesar's things" are overlapping or coexisting. So even a silver coin could simultaneously belong to God and Caesar. Caesar's things are external, but God's things are internal. Caesar's things are about money and personal interests, and God's things are about souls and worship.

66. At this point, Christ has separated two powers—although both of these powers ultimately are derived from his authority. One is "the power of the sword." It is what God has granted to states. Its purpose is for people to govern all things related to money and personal interests, to protect and encourage good behavior, and to punish wrongdoings for God's own glory and the public good. If the state abuses this power, thereby causing the church and believers to suffer many external losses in their rights, the church may fight and make legal appeals for its own interests if they only suffer physical or personal harm. But it does not deny the church and its members the responsibility to obey the government because these matters are not "things of God."

67. But there is another power of "the keys to the kingdom of heaven," and it is granted by God only to the church. Thus all that is required of a person's worship, faith, and the things of the conscience are what Christ calls the "things of God." The church is the community that preserves God's things and we are called "servants of Christ" (1 Corinthians 4:1). These things of God are the hope of all societies and peoples, including Chinese society and all individuals within it.

68. No government or social institution has the power to manage or judge a person's conscience, faith, and religion. Worldly power is limited to managing and protecting a person's outer body, properties, and the public good and order. By any definition, the Christian faith is not the affair of any national government. No government agency or its associates have the rights to interfere, monitor, or direct the church's doctrines, officers, or any gospel-related ministry. Also it cannot take away or limit the church's right to preach and administer the sacraments.

69. Although the things of the world and the things of God are hard to distinguish because they sometimes overlap, based on the freedom of conscience in Christ, the church can accept external losses of its interests. When it is necessary, and for the sake of the gospel, we encourage believers to have faith and courage to even accept the loss of life, because external loss and humiliation is the true meaning of the cross. As Christ once said, "Whoever finds his life will lose it, and whoever loses his life for my sake will find it" (Matthew 10:39).

70. The mystery of the gospel is based on Christ's death and resurrection. It turns this fallen world's principles, which make external, material, and military might as the highest power, on its head. Humanity's fallen and sinful state makes us indulge in these bodily and lustful powers; we cannot help ourselves. Only Christ's atonement can destroy the power of death, forgive the sins of those who believe in him, and give them freedom and life.

71. Therefore, the theology of the gospel is the theology of the cross. The kingdom of the gospel is the kingdom of the cross. In any age, any political realm, the cross has always been the message of the church, and the cross must be the means through which the church preaches this message.

72. Regardless of her circumstances, the church will always rely on the grace of our Lord to remain faithful to the end. We will not give up the power of the "keys to the kingdom of heaven" or offer it to any temporary political or economic power or in complicity with any political power confuse God's things with Caesar's things. Otherwise, the church not only offends and betrays our Lord, but she has also sold out the souls of humanity and any hope left in Chinese society.

AGAINST THE "THREE-SELF MOVEMENT" AND
AFFIRMATION OF THE GREAT COMMISSION

73. Regarding the power of "the keys to the kingdom of heaven," all the apostles have taught us, "We must obey God rather than men" (Acts 5:29). Because of this, we are opposed to the TSPM churches and their officers and their behaviors in China, which we have listed below, and we have to regard their behavior as shameful apostasy.

74. These behaviors include: accepting the state and atheistic political party's political censorship of, credential examination for, and monitoring, testing, training, registering, and financially contributing to any church officers; church officers simultaneously working for the church and the state, or a political party, or political agencies; churches ordaining those that are working in the government, in a political party, or political agencies as officers; organizing, joining, and preaching on behalf of the state, the party, or political agencies according to their political propaganda and agendas, even preaching these in the church and carrying out political movements within the church; accepting the state's, the Party's, or political agencies' limitations on age, location, methods, numbers, and content in the ministries of the gospel, public worship, and administration of the sacraments; accepting the state's, the Party's, or the political agencies' requirements or pressure in the primary ministry of preaching of the word, which results in altering, weakening, or self-censorship of the gospel message; denying the authority of the Bible or publicly accepting heretical behavior; working with or even joining in the persecution of members of the true church that upholds the faith of the gospel; working with or joining in the slander, accusation, and persecution of any missionaries in China and world missions; openly holding idolatrous worship gatherings or church ceremonies such as raising the national flag, singing communist revolutionary songs or secular music, public readings of political leaders' statements, and so on.

75. Those churches and officers who have or continue to betray the church's power of the keys of the kingdom of heaven confuse Caesar's things with God's things, join in the persecution of the true church, and compromise the gospel and its faith, should seek God's mercy to give them a faithful heart to overcome this world and repent and return to our Lord. Perhaps the Lord will have unfathomable grace, retract his anger, and still give

grace to his people. He may still enable them to be covered in the precious blood of Christ, remain faithful to the end, and win the crown of life (Revelation 2:10).

76. We believe that the Three-Self Patriotic Movement, which has lasted for more than half a century in China, is a result of some churches' active or passive cooperation with the atheistic government. It is a movement of the antichrist because it seeks to split the catholic faith and the catholic church, denies that there is a kingdom of Christ that is higher than the nations of the earth, and attempts to create a "Nationalistic Church" that depends on political power. This is a scheme of Satan for the destruction of Christ's church in China and turns true faith into a fake religion.

77. But the Lord's will is good (Genesis 50:20), and through more than half a century's political persecution and division in the church in China, it has resulted in the revival, fulfillment, and protection of the Chinese house church, and on three facets listed below, they remain faithful to the gospel and the way of the cross.

78. First, we uphold biblical inerrancy as the highest standard for the whole life of the church and believers, and as the judgment of all things. Second, we firmly uphold "Christ as the church's only ruler." We refuse any atheistic government's leadership or interference in our gospel and truth ministries. Third, based on the principle of the "separation of church and state," we uphold the dichotomy of the church's power of the heavenly keys and the government's power of the sword as coexistent. In the realm of government we submit to the rulers, but in the realm of the Spirit we uphold the freedom of conscience.

79. We believe that such religious agencies as the Three-Self Patriotic Movement and the Protestant Affairs Department are controlled and monopolized by the state. They are political agencies that have given themselves to political power, and they are agents of the antichrist. These two agencies are the "false church"; they belong as part of a group of secular national agencies, and they are not part of the church of Christ our Lord. The nature of a "church" cannot be controlled by any rulers or political religious organizations, but rather it is a community of people chosen by God among nations, peoples, and generations who proclaim and believe in a spiritual and covenantal kingdom of Christ that cannot be seen (John 18:36).

80. At the same time, even within the Three-Self system, there are only individual church buildings (places of worship) but no "local congregations"
registered as independent, corporate entities. All of the congregations are
controlled by an evil labor union that is loyal to Caesar. Only by being
part of such an agency can they obtain legal government sanctions. The
scheme of Satan is precisely to destroy the "local churches." Only by
taking away the local churches' autonomy and independence can they
establish a national "false church" and take away the church's keys to the
kingdom of heaven.

81. We believe that in today's China, only by completely parting with the
Three-Self system, completely ending cooperation with Caesar's con-
spiracy, solely relying on the Bible and the Lord Jesus' Great Commission,
proclaiming our faith, ordaining officers, reestablishing church properties, and recounting the remnants, can we restart building true and
independent "local churches" one by one.

82. The church must be willing to fight to the death, not for civil rights and legal
stature that are visible, but for the keys to the kingdom of heaven and the
power of the gospel that are invisible. The church should never give up her
most important assets. They are not church properties or financial deposits
but what God has given to us—the "mysteries," which are the holy doctrines
given to us by our Lord, the holy offices, and the holy sacraments.

83. Once the church capitulated to the flesh in holy doctrines, holy offices, and
the holy sacraments, once it began to depend on earthly powers and submit
to politics, then the church gave up her worship to idols. The church has
lost her beautiful and glorious nature as Christ's bride, which is her holiness; and she will become a whore and no longer a church of our Lord.

84. In summary, on the one hand, God has given the power of the sword to
the government (Romans 13:1-13) to administer worldly affairs, to ensure
physical order and peace. On the other hand, God has given the power of
the keys of the kingdom of heaven to the church (Matthew 16:19):
preaching the gospel, administering the sacraments, judging spiritual affairs, becoming "stewards of the mysteries of God" (1 Corinthians 4:1).

85. This means, on the one hand, the state cannot interfere or judge a citizen's faith and conscience, and it does not have the power to interfere
with a church's doctrines, offices, worship, and preaching of the gospel.

On the other hand, the church and her officers have no right to interfere or participate in state operations; it has no rights to take or execute any executive powers.

86. This does not mean that Christian citizens should not be like other citizens who do not believe in religion or believe in other religions. They can exercise their legal rights to vote and be elected and other political privileges. Christians should not be discriminated against or limited in school examinations, school applications, employment, advancements, awards, education, research, public speaking, service as officials, or leadership in any capacity. However, if an officer of the church starts to serve in the government or take on a government position, then the church has the right to ask them to give up or resign from their offices in the church. The church also has the right to ask Christians who work in government or take on any political position to resign and give up their government positions when they are elected to be a church officer.

87. Therefore, the church cannot accept an atheistic party's propaganda or accept the state religious department's interference with our religious freedom. We cannot accept that there could be state "administrative departments" above the church of our Lord Jesus Christ. We cannot accept that "religious affairs" constitute part of the government's function. We cannot accept limits on "self-propagation" on the national level and a scheme of "limited area, limited points, and limited people" on the local level.[4] These are nothing more than deception. We cannot accept the so-called political agenda of "religious autonomy."

88. Real "religious autonomy" is only with Christ as our Lord and the Bible as our foundation. Any "autonomy" outside of Christ is a betrayal to the Lord and comes from the Evil One. The real "self-propagating, self-sustaining" truth is that the faithful and unfaithful cannot be yoked together. "Do not be unequally yoked with unbelievers. For what partnership has righteousness with lawlessness? Or what fellowship has light with darkness? What accord has Christ with Belial? Or what portion does a believer share with an unbeliever?" (2 Corinthians 6:14-15).

89. In other words, religious affairs will never belong to China, and it does not belong to any temporary earthly political power. True religion

---

[4]See the "Three Fixed Policy."

(godliness) belongs to Christ the Lord, belongs to the whole world, and belongs to the conscience of all the faithful.

90. With regards to rulers and obedience to authorities, the church is willing and hoping that China will alter its religious regulations. We earnestly pray for the rulers and leaders of this nation and all its officers to receive the grace and forgiveness of Christ.

91. Once the Chinese government is willing to give up interference and control over the church's doctrines, offices, and proclamation of the gospel, the church is happy to accept the government's regulations and administrative limits for the sake of public order and public good, which may include the church being an independent religious organization and registering under a department of civil affairs.

92. When the state administers order and affairs outside of the church, as long as it does not interfere with the essence of our faith, then the church will have the responsibility to respect and obey. The church, being a part of society, is also willing to accept any state limitations on technology and material regulations, as long as these limitations do not contradict the Bible and are equally applied to other social institutions. Then it is the church's responsibility to respect and obey.

93. As long as the government insists on the "unity of church and state," continues to consider religious affairs as internal government affairs, violently interferes with the church's power of the keys of the kingdom of heaven, and refuses to allow any local church to independently register with any civil affairs departments, the church must hold firm to the above declarations of the house church. We will obey legal administrative regulations and respect the state's power of the sword, but on the other hand, through nonviolence, we will maintain our conscientious opposition, walk in the way of the cross, hold firm to the church's sovereignty and freedom of faith, and protect the believer's freedom of conscience.

94. Also, whether it is in season or out of season, the church will do her best to proclaim the gospel (2 Timothy 4:2). For individuals may be bound, but God's Word will not be bound (2 Timothy 2:9); servants may be killed, but the gracious Lord has resurrected.

95. In June 1955, a patriarch of the Chinese house church, God's servant Wang Mingdao, published a paper titled "We—For the Sake of Faith." It

was his public declaration, along with other Chinese churches', with regards to why he refused to join the Three-Self Movement. On August 8 of the same year, in the early morning, Wang Mingdao, his wife Liu Jinwen, and other coworkers were arrested. Later on, believers and evangelists who followed Mr. Wang Mingdao's example to hold firm to the ancient gospel and refuse to join the Three-Self were arrested, and the government called them the "Wang Mingdao Anti-revolutionary Organization." This year is the sixtieth anniversary of Wang Mingdao's arrest and the establishment of the "Wang Mingdao Anti-revolutionary Organization." Up until this day, the church of our Lord Jesus Christ in China has been under continuous political persecution for sixty years. Because of this, our church decided to publish these 95 theses, for the purpose of reaffirming the Chinese house church's positions on our faith, and before the government and society at large, with a fearful but humble heart, defend the church.

In the name of our Lord Jesus Christ, Amen.

Chengdu Early Rain Reformed Church

Pastors: Wang Yi, Wang Huasheng

Elders: Liu Huisheng, Su Bingsen, Xue Jiafu, Yan Xixia, Yu Tao

August 18, 2015

PART II

THE ESCHATOLOGICAL CHURCH AND THE CITY

On February 1, 2018, the New Regulations on Religious Affairs came into effect. They were announced by the State Administration for Religious Affairs one year prior and established SARA's responsibility to oversee all religious institutions and organizations in China, though it was generally unclear how heavily the regulations would be enforced. With their arrival, debate intensified within house churches regarding whether congregations should respond by preemptively breaking into small, private gatherings as they had done in previous decades or whether they should resist making any changes and continue with visible, public worship.

While Wang Yi's manifesto (part one) grappled with the theological significance of the history of the Chinese house church, part two turns to the development of his ecclesiology in the shadow of the New Regulations. In these chapters, compiled by the editors, Wang Yi seeks to answer the most fundamental question, "What is the church?" Part two reads differently from the previous section. Whereas the articles included in the manifesto were crafted as written texts, often for various human rights and democracy blogs or as chapters for books, the content in this section is mostly adapted from spoken contexts—sermons, conference talks, interviews, and so on. The reader will note a marked difference in tone between the two sections.

During this period, Wang Yi was involved with several large conferences, increasing his visibility within not only the Chinese house church, but also global Christianity. In 2013, Wang Yi preached on his first international stage at the Chinese Mission Convention (CMC) of Ambassadors for Christ (AFC) in Baltimore. In 2014, Wang Yi addressed a nationwide conference of twelve hundred house church pastors and leaders in Hong Kong. The first of its kind, the Grace to City conference was planned and organized by Chinese house churches and featured several prominent house church pastors as plenary speakers alongside Timothy Keller from Redeemer Presbyterian Church in Manhattan. Three years later, in 2017, Wang Yi spoke at Hong Kong 500, a nationwide gathering of house church pastors to commemorate the five hundredth anniversary of the Protestant Reformation. Three prominent American pastors—John Piper, Richard Pratt, and Paul Tripp—shared the stage with five important house church pastors who each preached on one of the five solas of historic Protestantism. Later in 2017, Wang Yi was scheduled to speak in Jakarta, Indonesia, at another Reformation anniversary conference hosted by Stephen Tong, a Reformed Chinese Indonesian pastor who has been significant in spreading Reformed theology among the Chinese diaspora. As the only house church pastor included among the plenary speakers, Jakarta would have been his most visible engagement of global Christianity; however, as with the Lausanne Congress, Wang Yi was not permitted to leave China to participate. Instead, his sermon was read in absentia by a friend.

In many of these chapters, Wang Yi discusses his own personal revival and reflects on his pastoral role. Wang Yi also demonstrates a growing belief in his eventual persecution and his sense of calling to publicly suffer for Christ. In each of these chapters, Wang Yi expresses his belief that the church is God's gift to the city. As such, he does not discuss persecution of either himself individually or of the church corporately as something to avoid. Persecution is ultimately problematic not because of the harm it does to the Christian but because of the harm it does to the church's ability to bless the city. The church is the city's watchman; without it, the city is left unguarded.

Beginning in mid-2018, government interference with large, public house churches increased significantly. Every year, Early Rain Covenant Church commemorates the Sichuan Earthquake of 2008 on its May 12 anniversary. On Friday, May 11, 2018, Wang Yi and fellow Early Rain elder Li Yingqiang (李英强) were arrested in advance of ERCC's tenth anniversary memorial service. The following day, roughly two hundred Early Rain members were also detained and government officials raided the church's building, hauling away close to ten thousand books from the church library. Wang Yi's wife, Jiang Rong, and church members searched for the pastors in local detention centers, but they were not able to find them. Posting online midday on Saturday, May 12, Early Rain called for global prayer for the situation to start at 10 pm Beijing Time and reported that churches across China, Asia, and North America gathered to pray in response. At 10:20pm Beijing Time, Li Yingqiang was released and Wang Yi called Jiang Rong to let her know he would also soon head home.

2018 also witnessed the closure of Zion Church in Beijing. Over the course of the year, government officials began prohibiting and closing Zion's many meeting places, and on September 9, 2018, approximately seventy police officers rushed into the final location, destroying the property, confiscating the church's materials, and blocking the entrance. Some church members were detained and taken away in police vehicles, fire trucks, and buses. The church was ordered to disband and never meet physically again. They currently worship together online.

These events heightened Wang Yi's belief in escalating persecution. In response, he and the leadership of Early Rain began to plan for further interference and harassment. They determined not to abandon public worship and street evangelism and to continue their aggressive church planting strategies moving forward.

9

THE MISSION AND LABOR CAMP OF THE GOSPEL

WANG YI

This sermon was preached to the Chinese Mission Conference (CMC) in Baltimore in 2013. It addressed conference attendees, most of whom were overseas Chinese, who were considering callings to ministry. The sermon clearly demonstrates Wang Yi's developing kingdom eschatology and its application to the pastoral calling. After the conference, Wang Yi's sermon was published in Church China, *the largest Christian magazine in mainland China.*

When I do premarital counseling, I ask each young couple to choose a book in the Bible for us to read and pray through together. We do this together in order to seek God's calling for them as they enter into their marriage covenant. I've always wanted someone to select the book of Job, and a couple actually selected this book a few years later!

I will usually ask the couple to share their thoughts and impressions after we study the book. I want to help them see the specific instances of grace and favor that Jesus has given them in their life stories. Finally, I work with the couple to identify a key verse that will serve as the theme for their wedding ceremony and the sermon I preach at their wedding.

Half a year ago, there was an engaged couple who selected the story of Joseph from Genesis for their wedding theme. The Lord used this story of bitterness and hope as his assurance and blessing for their marriage. This couple found a special comfort in Genesis 41:51-52 when Joseph names his oldest son Manasseh and says, "God has made me forget all my hardship and all my father's house" and names his second son Ephraim and says, "For God has made me fruitful in the land of my affliction."

The engaged brother that I was counseling said to me, "When we meditate upon these verses, we hear God's promise for our marriage."

Afterward, their wedding invitations were printed with the title of my sermon, "God makes me prosper in the place of suffering."

You'll most likely never hear this text preached at a wedding. However, isn't this the very nature of marriage? God makes us prosper in the place of suffering. And isn't this the gospel? God makes a way for his elect to prosper in the place where his Son suffered.

We tend to value and appreciate twenty-four-karat gold because of its superior quality. An eighteen-karat Christian can hardly be considered a Christian. What separates twenty-four-karat gold from eighteen-karat gold? It's gold that has been through suffering and high heat. In Proverbs 17:3, it says, "The crucible is for silver, and the furnace is for gold, and the LORD tests hearts." God also says to his captive people through his prophet, Isaiah, "Behold, I have refined you, but not as silver; I have tried you in the furnace of affliction" (Isaiah 48:10).

The Bible tells us that only men who have suffered are attractive men; only women who have suffered are virtuous women. Somehow, our standard for an attractive man has become about his riches and handsome appearance. When we were children, we were taught that the standard for the ideal man was Ken Takakura. His face looks like it was shaped by the Yangtze River, the Yellow River, and the Qinghai-Tibet Plateau. We wouldn't necessarily say that he was a very handsome man, but people were attracted to his tough guy persona.

Doesn't the gospel describe for us this type of man and woman? When does the gospel encourage or promise us that we will become beautiful and successful men or women?

1. Paul was not an attractive man, and the gospel he preached wasn't attractive to people either. Tonight, I want to specifically speak to a special group of people in our midst. This message is directed to those of you who have already been called by God, or will be called by God, to serve his people by preaching in a full-time capacity.

I want to preach what Paul preached based on the last two verses of Acts: "[Paul] lived there two whole years at his own expense, and welcomed all who came to him, proclaiming the kingdom of God and teaching about the Lord Jesus Christ with all boldness and without hindrance" (Acts 28:30-31).

The book of Acts concludes with this text, a meaningful open ending. These last two verses are full of dramatic tension. It is the mystery of the gospel which both creates and explains these tensions.

Paul is a prisoner, or more specifically, a prisoner who has made an appeal to Caesar for his case. However, Paul has been imprisoned for two whole years, and this length of time shows how long his case has been delayed. More than this, it also shows how the identity of being a prisoner has clung and stuck to him. He is also renting the house where he is imprisoned. This is just like the time period during the Cultural Revolution where if you were executed by shooting, you would have to pay for the bullet as well. Prison was not a place where you could eat and sleep for free. Prisoners were required to bear the cost of being imprisoned. This was truly unfair. Although Roman law was more civilized than ancient Chinese law, it's still considered uncivilized compared to our modern laws. Paul, at this time, had neither religious nor basic human rights. However, when Paul emphasizes the whole two years in which he was imprisoned, and the consequent boldness with which he preached and the fruitfulness of unhindered ministry, his situation doesn't sound like it's defined by suffering. Instead, it sounds like it's describing a type of opportunity. What Paul cares about, and even what the narrator, Luke, is concerned about, is not the way by which they came to Rome, but the purpose for their coming to Rome.

Therefore, the gospel creates a paradox in this situation. As each day passes, and being a prisoner seems more and more like Paul's permanent status, he actually becomes more and more like an apostle. His physical body is imprisoned, but the gospel is free and unhindered. This is exactly what Paul means when he writes, "For I think that God has exhibited us apostles as last of all." The apostles are compared to the prisoners of war who are paraded at the end of the triumphant Roman army. These captives highlight the glory of the victorious country. In this sense, the apostles are captives who reveal the glory of Christ's kingdom. If the gospel implies that this world is enemy-occupied territory, then the office of apostle is inseparable from the status of being a prisoner.

The way Paul entered the city of Rome is similar to the way our Lord Jesus entered Jerusalem. They both entered these cities in the midst of suffering. When you hear this, it doesn't sound like missions, but it sounds like a labor camp instead. If your son or daughter is called by the Lord to go on missions, a lot of parents may experience feelings and emotions that are similar to as if their child was going to a labor camp.

Recently, I heard that China has abolished the use of labor reeducation camps. Reeducation through labor (RTL) is imprisonment without trial and deprives citizens of their personal freedoms. RTL is a system that centered around the usage of forced labor to reeducate people into the Chinese communist ideology.

From the preparation stage in 1955 to the implementation stage in 1957 to its abolition in 2014, RTL lasted fifty-seven years. Like the seventy years when the Jews were taken into exile in Babylon, RTL lasted more than half a century.

Originally, Daniel, his friends of nobility, and the royal house of Judah were the first Jews to be taken into captivity. More of the social elites were taken among the second wave of exiles. Nebuchadnezzar put these exiles through a type of reeducation labor camp where they learned all of the knowledge of the Chaldeans. The Babylonian effort to reframe the exiles' understanding of culture and religion was an attempt to take the people of the Lord and make them belong to Babylon completely and teach them to be good children of the empire.

However, after more than half a century, the Jews not only survived this re-education labor camp, but they also raised remarkable descendants. Behind Nebuchadnezzar's efforts to reeducate God's covenantal people was actually the Lord's reeducation labor camp for his rebellious people. In a sense, when Adam and Eve were expelled from the Garden of Eden, this began the prolonged re-education labor camp for the entire human race.

The essence of the gospel is that this unfinished labor camp in the Old Testament has been completed in the New Testament.

Jesus' captivity in the New Testament became the hope for the captive Jews in the Old Testament. In the Old Testament, it is God's sinful and rebellious son, Israel, who is taken into captivity in Babylon. In the New Testament, it was God's sinless son, Jesus, who took the initiative to willingly be taken captive by Babylon, which is a symbol of our world.

The essence of the gospel is that unless the Son of God was condemned to the labor camp, then the labor camp couldn't be abolished.

The gospel means that since the Son of God was sentenced to the labor camp, and the servant cannot be greater than the master, and the student cannot be greater than the teacher, then we are also subject to being sentenced to the labor camps in this world. In fact, we must be forced into this world's labor camp.

The ending to the book of Acts means that Paul's mission is part of the prolonged continuation of this world's labor camp. However, unlike the exiled Jews, Paul and the other apostles (prisoners) began to preach a gospel of freedom while experiencing physical capture.

Missions is to preach about a labor camp that has been subverted by the power of the gospel. In other words, it is to preach about a labor camp that has already been made ineffective by the power of the gospel. Paul, while in bondage, preaches to those who are unbound to tell them that they are truly the ones who are in bondage. Paul, who is imprisoned, proclaims to the kings, the leaders, and all worldly powers that this world's labor camp has already been abolished by the power of the cross.

2. Regardless of what happens in the future and which city you serve God's church in, are you willing to enter that city in a manner of humility? Are you willing to be subjected to the suffering of the labor camp of this world in order to proclaim the gospel that abolishes it?

However, what I am worried about is today there are a lot of overseas Chinese churches who will not enter China in the same way that Paul entered Rome, and they will no longer enter China the way that Jesus entered Jerusalem. Choosing to work with a house church is the same as choosing the road which is forbidden by the government yet not forbidden by God. To choose the Three-Self church is to choose superficial glory and a road that is not forbidden by the government and yet leads to an utter dead end.

In these past two days, there have been co-laborers and believers who have asked me, "Is your church as public and free as the Three-Self church?" I told them, "No, no. We are actually more free than the Three-Self church." Why did I say this? Because we are the same as Paul—we are completely "unlawful" so the gospel that we preach is not hindered or changed by anyone, whether it is the Religious Affairs Bureau, Ethnic Religion Committee, or the United Front Work Department.

Last year, I was in Taipei attending a seminar, and we were talking about setting up a school for church planting. There were some Taiwanese co-laborers who asked in surprise, "Doesn't the Chinese church not have religious freedom? How can you still set up a church planting school?" I told them, "We can do this precisely because our house churches are underground and completely 'unlawful.'" So praise the Lord! We are living in the midst of the gospel, and we actually have more religious freedom than the Chinese churches in Taiwan, Hong Kong, and North America. We have more freedom just as the apostle Paul, though bound, had greater religious freedom than the Jews who worshiped in the synagogues. It is precisely because we are completely "unlawful" that God, in the midst of a rising superpower nation and a type of decaying social order, can open up unreached and unknown places for the gospel to flourish. This is just like what God did at the height and fall of the first century Roman Empire.

I'm also worried that within our house churches today, there are those who desire to enter mainstream society by actively participating in its activities.

These individuals no longer seek to enter Rome and Jerusalem by the ways of Paul and Jesus. To become a "public church," you must first be a publicly persecuted, marginalized, and openly rejected church. Paul's approach to evangelism and church planting were the same as Jesus'—they were both public. When we read Acts and the Epistles, we do not see the apostles carefully avoiding any hard topics or hiding themselves and their ministries from the public eye. In fact, the disciples were always committed to their ministries especially in the midst of greater and more widespread persecution. I'm not saying that the disciples were looking to be publicly persecuted. Instead, once you realize that missions is missions in a labor camp, or missions includes suffering, you won't be confused when you suffer in ministry. Just like what Paul and Luke said, the gospel had unprecedented growth and had an impact like a nuclear explosion in the Roman world. Unprecedented bondage became unprecedented joy.

The very essence of the gospel causes evangelists to experience an upside-down way of life and fundamentally changes how they measure their own success. In the last two verses of Acts, we see the nature of this upside-down witness.

3. In his *Republic*, Plato recounts Socrates's dialogues with different individuals regarding what justice is and what a just city-state looks like. One of these individuals said to Socrates, "Most people obey the law and do justice because, in most cases, it is to their advantage to do so." In response, Socrates said that unless you can prove that justice is worthy to attain and trust in of itself, the unrighteous will get everything they want. That is, when absolute justice is infringed upon by absolute injustice, the righteous and just person will lose everything. However, people today still believe in a sense of justice and will abide by justice. Therefore, only justice can justify itself and allow a just city-state to be possible.

In actuality, Socrates's argument encounters its biggest challenge here. In the end, Socrates was unjustly put to death by an unjust city-state. However, we know that he could have fled from his captors and died in peace. Socrates, in this way, answered the questions which he couldn't fully answer in the *Republic*. In other words, Socrates chose to use his death to bear witness to the justice of the city-state that he spoke about. In Socrates's mind, justice must be just in and of itself, even in the midst of unjust circumstances.

This is actually Jesus' Great Commission. Socrates became a missionary for his own ideals just like the heroes in Chinese history who sacrificed their lives for the sake of justice. They were all missionaries who spread their own ideals.

Jesus also called his disciples to be missionaries, but on account of the gospel. All missionaries and evangelists who preach salvation outside of Christ are witnesses unto death. Suffering is guaranteed in this life; however, missionaries in Christ are witnesses unto the resurrection. Suffering is necessary among both types of missionaries, but it does not have the final word for the Christian.

In a sense, the books of Daniel and Job both answer the pressing question in the *Republic*, which is, "Is there a value in righteousness that overcomes suffering? Is justice worth laying our lives down for?"

However, in the ultimate sense, only the Gospels thoroughly answer this question. Pastor Timothy Keller points out the difference between the Passion of Christ and the passion of the saints. From the surface, the Passion of Christ is not as stirring and fervent as the passion that Christians face. Even the heroes of the Liangshan Marsh and of the Chinese Communist Revolution had powerful last words as they faced their deaths.[1] However, Jesus on the cross is the upside-down hero. He is silent and sometimes wails. He mourns and does not rejoice. He suffers and does not experience peace.

Because of Jesus' suffering, his disciples can experience the most supreme joy. In the history of humankind and all of our suffering we cause and bear our own suffering. There is no redemptive meaning in our suffering which could save others. We give up because the cost to redeem others is too high. The Passion of Christ is the only redemptive suffering that can save. Therefore, Jesus bore the root and essence of suffering for all of those who suffer in him, which is separation from God's holiness, righteousness, and love. And all of those who suffer in Christ, in turn, receive the full privilege of their suffering in Christ, which is their renewed union with God's holiness, righteousness, and love.

In other words, the reason why our suffering in Christ is joyous and glorious is because our suffering allows us to experience union with Christ. And the reason why Jesus' suffering is so painful and meek is because on the cross, at a specific moment and in a certain sense, the Holy Son experienced a complete legal and emotional separation from his heavenly Father.

This is the mystery of the gospel, and the secret paradox of Paul's simultaneous freedom and bondage. This is God saying, "Whoever finds his life will lose it, and whoever loses his life for my sake will find it" (Matthew 10:39). God says again, "Whoever loves his life loses it, and whoever hates his life in this world

---

[1]The Liangshan Marsh heroes are found in the *Water Margin*, one of China's Four Great Novels. It tells the story of a band of outlaws who rebel against the government but are granted amnesty in exchange for their aid in countering other nomads and rebels.

will keep it for eternal life" (John 12:25). As D. A. Carson said, "The cross is not only our creed, it is the standard of our ministry."[2]

This is the call of gospel-centered preaching. Although every Christian is called to live according to the principles of the upside-down kingdom, preachers are particularly called to become representatives of this upside-down way of life among our brothers. Your lifestyle needs to be a model room for the kingdom of heaven. Your family needs to be like a flagship store for the gospel. If you will not die for your faith, then you will not live for it. If your faith is not something you're willing to die for and live entirely for, then it's nothing. What kinds of situations will help us witness to such a gospel? What kinds of situations are preachers joyful to be in and should we desire to live in? We eagerly desire the "without hindrance" result so that, like Paul, we completely forget about our outward circumstances. The one who pursues marriage in the midst of a famine forgets that he is in a famine, and the one who returns home in the midst of a storm forgets the storm outside. It is just like Su Dongpo's words, "It is neither stormy nor clear."[3] For him, it was his ideal of a simple life which finally ended any potential for pursuing lofty goals. For Paul, it was a fervent commitment, which even if it looked crazy was worth it for God.

In Genesis 41:14, "Then Pharaoh sent and called Joseph, and they quickly brought him out of the pit. And when he had shaved himself and changed his clothes, he came in before Pharaoh." Chrysostom, one of the early church fathers, said that Joseph endured through his suffering and was thoroughly purified, like a piece of gold.[4] When he was brought out of prison and before Pharaoh, he shined brightly.

What is our calling in the midst of the gospel and the ministry of preaching? When my child has a high fever, I long to have a high fever with him. When I first started pursuing my wife, I dreamed about having the same illness as her so that I could be more intimate and know her more deeply. I even longed for the chance to faint in front of her so that she would pity me. I was so committed to that hypothetical situation that I would have been okay with even dying in that moment.

In the gospel, God's only Son "faints" in our presence. He doesn't beg us for love, but he shows unimaginable love to those of us who have been begging for

---

[2]D. A. Carson, *The Cross and Christian Ministry: Leadership Lessons from 1 Corinthians* (Grand Rapids, MI: Baker Books, 2006), 40.

[3]Su Shi (1037-1101) was a Song Dynasty official, poet, and artist. He is the author of many famous classical literary pieces, which Wang Yi here paraphrases.

[4]This is likely referring to John Chrysostom's *A Treatise to Prove That No One Can Harm the Man Who Does Not Injure Himself.*

love our whole lives. The call to full-time ministry is for those who have been conquered by this love. Are you willing to experience the same disease as the one who loves you? Are you willing to endure a fraction of the contempt that the Lord endured and to walk a small segment of the harsh road that our Lord walked?

The gospel doesn't eradicate suffering and loss in this world, but it does wrap all of your suffering and loss in mercy and goodness. It's just like the words in a song, "I'm willing to be a little lamb and snuggle up beside her. I'm willing to be lightly whipped by her every day."[5] When you hear this calling from God, are you willing to be daily struck by his rod and staff? Are you even willing to allow the Lord to use his church, whether a group of Christians you know or don't know, to gently strike you every day?

4. Luke provides two clear definitions of the gospel in these last two verses of Acts.

First, the core of the gospel that Paul preached was the kingdom of God. In the Chinese translation of verse 31, the literal translation says that Paul preached "the way" of the kingdom of God. This was an added interpretation in the translation. In Acts 1, the resurrected Jesus used multiple methods to prove that he was alive to the disciples and spoke to them about "the matters of the kingdom of God." The Chinese translation adds "the matters" into the text. Luke, the author of Acts, carefully focuses the message of the gospel upon the kingdom of God throughout the book. This kingdom of God is the new world where God's reign comes into the old world, and the formation of a new society where God's reign replaces the old society. In other words, the purpose of the gospel is not to establish individuals in a new position within their old society, but to place God's covenant community in a new world to contrast and subvert the old way of living. The difference should be as stark as a fat man standing next to a skinny man, or a tall man standing next to a person of short stature. If this old world was poor, then the gospel would mean riches and prosperity in this life. However, if this old world is full of riches and prosperity, then the gospel means poverty in this life. Likewise, because Rome is powerful, the gospel is powerless. Because Rome was free, the apostles were in bondage.

The gospel implies that the purpose of how we live is to clearly define the boundaries between two overlapping, yet completely different, kingdoms. The

[5]"Zai Na Yaoyuan De Difang" (在那遥远的地方,"In That Faraway Place") is one of the most well-known and widely recorded Chinese pop songs. It was written in 1939 by Wang Luobin.

preacher who is called by God is called to make his entire life a boundary marker among people and to become a landmark in the kingdom of God. By looking at his life, people can discern that there are two kingdoms, and they can redefine shame and glory, and bondage and freedom; all of their circumstances and assets can be redefined.

Second, the core of Paul's gospel message was "teaching about the Lord Jesus Christ." What this means is that everything he preached was related to Christ. More specifically, he preached about the person of Christ and his works.

Chinese people are very hard-working—we read and conduct business, and this is almost how the entire world views Chinese people around the globe. It seems that the harder we work, the more capable we are of receiving blessings from heaven. Therefore, we seem to be only second to the Jews as a people who are blessed by God's favor. If this moralistic claim is true, then China really doesn't need the cross of Christ. If this moralistic claim is true, then Chinese people only need to know more about ourselves, and we don't need to know more about the things of Jesus Christ.

If you have both a master's degree and a PhD, then your title must be PhD. If you've attended college, then you must have also been in kindergarten. But on your business card, you must not write that you graduated from kindergarten. Yet, when the Son of God came into this world, his business card read, "baby in the manger," and he called himself the "Son of Man" on his banner.

This is what it means for those of you who have been called into subversive, full-time gospel-centered ministry. If you hold a doctoral degree or if you're a CEO, would you be willing to change the title on your business card to "evangelist" tonight?

When we watch soccer, we will often see some very discouraged players on a team play frantically and even get hit with a red card with just a few minutes left in the game. However, if this player's team wins in the end, he will be just as ecstatic as his teammates, and he is allowed to return to the field and run wildly, hugging his teammates, and soak in the cheers of the audience. This is because the team's victory belongs to every player.

This is a gospel-centered alternative calling to the secular workplace. If you think that you're really suited to being a minister, and you feel like you're better than many preachers today, if you want to dedicate yourself to the ministry because you don't want to listen to your pastor's sermons anymore, and you want to plant churches because you can't stay in one specific church, then I pray that the Lord stops you from pursuing ministry. May you flee from your heart's expectation to preach just as you would desire to flee from the fires of hell. Unless you understand that the Lord is not calling heroes of the faith, but he is calling saints; not victors, but failures; not the mighty ones, but the incompetent. Unless you grow in the realization that the defining moment of our lives was Jesus' crucifixion, and how you were not there.

5. The greatest tragedy in our lives is that we all love ourselves.

In many works of literature, people often experience a type of tragedy. That is, the character only realizes and notices that he missed out on all of the people who cared about him at the end of his life. It turns out that the only person who truly loved him was the person he either ignored, didn't care about, or didn't believe in. These sad stories actually all point to the greatest and truest tragedy in our lives—that God's love for us, or the person of the Lord Jesus Christ, is usually the last thing we notice and fully commit ourselves to.

Even after we follow God for many years, we say over and over again, "Oh Lord, I know that you love me, but Brother Zhang doesn't love me, Sister Li doesn't love me, or my pastor doesn't love me."

I have a congregant who wants to marry her boyfriend, who is a nonbeliever. They came looking for me, and the young man very angrily said to me, "Why can't Christians and non-Christians marry? You're not her father. What does this have to do with you?" I responded, "The truth is, if you two get married, have you decided which of you is going to be crucified? Because marriages are covenants, blood must be shed for marriages to be established. If the gospel is not the source of your identity, security, and all of your satisfactions, then you two will surely crucify each other." There are even some unmarried young people who have already crucified their parents!

The heart of the gospel is the kingdom of God and its coming, and the foundation of the kingdom of God is the personhood and work of Jesus Christ himself. The gospel must be relevant to your current life, it must envelop every nook and cranny in your life, and it must be interposed in the midst of all your internal thoughts. The gospel means that Christ is your Messiah in every situation and circumstance of your life.

The gospel is not a conduct record that we provide to the Lord. Instead, the gospel is the Son of God providing us with a perfect and sinless record. To be a Christian is to refuse to trust in your own works or personhood in any way and to trust in this perfect and sinless record for everything.

The gospel allows for everyone's story to be retold, and it answers all of the questions which could not be answered within the story itself. The gospel means that the stories about our lives have no real substance without the story of Christ. The gospel means that once we have Christ's story, all of our stories become one story. To be called as a preacher is to be called into the gospel story and to carry this story into others' lives. It is to tell those who believe that they have meaningful stories that what they have compared to the gospel is really nothing. It is to tell them that everything in their lives depends on the "personhood and works of Christ."

In the book of Acts, Paul is described as a "disturber of the peace." If we use a Chinese idiom, then we could say that he turned the whole world upside-down. The gospel is a story that turns the whole world upside-down. It's upside-down because Christ became flesh. The meanings of "rich" and "poor" are upside-down because the king of the universe became poor. Life and death are upside-down because the Lord of life died on the cross. The inside-out is reversed because the Holy Spirit has come. In Christ, all debts are paid; outside of Christ, all wealth amounts to nothing. In Christ, all failures become successful; outside of Christ, all who succeed become failures.

The gospel is not only what Christ has done for us—the gospel is Christ himself. The gospel is not only the gift of salvation that God gives—the gospel is God himself. To use the famous phrase from the communication theorist McLuhan, "The medium is the message."[6] In regard to the gospel, Christ is the only medium, and he is the only message.

The gospel tears down our pride because the Son of God had to die for us. There is no way to salvation in this world except through the bloodshed of the Son of God. The gospel also eradicates our fears because when we are still enemies of God. He died for us. Therefore, no enemy can ever overcome us.

Tonight, God wants to call those whose pride in this life has been completely destroyed to be full-time ministers of his gospel. Tonight, God will also eradicate the fears of those who hear his calling. He will eradicate the fears of the future, fears of lower standards of living, fears of their children's futures, fears of the weaknesses in the church and in brothers and sisters, and fears of unfamiliar peoples and cultures.

6. Like Paul, you will need to be a prisoner who freely enters a city under bondage. On the one hand, you must have already entered or seen the city of God. On the flipside, you must despair for the city in which you enter.

We once heard the news that a new ambassador to China liked Chinese culture very much. If this news was true, then this was a very stupid thing for

---

[6]Marshall McLuhan, *Understanding Media: Extensions of Man* (Cambridge, MA: MIT Press, 1994).

the other government to do. Think about it: Do you think God would send a person in love with Roman culture to be an ambassador to Rome?

Faith is turning to God with despair in this world. Those who are called into full-time ministry must be people who despair for themselves and the people of this world. They must be like the prophet Daniel, who despaired when he saw the vision and collapsed to the ground like a dead man and became very ill. They must also be like John, who saw the vision of the coming Christ on Patmos, and fell on his face full of terror and became still like a dead man.

I had a conversation with a brother who wanted to get a divorce. I asked him whether he wanted to get married again if he got a divorce. He said, "If the Lord permits, then I am willing." I told him, "People who want to be divorced are still looking for their hope in this life. You are still obsessed with yourself, with the world, and with wishful thinking outside of the marriage which God has established." People who despair in this world will not divorce. People who despair of this world depend on the gospel and serve the gospel.

In other words, if you haven't yet divorced from this world, then you will inevitably be divorced yourself. The servant who is called by God is the bride who is willing to serve him. Therefore, you must be careful. There is no one more wicked and adulterous in the world than the preacher who has not divorced from this world. This type of person, with various motivations, is sometimes willing to serve the church. However, this type of person never wants to enter their appointed mission field in the same way that Paul entered Rome.

7. Everyone wants to meet another person in their best season of life and condition.

On our own terms, we don't want to be treated by the doctor-in-training at the hospital, have our hair cut by the new apprentice in the barbershop, or even listen to the sermon preached by the new intern preacher at church. We don't want to be serviced by someone who is in the midst of their learning process, commit to an immature church, or live in a corrupt and unfree society.

If most of you go to America to escape these things, then how can I call you to leave your comfortable homes to come back to a home filled with mice to serve God?

In a relationship, we hope that the other person is ready. We believe that the most romantic thing is to meet someone who is living their best life. This is how most people define happiness and romance. However, this is not love. This is a consumer's idea of love. A consumer's idea of love doesn't include the desire to grow up and suffer with the other person. They want to jump straight into maturity. We have this consumption-driven sense of love because we don't have the gospel, the kingdom of God, and the works of Jesus Christ. Therefore, we don't have a hope for the future.

There was a pastor who said that people's natural impulses are to only love those who we find worthy of our love. However, it is only God who has the right to love those who he deems worthy of his love, and he has forfeited this right. This is the mystery of the gospel. This is the mystery that creates and explains the tension found at the end of the book of Acts. The one who has his rights lays down his rights. The one who does not have any rights demands such rights. We suffer because we continue to pursue those rights which don't belong to us in the first place.

This ending to Acts doesn't seem to be an impressive turnaround. It just depicts the transformation of a life without rights but demanding rights to a life with rights but laying them down.

However, it means that we need to have encounters with people who are still just learning to commit to the church when it is still immature; to stay in a country when the government is corrupt; to serve the world before it falls apart because the church is the mother of believers, the manifestation of God's kingdom, and the cradle that keeps us nurtured and safe. Our mothers are not perfect, and perfect people do not need grace. The church is not perfect so it is exceedingly full of grace. You cannot enjoy the fullness of grace in Christ without committing to the weakness and imperfections of the church.

The gospel is grace for the weak and not a reward for the strong. The call to full-time ministry is also God's grace for the weak and not a reward for the strong.

Tonight, God wants to call a group of weak people who have turned to him to be examples and representatives of this upside-down life in the church. Are you willing to serve the church not only through your strengths but also through your weaknesses? Are you willing to demonstrate God's extraordinary grace through your failures? Are you willing to let others know about your incompetency and step on your body in their journeys of difficulties and hardships? Are you willing to, one day, in order to add another full-time co-laborer, decrease the amount of support which you receive from the church, to be like Paul, who had the authority but didn't use it to the fullest?

If you are willing, please walk up, and in the presence of Jesus, say, "I am willing."

Sacrifice is laden under every reward. Have you received this reward? God has given you his only begotten Son, and he has rewarded you with an eternal inheritance and everlasting crown in his Son. Do you see that full-time ministry itself is part of this great reward? Do you believe that God's calling for you is his reward for you? If you do, then please come up. If you are not filled with joy, or if your heart is full of sadness, please do not come up because God has not called you tonight. At least, not the person you are right now.

Finally, I would like to use this passage written by one of the elders at my church to make a final call to the workers whom God has called tonight. I would also like to use this passage to speak specifically to the full-time laborers, missionaries, and seminary students who are willing to return to China to serve:

> The most romantic thing that I can think of is to grow old with you in the smog and pollution and share the gospel of Christ alongside you. The most romantic thing that I can think of is to have chemotherapy with you years later and to pray to God with you. The most romantic thing that I can think of, oh, my flesh and blood, is to share the same fate as you and to preach and live according to a true understanding of the gospel.

10

THE CITY OF GOD ON EARTH

WANG YI

This is a transcribed and edited sermon delivered by Wang Yi to Grace to City, a nationwide conference of twelve hundred house church pastors and believers in Hong Kong in 2014. It begins to flesh out Wang Yi's ecclesiology, as well as his theology of the city. He argues that the church is not simply a gathering of Christians for their individual, personal edification. The church is the city of God on earth, the promise of God with us, and salt to preserve a dying world. Speaking to those flocking to China's booming urban centers, Wang Yi seeks to declare the true city that humanity is created to desire—God's city, which is his church.

¹God is our refuge and strength,
  a very present help in trouble.
²Therefore we will not fear though the earth gives way,
  though the mountains be moved into the heart of the sea,
³though its waters roar and foam,
  though the mountains tremble at its swelling. *Selah*
⁴There is a river whose streams make glad the city of God,
  the holy habitation of the Most High.
⁵God is in the midst of her; she shall not be moved;
  God will help her when morning dawns.
⁶The nations rage, the kingdoms totter;
  he utters his voice, the earth melts.
⁷The LORD of hosts is with us;
  the God of Jacob is our fortress. *Selah*
⁸Come, behold the works of the LORD,
  how he has brought desolations on the earth.

[9]He makes wars cease to the end of the earth;
>   he breaks the bow and shatters the spear;
>   he burns the chariots with fire.

[10]"Be still, and know that I am God.
>   I will be exalted among the nations,
>   I will be exalted in the earth!"

[11]The LORD of hosts is with us;
>   the God of Jacob is our fortress. *Selah*

(Psalm 46)

This psalm has a very simple structure: "God is our refuge" is mentioned three times, in verses 1, 7, and 11.[1] You may know Martin Luther's best-known hymn "A Mighty Fortress Is Our God." It is just a paraphrase of this psalm. Our mighty fortress is the Lord who we have praised, worshiped, waited on, and trusted in again and again. It is interesting that here the Lord is not only called a protector or refuge giver but also a *place* of refuge, a city, or a holy place.

I have observed the vicissitudes of Chinese society for the past thirty or so years, and there are two things I have noticed.

First, there is a pop song, "Where Has All the Time Gone?" Where has all the time gone over these past thirty years? China rose sharply and became rich, but we did not have many chances to look around before we were dazzled. There is a Chinese saying, 逝者如斯夫 (*shi zhe ru si fu*), which means time passes like a river.[2] Time rushes by and we can do no more than sigh. We can build up prosperity on earth, but there is no way to stop time. If we cannot rest peacefully in the time we have, we are doing nothing more than simply moving in circles.

Second, I recently read a novel written by a young man who worked in Shanghai. This novel attracted a lot of attention. The author talks about life in the major cities and the struggles of younger generations living in Beijing, Shanghai, and Guangzhou, especially compared to the living conditions in minor cities. He tries to speak up for those drifting or living in major cities and is proud to tell his story of a young man from Shanghai struggling to pursue freedom and his own dreams.

His novel shows us that, in China's major cities today, a new lifestyle and a new society is rising. A new system and an exciting individualistic ideal are emerging. This young man disdainfully looks down on those who, in contrast

---

[1]In Mandarin, only one word is used for "refuge"/"fortress," but the Hebrew uses both refuge and fortress as does the English.

[2]Wang Yi is quoting from the analects of Confucius.

to him, stay in small towns and get jobs in the government or public institutions with their parents' help. Those young people will probably be able to buy their own apartments earlier than their classmates who live in major cities, but the author concludes that they are fallen people, people without dreams. In today's China, the young people with dreams live in major cities.

Dear brothers and sisters, the gospel is not only about individual salvation, but rather, it is more concerned with heaven and earth. The gospel is about redemption in time and space. Modern cultures stress individual stories. To some extent, each person's story deserves to be heard. But after listening to these personal, inner-heart stories, why do we still feel empty? Because the gospel is a story of God's salvation and grace that occurs within time and space.

We see many grand narratives in Chinese society, stories that seem likely to turn the "Chinese dream" into an even grander narrative. This story of the "Chinese dream" enters our dreams of time and space, conquers those dreams, and sweeps them away. Meanwhile, the gospel, the only real grand narrative which has happened in human history, is narrowed down to a single story of the inner heart.

A key word turns up over and over again in Psalm 46: "earth." In eleven verses, "earth" appears five times. The Lord wants to be a refuge on earth for his people, to be with his people on earth, and to make his people at rest on earth. We see a dream that one day, God's will will be done on earth as it is in heaven.

If we believe heaven and earth were created, then heaven and earth are like a building, or a landscape. Houses are built by human beings, but all things are created by God. The whole world is God's building. As the psalms say, the purpose of this building is for God to live together on earth with his people and to govern them by his grace and righteousness. Heaven and earth, as well as time and space, are like a city—the city of God. Genesis showed us the initial stages of creation, when earth was a construction site and Adam the foreman. After Adam fell and was chased out, where can we find the final architectural rendering of this construction site?

There is a construction site next to the building where I live. The site has been there for five years. Recently, they finally started to dig a big hole. But there are no large blueprints or company slogans on the exterior fences to show what they are building. I have passed by that site several times. Each time I ask the exiting workers, "What on earth are you building?" Each time they answer, "We don't know." You see, the entire human race lives in heaven and earth. Even many Christians—called, born again, and saved—live in this land and do not know the final rendering of God's construction site.

This final rendering is recorded in the psalms of Zion and in the books of Revelation and Ezekiel. It is the city of God, which will fill the earth. There are some terms—"to the ends of the earth" and to "fill the earth"—which are used quite similarly in Psalm 46 and in the book of Genesis. There are similar terms in the Great Commission: "to the ends of the earth" and "to the end of the age." Psalm 46 tells us that from the time Abraham was called by God, the dreams and hopes of the Israelite nation and their relationship with God never rested on individual salvation. They dreamed of a city of God. In this city the Lord would live together on earth with his people, be with them, and bless them with peaceful rest. The Lord sends out an announcement to a turbulent world that betrayed him: "Cease striving and know that I am God." In the same way, Jesus Christ rebuked the winds and the sea: "Be still, and know that I am God."

In Revelation 11:19, when the seventh angel sounded the trumpet, "God's temple in heaven was opened, and the ark of his covenant was seen within his temple." This is very interesting. After captivity in Babylon, the Israelites returned to Jerusalem. They rebuilt the fallen tabernacle of David, the walls of the city, and even a second temple. But in this second temple, there was no ark of the covenant, no Urim and Thummim, no tent of meeting used in the wilderness. The glory of the Lord, which appeared when Solomon dedicated the temple, did not appear. This was an empty temple, a holy city without the ark of the covenant. The glory of the Lord did not show itself among them—at least not until John 1:14, when the "Word became flesh and dwelt among us."

"To dwell" means to pitch the tabernacle and the tent of meeting among us. When the ark of the covenant is revealed in heaven at the end of history, the whole world will become the holy temple of the Lord, the entire universe will become a city of God. The church should be this city of God.

In Kunming's terrorist attack, we saw how the conflict and hatred between a Rome-like empire and the tribes it conquers make a city totter.[3] Then at 4 p.m. on March 14, 2014, there was a mass panic on Chunxi Road in Chengdu. Hundreds of people ran wildly in the streets, because a rumor had spread saying someone was killed. Perhaps someone saw a few people who looked like they came from Xinjiang. This panic showed us a defeated city and a divided people.

---

[3] In 2014, a group of men and women carried out a terrorist attack on a train station in Kunming, Yunnan Province, killing 31 people and injuring more than 140. It was reported that the attackers were Uyghurs, an oppressed Muslim minority group in Xinjiang Province; however, no group has claimed responsibility for the attack.

Over the past few decades in China, we have heard news of defeated cities and divided peoples every day.

But every day we preach the gospel of the Lord Jesus Christ in those defeated cities. We hear that one more city has been gathered up and taken in by the Lord himself. Every day, in each city in China, people flee and regather. Meanwhile, each day, in each city in China, the Lord counts his towers, considers his ramparts, and goes through his palaces: his church in that city.

In the Old Testament we see that the captive Israelite people—who continuously failed in God's grace—changed Jerusalem into a Babylon, into a Sodom and Gomorrah. But in the New Testament, we see the real people of Israel, the real sons of Abraham who are blessed with God's promises. They came to Babylon and turned Babylon into Jerusalem.

We saw something exciting when the Holy Spirit came at Pentecost. All the VIPs of Jerusalem had gathered in the city. On that day there would be sacrificial offerings, ceremonies, and celebrations in the temple. But the Holy Spirit did not come to the holy temple. He came to a group of nobodies, of Galileans. God fulfilled the prophecy of Psalm 46. He is with his people on earth, through the salvation made by his son, Jesus Christ. God made his lowly people into a holy place, the city of God on earth.

The gospel itself means a city of God, which is built and expanded among the cities on earth. When you read about Jews from every nation under heaven gathered in Jerusalem on the day of Pentecost in Acts 2:9-11, you find something very interesting: the huge Roman Empire appears in that list very quietly. Without the Lord's presence, the city of Rome was accurately described in Psalm 46 and Acts 2 as "the end of the earth" or "the desolation of the earth." The commission of the gospel is to make the church the city set up by God and to usher it into every city, until the ends of the earth.

Sometimes, I cannot find the things I need, even in my home; sometimes, this includes very important items. I search everywhere, but cannot find them. Later, I find a pile of things. As I clear away the pile—napkins, magazines, and books—I finally find what I need. It was buried at the bottom. In our lives and in the churches of Christ, often the last thing we find is the gospel. As we look at our relationships with our cities, we need to be renewed in the gospel.

A few weeks ago, I went to church on my electric bike. As I passed a bus stop, a bus rushed by and pushed me aside. As I fell, I knocked an old lady off the nearby step. I am a pastor, and I knocked down an old lady. That could be a very serious issue. At the time, I felt my behavior over the next ten minutes was quite good. But when I arrived at church, I shared with my fellow workers that I realized I had behaved like a Pharisee, because I only accepted my exterior responsibility. I kindly raised the woman to her feet, stayed with her, told her I would provide any help she needed, and asked if she needed to be sent to the hospital and where her home was.

What does it mean to be a Pharisee? It means that you take responsibility if you can be regarded as a moral person. But in my heart, in those ten minutes, I was not focused on the Lord. My first thought was: "Something is wrong!" I was worried about myself, not about the woman: *I* messed up, *I* was in big trouble, *I* would miss the morning's meeting with my fellow workers. My relationship with her was not a gospel-centered relationship but a morality-centered one. Morality can define our responsibilities and evaluate our performances. Based on morality, maybe I could receive a good evaluation as a pastor. But the gospel does not put boundaries on our relationships with others. I found out that when I, a pastor, knocked down an old lady on the street, the matter did not become a means of expanding and presenting the city of God in Chengdu.

Why? There was fear in my heart, which made me lose the power and mission of taking Chengdu as my parish. When I knocked down the old lady, I forgot the city of God, the city announced and prophesied in Psalm 46. I forgot Pentecost, when the city of God became present in a city on earth, when a new society appeared suddenly in the midst of an old society. In that moment, I almost did not believe the city belongs to Jesus Christ, the God of resurrection. In that moment "though the mountains be moved," I also moved; "though the seas shake," I also shook.

Brothers and sisters, when I examine myself seriously, I see that when I knocked the old lady down, I faced an identity crisis. I was not acting as a pastor or as a Christian but as a knowledgeable and cultured person, a respectable person. Although I am fat, I am still a gentleman, a glasses-wearing intellectual. That identity faced a challenge: I was a perpetrator, a troublemaker. I had to face the crisis. In the ten minutes after I knocked the lady down, I helped myself out of the situation through good deeds but not by the gospel. I did not allow it to be a chance to make the city of God known in my city. God allowed it to happen "for those who love God all things work together for good" (Romans 8:28), for me to believe the gospel more, for his gospel to enter the city more deeply. He did not allow it to happen so I could keep up a respectable image. Unfortunately, I failed.

This psalm responds to the issues faced by Chinese society. How can we answer the questions Chinese society faces about the passage of time? Time's passage is a fate the Scriptures sum up as "in the morning it flourishes . . . in the evening it fades" (Psalm 90:6) and "he comes out like a flower and withers" (Job 14:2). Psalm 46 tells us the Lord is our dwelling place, that our entire hope and faith is placed on the Lord dwelling in a city, and that "the LORD of hosts is with us."

Facing the lapse of time, the deaths of family members, and the fading away of life reminds me of another psalm of Zion. Psalm 48 says that in the city, God will be our God forever and ever. Another psalm tells us, "Lord, you have been our dwelling place in all generations" (Psalm 90:1). Jesus fulfilled the promise and hope of dwelling together with us. "In the beginning was the Word, and the Word was with God, and the Word was God" (John 1:1).

Jesus came among us from the very beginning of time, and all times are in his hands. In Romans we see a response to the fears Chinese society faces about the passage of time: time is "from him and through him and to him" (Romans 11:36). Jesus is Immanuel, "God with us." The dream of God and people living together on earth was realized in Jesus. The Holy Spirit's coming poured out his salvation on a group of lowly but powerful people who belonged to him. At that moment, the future Jerusalem appeared in the earthly city of Jerusalem. In a spiritual sense, the church became the capital of a whole new world. The church became the city of God. Israelites from every nation under heaven are representatives of the whole earth, representatives of God's plan to "be exalted in the earth" (Psalm 46:10).

Chongqing is called a city of mountains; the church in today's China is a city of mountains. Jinan is called a city of fountains, because there are fountains of living water flowing out from under the city; so the churches in each city of China are cities of God where fountains of life flow out from underneath our feet. Zigong in Sichuan Province is known as a salt city, but the church in each city of China today should be the real city of salt. We are the salt of the earth and the light of the world. Beijing is called the capital, but the church should be the real capital in each city of China. Psalm 46 is a response to contemporary Chinese people's desire and pursuit of the major cities.

As cities of God and capitals of the world, the church is found in each city of this world. People's dreams climax in the city. Without the gospel (which has already entered and will continue to enter each city in China), the commission to preach the gospel, to build the city of God, and to expand the Lord's kingdom, our society will be anxious to build more and bigger cities.

To some extent, people think only major cities matter or that it is only worthwhile to live in major cities. But the gospel tells us the church is the biggest city in the world. The church is the real "Beijing, Shanghai, and Guangzhou." The church is the capital of human souls. The gospel made a group of apostles from the backward province of Galilee into the center of the new world.

The gospel turns on its head the desire Christians feel for major cities, but it also motivates the Christian commission toward the city. If you live in the gospel, wherever Christ's church is being built is the capital of the world. You can bring the gospel to the biggest city—a metropolis of tens of millions—or to a small town with only fifty thousand souls, because the Christian's dream for a greater city has already been fulfilled.

May God raise up more of his servants in this generation to be coworkers and gatekeepers at the entrances of the city gates. Through the gospel, these gatekeepers, these pastors, open the doors to the kingdom of heaven for our cities.

As for myself, Christmas Eve of 2010 was a special night for me to see again my commitment to the city of Chengdu. At 3 p.m. that afternoon, the police captured me in front of my coworkers and the members of my church. It was a busy evening; all the police were on duty in the streets. There was just one policeman and me in the police station. Around 8 p.m., a prostitute was brought into the office. She was captured in the process of a police room check at a hotel. The police left her and went out again. At 10:30 p.m., a thief from Xinjiang was captured and brought into the room. It was a very peaceful night: a pastor from Santai, Sichuan, a prostitute from Zigong, and a thief from Xinjiang, all gathered together in the city. It was Christmas Eve in Chengdu. Our churches are becoming crowded with middle-class professionals. The gospel needs to enter the city more deeply. It must enter the drains, enter in with the petitioners and the marginalized peoples.[4]

Dear fellow workers, maybe you are a part-time minister in your church.[5] Maybe in the past you pursued the Lord's calling for full-time ministry. Perhaps at one time the city of God motivated your heart. If your church still has no pastors; if there are no pastors in your city, your community, or even your street; if your company has a GM but there is no pastor there; if the university you work for has a Party committee secretary but there is no pastor, then I must ask: do you know the average ratio of prostitutes to pastors in China? Do you know the ratio of thieves to pastors, of corrupt officials to pastors?

May God bring you back to respond to his calling to serve in his house, where he is with his children forever, and to serve in the churches which represent the

---

[4] See "National Public Complaints and Proposals Administration."
[5] It is still common for house church pastors in China to serve the church bivocationally, without receiving salaries from their congregations.

living and visible body of Jesus Christ. He is calling you to respond to him, to respond to the city of God, to build the city of God in your own city, to be a doorkeeper in his city. Let this become the biggest dream of your life, the calling that God has given you. But know this road will be very hard.

During the Reformation, every time Martin Luther received depressing news, he said, "Let's sing Psalm 46." I want to call you through this psalm. In the Lord's name, I want to ask anyone among you who is willing to fight for God, with the grace of the gospel and the victory of the Lord, to preach his gospel and to build up coworkers and members in his church. If you once received or pursued this calling, but doubted and ran away from it or never dared to take the first step, I ask you to stand up and say, "I have heard God's calling for me to offer my whole life to be a full-time minister in this era, in each city of China, in the major cities and in the small towns to which I am committed and to which the Lord will send me."

I want God himself to talk to you. Hold the church you serve and the church members you serve in your heart. Think even of brothers and sisters you do not yet know who are in a place where the Lord will send you. If you have heard this call, I ask you one more time: respond.

11

THE WAY OF THE CROSS, THE LIFE OF THE MARTYRS

WANG YI

Shortly before the Early Rain's commemoration of the anniversary of the Sichuan Earthquake, Wang Yi was arrested and detained. This is an edited translation of Wang Yi's sermon to Early Rain on Sunday, May 13, after his release. Wang Yi's sermon was posted publicly on Early Rain's now defunct website. It is an emotional and prayerful sermon based on a traditional Korean hymn about faithfully serving while following in the sufferings of Jesus, and italics are here used to indicate moments in which Wang Yi turns to address God directly in prayer. Wang Yi asks his church to make a commitment to "walk the way of the cross" and to participate in filling up the incomplete number of martyrs so that the church might intercede on behalf of Chengdu and China before God's judgment throne.

When he opened the fifth seal, I saw under the altar the souls of those who had been slain for the word of God and for the witness they had borne. They cried out with a loud voice, "O Sovereign Lord, holy and true, how long before you will judge and avenge our blood on those who dwell on the earth?" Then they were each given a white robe and told to rest a little longer, until the number of their fellow servants and their brothers should be complete, who were to be killed as they themselves had been. (Revelation 6:9-11)

Peace be with you, brothers and sisters.

Praise the Lord. This Sunday seems especially precious in the presence of the Lord.

The night before last I was taken away to the central investigation area of the Qingyang branch of the Chengdu Police Bureau. This time I went through the formal procedures. I had to take off all my clothes and they took away all my belongings. Finally, they even took away my wedding ring. What was I thinking at the time? It felt like the chief priest going into the most holy place—he had to leave behind all his belongings and relationships, because he must face the Lord by himself. Therefore, with all my prior experiences being taken to the police station all over these years, this time my heart was unprecedentedly calm. In my previous experiences inside the police station, I worried about our church and my family. What could happen to them? Yet when the police asked me to take off my wedding ring, I was able to put everything aside all of a sudden.

Lord, I turn my family over to you, as well as your family, the church. You are responsible now because I can't control it anymore. Now I only need to face you alone; I will face the almighty God alone with my conscience. Everyone will have to fight his own battle.

When I came out of the police station and read all the messages, I thanked God for the great things he did among you. I thank God for being with you.

I read many messages and was particularly moved by the prayers of churches all over China. Many have expressed a similar idea that this was originally only a prayer meeting for a church of two to three hundred people, but it turned into a prayer meeting for believers all across the country, then a prayer meeting for believers all across the world. Praise the Lord. I found out that one social media account drew sixty thousand viewers who were praying for our Early Rain church within two hours. One pastor told me that over a hundred people gathered at his church to pray for us last night. This morning another pastor said the attendance at their morning prayer meeting today was the highest in years. I thank the Lord, he has not only done great things among us but also through us in all the churches in China.

We ask the Lord to test us for the sake of the gospel. While we are not worthy to be tested by God, what will come, will come. We cannot even say we long for its coming; there is never a day in which we look forward to its coming, yet nor do we hide from it. We have not been hiding; we have been preparing ourselves.

Today's sermon was chosen two weeks ago as I was scheduled to preach on the topic, "The Way of the Cross, the Life of the Martyrs." Who would have thought that God's plan was for me to preach this sermon among you today? In fact, I had not finished writing it on Friday, but I was able to finish it inside the police station. There I read through Revelation, and then Esther, and God has been leading us along the way.

We thank God and praise God. Let us pray together:

Lord, you are the king of kings, you are the head of the church, you are the Lord of our lives, your ways are just and true. O Lord, your honor and glory and grace are great and amazing. O Lord, we praise and thank you! You are not only the head of the church but also the Lord of all the earth. We pray today that not only will you pour out onto us the power of your gospel and resurrection, you will also pour out the fire of the Spirit and the fire of revival on all flesh in church gatherings all over China. We also place in your hands those brothers and sisters who cannot be here today, because you are with them as we are with them. Lord, may the universal church be with them! We thank you and praise you!

Lord, reveal to us the final scenes according to Revelation, the spiritual war at the end of times. Lord, we are unworthy to fight in this war, but you are our head, and you are the commander of the army of the Lord. Lord, lead us as a spiritual band of brothers, lead us as the spiritual 101st Airborne Division. Lord, make us into an arrow shot from your hand, never missing the target, never hanging in the air, never turning back, never to the left or right! Lord, submit us to yourself as the arrow submits to its master.

We thank you and praise you for listening to our prayer. We pray all this in the holy name of our Lord Jesus Christ. Amen.

God has done great things among us as we commemorate the Sichuan Earthquake of 2008.

The whole country, especially those of us who live in Sichuan, shares in the suffering of this earthquake. When we come here, we share and we pray as the suffering goes on. Suffering is not in the past; suffering is a continuous situation. To commemorate suffering we will have to bear the burden of suffering, as we share the burden as God has instructed us to do.

Since 2009, our church has adopted May 12 as a day of prayer for the nation. Yesterday I saw many pastors calling to adopt May 12 as a national day of prayer for all the churches in China.

How do you convert a day of prayer for one church into a day of prayer for the nation that many churches will participate in? It's not something that will automatically happen when you call for it. It is because you have prayed for this year after year, and you have paid the price for it.

When I was reading Esther in the police station yesterday, I wrote this down: "Lord, make May 12 Purim for the Chinese church and let your children gather all over China.[1] Of course, we gather not with real swords but with the whole armor of God, with the sword of the Holy Spirit, with the sword of the gospel. We gather to claim victory over the enemy. The day when your enemy plots against your church will be the day your church prevails. Amen! It will be the day when the Lord Jesus Christ crushes death. Amen! May the Lord give us such power."

The entirety of Revelation 6 is about the catastrophes brought on by the seven seals. What we see here is the opening of the fifth seal. What did the first four seals bring? We see one red horse, one black horse, one white horse, and one pale horse. The first horse stands for wars all over the world. It points to one ruler at the end of the age, one king who will bring war and suffering all over the earth, as well as the prince of the power of the air behind this earthly king. The second horse represents all conflicts, coups, rebellions, and revolutions among the peoples of the world. The third horse represents disease, poverty, economic chaos, financial crisis, inflation, and the collapse of the whole economic order. The forth horse carries a rider whose name is death, but the name in the original language is pestilence and its rampage can kill a quarter of the earth. Revelation is not intended to tell us when this will happen, nor will it give us a detailed roadmap of events. It tells us one thing: before Jesus comes again, this world by nature is against the gospel. Human evil will worsen over time. Therefore, the first four seals represent all kinds of suffering that permeate the end times—suffering from politics, from wars, from diseases, and from nature.

After the fifth seal, the sixth seal brings an earthquake, which is an apocalyptic earthquake that is one hundred, one thousand, or even ten thousand times stronger than the Sichuan Earthquake. "The sun became black as sackcloth, the full moon became like blood, and the stars of the sky fell to the earth as the fig tree sheds its winter fruit when shaken by a gale" (Revelation 6:12-13).

About six o'clock last night, just as I was finishing up my notes, two officials from the enforcement unit of the Bureau of Cultural Affairs came to me. They told me what they had done in our church and what they had confiscated. I said to them, "What you have done is illegal; I was taken here under the allegation of 'disturbing social order,' which is not related to your case. You will have to wait and make an appointment with me after I am released. I reject your enforcement." He said, "No problem. We will just ask a few questions." I said, "You can ask and answer them yourself." Then I went back to reading the Bible.

---

[1]Purim is a Jewish holiday that commemorates the saving of the Jewish people from Haman, an official in the Persian Empire who was planning to kill all the Jews, as recounted in the book of Esther.

Then he started to question me and I started reading Revelation 6 aloud. By the time I got to chapter eight, they had already left. Before they left, he said to me, "You read very well; I used to like reading aloud, too." Then I read aloud to them, "When he opened the sixth seal, I looked, and behold, there was a great earthquake" (Revelation 6:12). In the Gospel of Matthew and the Gospel of Mark, when Jesus talks about the end times, is it a lot like this? The four horses coming out of the first four seals represent the four corners of the world, which also appear in Zechariah. When Jesus describes the end times, what else does he mention besides famine? A great earthquake.

Let us look at the one in the middle, the fifth seal. "When he opened the fifth seal, I saw under the altar." Let me ask you, where is the altar? It is in heaven. Notice one thing here: the first four seals—and also the great earthquake of the sixth seal—all happen on the earth, but the fifth seal is in heaven. He sees the heavenly king of glory, the Lamb that was slain, and the altar in heaven. "The souls of those who had been slain for the word of God and for the witness they had borne," meaning the souls of the saints, the souls of the martyrs. "They cried out with a loud voice, 'O Sovereign Lord, holy and true, how long before you will judge and avenge our blood on those who dwell on the earth?'"

When we share the gospel, we usually want people to know that God is love, that on the cross Jesus has the power to save, but we also hope people will know that God's wrath and the final judgment are real. Because the judgment is real, the Lord Jesus Christ had to bear on the cross the suffering that we should bear.

In the final judgment, what will the earth give up for all those who were innocently killed for the sake of the Lord? The earth will give up the dead and the sea will divide and also give up the dead. For those martyrs, how long will they have to wait? The sword of the Lord has been hanging in the air, but why has it not come down? The sword of the Lord has been hanging over China for a long time, but why has it not come down? Because the Lord is still waiting, because he is still giving time to his church, to his gospel, and to the opening of the gate of his grace. In him there is a time that has not yet been fulfilled; in him there is one number that has not yet been reached; in him there is one part of the journey that we have not yet finished.

Therefore, my brothers and sisters, on earth we are like Abraham interceding for Sodom and Gomorrah. The church is the watchman for today's world. If the church does not point out the evil of the world, the church will be condemned along with the world. The church is the intercessor for today's world. The church prays in the presence of God, saying, "God, do not destroy this great city of

Chengdu, which has a hundred righteous people, fifty righteous people, or even one thousand righteous people. O Lord, do not destroy this city."

Seekers do not know this; they do not believe this. But we will say to you, dear brothers and sisters, Chengdu exists because of you. Chengdu has not been destroyed because in this city there are faithful children of God. The people of China have not been destroyed by God. They should have been destroyed a long time ago; it is against God's law to omit China from destruction. But this deeply sinful people exists today because in its midst there are God's people, because in its midst there are faithful children of God, because in its midst there are people who intercede for the people and for the nation, people who intercede and negotiate with God like Abraham, saying, "If the number of those attending our churches decreases, will you still save the city? Will you still destroy the city?"

"What about two hundred righteous people?" Two hundred righteous is okay.

Then they boldly ask, "What about fifty?" Fifty is okay.

Even when there is only one.

It is not you, nor me. Our Lord Jesus Christ is the only righteous one. Is Christ in Chengdu? Is Christ in China? If he is in China, if he is in Chengdu, Christ is the only mediator.

When I was in the police station yesterday, I let go of everything. I thought about what is in front of us, and how I did not know we had been preparing for this over the past two years. I was certain of one thing: as long as this church is still proclaiming the gospel, as long as God's Word is still in the mouths and hearts of our brothers and sisters, this church cannot be destroyed.

I talked to a police officer last night and told him about an article written by an unbelieving Chinese religious scholar. Why does Christianity continue to spread? Why is it spreading faster and faster? He said the most important reason is the government's restriction of Christianity over the last few decades, which has actually led to its fast growth. I said, "Each time you take action is foolishness, because each time your actions lead to the church's revival."

Every time is the same. It has been the same over the past half century, it has been the same in the last year, and it is the same in this day. Amen! Therefore, when we look at the future, it will also be the same. Amen!

Do we long for the Lord's second coming? Do we long for the end of history? There is tension in the end times. There is a tension between what has come and what is yet to come. I belong to the current age and to the age to come. I belong to earth and to heaven. Therefore, we live in this reality.

They asked, how long? God told them, rest a little longer. Until when? Till the number is complete. There is a tension between this waiting and this incomplete number. If we ask what we are waiting for, what has not yet been accomplished, then we see something very surprising. It suggests there is a reason history has not yet come to the end, that Christ has not yet come, and that we will have to wait and rest a little longer: the number of martyrs has not been reached.

Oh! In God there is a number for martyrs. Revelation does not intend to tell us what that number is. We do not know. But God has a number, which has to be completed through history. We return to what Jesus says, "If anyone would come after me, let him deny himself and take up his cross and follow me" (Matthew 16:24).[2] The number of those who take up their crosses and follow the Lord, those who fill up what is lacking in Christ's afflictions, those who bear the mark of the cross by God, has not been completed.

They are instructed to wait a little longer. "Until the number of their fellow servants and their brothers should be complete, who were to be killed as they themselves had been." Brothers and sisters, what are they waiting for? They wait for their fellow servants and brothers, who were to be killed as they themselves had been killed. These people were all killed. They are the saints who were killed in the past, the martyrs who wait at the table for their fellow servants. We see a passing on of martyrdom. We see a history of martyrdom. We see the continuation of martyrdom in the Lord's church until the day Christ comes again.

Therefore, how do we understand this waiting and this incomplete number? It suggests a few things:

First, it suggests that martyrdom is not exceptional, it is not accidental. Martyrdom does not belong to a certain short period; it is widespread and continuous. For the churches of all ages and over all the earth, martyrdom is widespread and continuous, even a glorious inheritance and cycle, not accidental, not exceptional, not temporary. The church will be filled with martyrs and witnesses of the martyrs from the time of the Lord Jesus Christ's ascent to heaven until the day he comes again.

Second, you, your fellow servants, and their brothers represent the cycle and passing of three different groups of people. This could mean three generations of martyrs—saints of the past, saints to come, and their descendants. Therefore, martyrdom is the common experience of churches of all eras and all peoples, a

---

[2]See also Mk 8:34; Lk 9:23.

life experience shared by all of us. It does not happen to every church. Not every believer will be a martyr. But in churches of all eras, as long as you belong to the church, the life of martyrdom is a life we share in common.

Many years ago I met a Korean missionary and he asked me, "Why do so many Korean missionaries go to China?" Korea is not a big country. Do you know what the total population of Korea is? Do you know how Korea compares to Sichuan geographically? It is much smaller than Sichuan. Korea is not even considered a midsize country in the world. It is such a small country, but its missionaries are all over the world. Even with so many missionaries they are just a little matchstick, but China is like a room full of firewood. Their goal is to light a fire under you. "If we do not light you up, we cannot burn very long as a matchstick, but you are like huge piles of firewood."

Dear brothers and sisters, may the Lord light the fire among us. May the Lord light the fire in the Chinese church through the missionaries of all ages, including the many Korean and American missionaries who are still among us today. Amen!

This Korean hymn "The Way of the Cross, the Life of the Martyrs" is not about an exceptional few or the lives of a small number of martyrs in the church. It suggests that the life of the martyrs is the treasure and glory of the whole church. If the church is one body, if the church is one in Christ, one connected body, then the life of the martyrs is the life of believers. Every believer shares in not only the crucified life of Jesus Christ but also the life of the martyrs in Christ through the ages. We hope that the life of the martyrs is also flowing in and among us. Amen!

After I came back from the police station last night, a former elder at Shouwang Church called me and said, "What happened to you today was like what we experienced on the first day when hundreds of brothers and sisters were taken away in buses. Then they blocked people from coming to gatherings."

This may become more and more likely, and they could mobilize a thousand, even thousands, of civil servants to come and block us from gathering. Gradually you may see that in your community or at your job or from your local police station three to five civil servants may be mobilized to deal with just one person. Last Monday, I invited you to pray with me that Early Rain could bring many civil servants to God in this city. Then God did bring a lot of civil servants here. Hallelujah! The Lord is a God who hears our prayers, and he has his own ways. He says, "Work with this first batch; work as you go. Keep in touch with them and share the gospel with them; when they are almost done, I will send you another batch. Don't you want to bring civil servants to me?"

Lord, lead us on.

When that former elder of Shouwang Church called me, I said, "You are right; you have persevered for so many years, and now it is our turn to pick up the baton." He said, "That's why I called you. You are taking over the baton now." This incident at Early Rain is just the beginning.

Lord, lead us on.

Martyrdom is the mark of Christ's second coming, because in this text the Lord connects martyrdom, the life of the martyrs, the number to be completed, and his encouragement to the saints to wait patiently for his second coming with the judgment of the end times. Therefore, just like the great earthquake is a mark of the end times, martyrdom and the life of the martyrs is also a mark of the end times. There is hope that redemptive history is approaching the end.

You may be surprised and ask, "How can martyrdom turn into hope?" A hope for the end of redemptive history? For believers, we hope for the Lord to come again. Amen! Therefore, we hope for the life of the martyrs.

When we see the martyrs, when we see their testimonies, we know that redemptive history is progressing. We know that the end times are near, although we do not know which day it will be. Our hearts will then be lightened; we will no longer think so much about the things of earth but more about the things of heaven. We will no longer think so much about the things of the present age but more about the things in the coming age. We will no longer think so much about ourselves but more about others. This is the life of the martyrs. This is a mark of Christ's second coming in the end times; this is a mark in the life of the pilgrim.

Lord, through the events of yesterday, reveal to this church and our brothers and sisters that we are a group of pilgrims.

We didn't ride the police vehicles to the police stations; we were on our way to Zion. Amen!

Lord, lead us on.

Therefore, I have come to the conclusion that the life of the martyrs is the glory of the church. We can even say that the life of the martyrs is what every believer longs for, what the church of every age longs for. Let us courageously tell this world that all it pursues is vanity; all is vanity. Let us proclaim to the world, as pilgrims on our way to Zion, that the ways of the world are all dead-ended and dark and hopeless.

In Ephesians, Paul said to the Ephesian church, "I, Paul, a prisoner of Christ Jesus on behalf of you" (Ephesians 3:1). Paul wrote this while suffering as a prisoner, encouraging the Ephesian church not to lose heart or be discouraged over what he was suffering for them.

Brothers and sisters, when we see a rise in illegal activities, when we see persecutions, when we see many brothers and sisters being taken away to the police station, is it possible for us to lose heart? It is possible. Will we be weak? We will. In the days to come, may the Lord be with us, whether we are strong or weak, let us walk down this path together. I know in our sinful nature, hearing these things may make you weak. According to your human nature, this will make you weak and discouraged.

But Paul told the brothers and sisters in the Ephesian church, "You shall not be discouraged or weakened over what I am suffering as a prisoner." Because this is your glory. Paul said that his imprisonment was the glory of the Ephesian church. He built the Ephesian church; his life was tied to the church in Ephesus. Therefore, he said, my imprisonment is your glory.

Let us return to a focal point of our application: In what should a church glory? In whom should a church glory?

We have many rich brothers and sisters in our church. We have quite a few powerful businesspeople in our church. Some people in our church have received prestigious awards. One brother in our church invented a very powerful tool. One brother in our church is very powerful and his company is ranked in the Fortune 500. I am not saying these things are not good, but none of these shall be the glory of a church.

The church does not become good because we have some capable members, some powerful members, some influential members, some rich members, or some accomplished members. No. What should a church glory in? It should glory in the suffering of Christ, the body that suffers for the sake of Christ, the life of the martyrs. What a church glories in, who it glorifies, and what kind of life it glories in will demonstrate whether it is a faithful church that is filled with longing for the end times. Amen!

Let me say this, those of you brothers and sisters who were taken to the police station yesterday, you are the glory of the church, you are my glory. As Paul said to the Ephesian church, you are my glory. Even the Lord Jesus Christ said that he is willing to wear you on his crown of glory.

Lord, let us pursue this glory.

A lot of our books, including the Bibles and hymnals in our sanctuary, were taken away yesterday. Including the books in the seminary library, we lost about fifteen thousand books. Therefore, you should repent in the presence of the Lord, saying, "Why didn't we buy more books? We should have bought more books for them." We might be able to get the books back, we might not. But for our Early Rain Covenant Church, at least fifteen thousand books have been martyred before us.

But we touched them with our own hands. And we read them with our own eyes, so there is no regret. A brother asked, "The police came and took away our money. What are we going to do?" I said, "Are you complaining because our money has been martyred? The money belongs to God. Our tithes belong to God, and what is God's purpose behind every penny? To glorify himself. The ultimate purpose of God using every penny is to proclaim his gospel and testify for his glory. Now all of the church's money has testified to the glory of God. What are you worrying about?" Therefore, we do not care that the books have been martyred.

One coworker was worried that the brothers and sisters of the church were so passionate that they were distributing tracts on the street. Praise the Lord, we are encountering this trial in the middle of a revival rather than in the midst of a retreat or spiritual depression. That coworker was worried that many from our church and from our college were young people.[3] What if they were taken into custody or died at the police station?

We do not ask for these things; we ask for the Lord's protection. This definitely is not what we want, but if such things happen, it is the glory of this church, the glory of his family, the glory of his life, the glory of the whole Chinese house church today. Amen! Neither would the church avoid these things. We do not pursue them, and we won't ask for them, but we will not avoid them either. Which one of us is worthy to be a martyr? Which one of us is worthy to be shamed for the name of the Lord? How much shame have you suffered in your life? Most of the shame comes from our own sins or the sins of others. Woe to me, for I am a man of unclean lips, and I dwell in the midst of a people of unclean lips (Isaiah 6:5).

Like Paul, who testified every time that his imprisonment, arrest, and beatings were solely because of his faith in the risen Christ who gives new life, if you are shamed or mistreated, and you know clearly that you have not committed any sin, that you have a clear conscience in the presence of God on this matter, and you know clearly that the reason you encounter opposition is solely because of your faith in Jesus, then may the Lord give us joy in our

---

[3]ERCC supported an underground Christian liberal arts college founded by a group of house churches.

hearts. Amen! May we say, "Lord, we are unworthy servants and yet you have given me such glory."

Brothers and sisters, yesterday in the police station I said to the police chief of the Qingyang branch, "You don't believe in the Lord and you don't understand that if you arrest me and put me into prison, it will be a great glory for me. I have been waiting for this for years." I said, "You won't understand that if you persecute this church, you are adding tremendous glory to this church, you are adding to the brothers and sisters of this church things they are unworthy of. You cannot understand this unless you come to know Jesus."

Lord, lead us on.

Let us pray for the road ahead. I invite you to sing this song with me, "The Way of the Cross, The Life of the Martyrs":

Lord, fill my heart with your love

Lord, fill my mind with your truth

My eyes are full of tears because of your saving grace

Lord, fill my mouth with praise

Make my two hands serve humbly just like you

I deeply wish the marks of Jesus remain in my whole life

The way of the cross, the life of the martyrs

What a blessed way this is!

Lord, I want to follow the footsteps of Jesus

Lord, make me your pure bride

With victory over all temptations, difficulties, and mockeries

I gladly offer my life to you

Let us come together and pray in the presence of the Lord:

May the way of the cross lead us. May the life of the martyrs manifest in our lives. Lord, lead us into this blessed way that overflows with abundance. Lord, lead us to follow you and let us say, "Lord, where you go, we will go. Where your apostles have gone, we will go. Where your power led the apostles and the martyrs, we will go. Where Wang Mingdao has gone, we will go."

Together we offer our lives in the presence of the Lord. We look upon you for the unity of this church. We look upon you for this church's power in the gospel; we look upon you for this church's love in the Lord. Lord, cleanse us with your precious blood for the sins that we have not confessed. Make us, the holy bride, worthy of fighting the holy battle. Lord, reconcile those who have complaints against each other and make us love each other, as only those who love each other can come together and fight the good fight.

Lord, make us despise the scoffing, suffering, and temptations of the world. O Lord, while we are seen as garbage among the people, reveal to us that you have lifted us from the ash heap. Let us pledge in the presence of our Lord, "I am willing to offer my life to you, my family to you, my sons and daughters to you. All my family and my descendants are in you."

Let us pray together in the presence of the Lord:

O Lord, we look upon your grace. Lord, lead us. Lord, you have done great things among us, you have been glorified among us and you will continue to be glorified among us. O Lord, lead us even though we are unworthy of it.

O Lord, use us. O Lord, lead us with your nail-wounded hands and let us touch your wounds. O Lord, let us touch the wounds of this age and the wounds of this city. Reveal to us all the lost souls in this city. Lord, revive your church.

O Lord, the cross is forever my glory. O Lord, lead us on that road of glory. What the world takes as shame, we take as glory. O Lord, let us count all things as rubbish, and suffering as trivial.

O Lord, lead us down this way in this city. Bring us into a revival that this city has never experienced, never seen, one that the world is unworthy of.

Lord, we thank you and praise you for listening to our prayer.

Lord, in your presence we pray for revival. Lord, in this city you once enjoyed the glory of the gospel. During World War II when many Christian schools gathered at Huaxiba, Pastors Ji Zhiwen and Yu Ligong led a college revival that ignited the spiritual fire of the colleges in Chengdu.[4] O Lord, that was over half a century ago.

O Lord, revive your churches in Chengdu. Lord, show this city something it has never seen, reveal to it the churches of the city. Lord, this world is unworthy of your children; what others treasure, we take as rubbish. What they fear, we take as precious. O Lord, let our faith overturn this city's way of death, the life bound and controlled and enslaved by wealth. O Lord, may we shake Chengdu awake. O Lord, shake Chengdu awake through your churches in this city. Lord, shake the lost souls awake. O Lord, awaken all the big and small churches in this city, those believers gathering in the name of the Lord in communities and families.

O Lord, revive us. O Lord, lead us.

---

[4]Yu Ligong (于力工, Moses Yu, 1920–2010) was a preacher, university minister, and seminary founder. During WWII, many of China's leading universities relocated to southwest China. Many Christian fellowships were established during this time and in 1945 InterVarsity's First National Congress of Christian Students took place. Yu served as a speaker for InterVarsity's summer retreats and revival meetings on college campuses.

O Lord, we have nothing to seek in our lives except to be in your presence and for your kingdom and your righteousness, and you will add all other things to us.

O Lord, may the life of the martyrs be with us. Lord, if you have mercy on the Chinese church today, give to the Chinese church today those who are ready to be martyred, those who are willing to follow you and offer their lives on the altar.

O Lord, we pray for the Chinese church. We look upon you for the churches all over China. We look upon you particularly for all the church leaders and all those whom you have called to proclaim your gospel. O Lord, make them strong and courageous. O Lord, raise among them a great army of the Lord.

O Lord, we thank you and praise you, and ask you to revive this church. Revive your church by reviving me.

O Lord, your church had ten years of great revival from 1927 to 1937, which still impacts the church today one hundred years later.[5] *Lord, we ask for another great revival. Lord, impact the Chinese church for another one hundred years and bless Chinese society for a hundred years. When the Communist Party no longer reigns in this country, your grace will reign in this country. When all the powers of the world collapse, your churches will still stand on Calvary. I believe in Calvary, I believe the glory of the cross will forever be with your church.*

O Lord, we place in your hands the 2008 Sichuan Earthquake, the city of Chengdu, the province of Sichuan that has been through the earthquake, and those who cannot help themselves—those who are still in pain, those who cannot let go of their sorrow and anguish. Lord, give them to your church. O Lord, let all who labor and are heavy laden come to you, for all who come to you will be fulfilled and forgiven.

O Lord, let us pray and ask boldly in your presence, as John Knox did. Lord, give China to us, give Chengdu to us, give Sichuan to us. Give them to your church and be glorified through us. Otherwise, Lord, take us to your heavenly home, as our lives would be meaningless in this world.

Lord, we have no need or desire in this world. All we want is to have our lives burn for the gospel of the Lord and for great revival. O Lord, hear our prayer. What you did among the Chinese church before, do it again among us. Do it again among the Chinese house churches today. Lord, we thank you and praise you. Raise up

---

[5]Waves of revival took place across China in the 1920s and 1930s. There was a convergence of influential preachers and pastors, including Wang Zai (王载, Leland Wang), Ji Zhiwen (计志文, Andrew Gih), Zhao Junying (赵君影, Calvin Chao), Song Shangjie (宋尚节, John Sung), and Ni Tuosheng (倪柝声, Watchman Nee), as well as the founding of institutions such as the Bethel Mission in Shanghai, the Bethel Worldwide Evangelistic Band, and Wang Mingdao's church in Beijing.

the Wang Mingdao of this age, the Ji Zhiwen of this age, the John Sung of this age—wave after wave of faithful children in this age.

Lord, we thank you and praise you. Lord, hear our prayer and let our worship and praise shake the gates of hell. Reveal your wisdom through your church to all the powers and authorities in China. O Lord, make the prince of the power of the air flee. Those who persecute your church with swords, let their feet be caught in their own net. Make the day they gather to persecute your church a day that they themselves will be shamed. The scaffolds they make for the church, let them be hanged on them.

O Lord, we thank you and praise you. Every age has Haman's scheme and Haman's cunning. Lord, defeat all those schemes for your own victory, because you have been crucified on the cross. O Lord, you are risen. Lord, the one we follow is the risen Lord Jesus Christ. The cross will forever be our glory. We thank you and praise you, Lord, as the army of God and as one church.

Lord, if you approve, send us.

If you see us as worthy, use us.

If you see us as ready and pleasing to your eyes, send us.

We thank you and praise you, Lord, for listening to our prayers in your presence.

We pray in the precious and holy name of our Lord Jesus Christ.

12

THE CROSS AND THE LANDFILL

WANG YI

In this pastoral letter, Wang Yi engages the question of eschatology. What is this world destined for and how are Christians to live in the light of eternity? In response, Wang Yi declares that the church is like the most beautiful ballet dancer who must dance on a garbage dump as her stage. The dump does not diminish the beauty of her dance, rather the contrast enhances it. For, according to Wang Yi, the garbage dump is not meaningless; it has been given meaning through the incarnation of God into its reality.
Wang Yi sent this letter to his congregation in October 2017.

The Lord's Servant, Wang Yi,

Peace be with you, brothers and sisters in all the churches that are filled with "the fullness of him who fills all in all."

This has truly been a busy and eventful month. From the start of Camp Shiyi, the "theology of the cross" has been in our midst, and everything seems to have picked up pace. I apologize that there has been a lull in the release of pastoral letters; however, there are many words I would like to share with you. I am filled with both a sense of the shortage of time, as well as with an unspeakable excitement. Since 2009, the Lord has often used Ezra 9:8 to motivate and inspire me: "But now for a brief moment favor has been shown by the LORD our God, to leave us a remnant and to give us a secure hold within his holy place, that our God may brighten our eyes and grant us a little reviving in our slavery."

At that time, Israel was rebuilding the temple and the city walls. During the 2008 earthquake and the ensuing rebuilding in 2009, which the church continued amid suppression, this verse became for me a vision from the Lord of a small revival of the church. In fact, over the last few decades, house churches have often drawn encouragement from the postexilic accounts of the Israelites. Early in my walk with God, the Xiaomin hymns, such as "In These Remaining Years" and "Treading the Remaining Miles," overturned my knowledge of reality.[1] The tradition of the house church emphasizes the "eschatology of the gospel" or the "eschatological gospel."

The church usually has three ways of viewing reality. One view is that the ship is sinking, and thus there is no value in doing anything other than endeavoring to save souls. Another views the ship not as sinking but as damaged. Regardless of how tattered the ship may be, those who hold this view believe that the power of redemption will uphold the ship and that the kingdom of God will eventually be established on the ship. The third view says that the ship is sinking, but the instruments on the ship must still be cleaned, even played at least one more time as in a performance. There will be a brand-new ship in the future, but life on the new ship will not be completely unrelated to our life on this currently sinking ship.

In a way, our present reality has in fact become meaningless in the light of the gospel. As such, if we were to die immediately or if time were to instantly come to an end, we would have no regrets. However, in another sense, this meaningless reality has become meaningful because of the gospel. We must cherish every second as long as we are still alive and time has not yet come to an end, for it is only through faith that this meaningless reality is connected with eternity. The present reality is an inverted image of eternity.

Therefore, our view of reality is of the third kind. The world is a damaged ship and really is sinking. As such, you cannot build the kingdom of heaven on this ship, nor can you treat this ship as your eternal home. But all that is on the ship is an inverted image of eternity, and it is only on this old ship that we can understand the form of the new ship.

The key is faith, and faith needs a stage. Faith is like a master ballet dancer dancing gracefully on a dilapidated stage. On the one hand, as long as the dance is beautiful, what does it matter if the stage is in tatters? Alternatively, imagine how glorious and resplendent it will be the day this master dancer performs on a magnificent stage. For now, however, God says that the value of the dance must be expressed on a dilapidated stage.

Let me give you another example. Many have read the story about the experiment where Joshua Bell performed six Bach pieces while standing in the subway. He is the greatest violinist in the world and he plays a violin that is

---

[1] Lü Xiaomin is a popular Chinese hymn writer. See note 3 in introduction.

worth 3.5 million American dollars. The average price of a ticket to his concert just two days prior to the experiment was $200. However, in this experiment, of the two thousand people who walked by during Joshua Bell's forty-five-minute performance in the subway, only twenty stopped to listen, earning him $32 in his hat.

Beloved brothers and sisters, what I am trying to say is that you are a group of the greatest artists in the universe performing in a subway station. The world does not recognize you, but your value is, ironically, manifested through their ignorance and lack of recognition. Put another way, you are a group of master ballet dancers performing at a landfill. And this is the meaning of the landfill—that although you will be deemed lunatics by those who stay near it, because of you, the landfill has become an image of the new heaven and the new earth.

This is how the author of Hebrews describes your value: "Of whom the world was not worthy—wandering about in deserts and mountains, and in dens and caves of the earth" (Hebrews 11:38).

Our power and water were cut at the camp, thus showing that we are people of whom the world is not worthy.[2]

The brothers and sisters heading to the Hong Kong theological conference were questioned, threatened, and investigated, proving them to be people of whom the world is not worthy.

Brother Ding Shuqi was pinned to the floor by the airport police and, over the course of twenty-four hours, subjected to dreadful and agonizing interrogation techniques that included being detained, handcuffed, having a bright light shone on his face, and being deprived of sleep. All of this shows that the world is not worthy of him.

But what is amazing about the gospel is that Jesus Christ came to the landfill and gave the landfill meaning. Jesus took the form of a servant and in so doing made servanthood meaningful. Jesus entered shame and death, so that the shame and death of this world would now have meaning. This is the reason I say that first, the ship is sinking, and second, the sinking ship still has meaning.

Beloved brothers and sisters, I particularly want to remind you that spiritual warfare is intense. The works of Satan are putrid and diabolical. For many years, the government has been searching for holes in this church and scrutinizing my mountain of materials. It has even tried to secretly provoke or create holes in the church. I am paying attention to all the rumors and traces of this. The church

---

[2]ERCC was participating in a church retreat.

has also recently confirmed that a former member (who has since left) was a spy from a related government department and had been spreading lies among the believers.

Some things will be revealed when the time is right. But there are many things that will only be made known when we see the Lord. The goal of all of this is to make manifest, on this dilapidated stage, the value of faith. Therefore, it is critical for you to realize that if you do not have love in your heart, you will become an instrument of the devil. And if you are filled with complaints and grumble against the church, its pastors, or its coworkers, and are unable to come to them in light of the gospel, then someday you will become an instrument that Satan employs to destroy the church.

In *The Compelling Community: Where God's Power Makes a Church Attractive*, an author writes about how much he missed Pastor Mark Dever and Capitol Hill Baptist Church while he was serving elsewhere. But he went on to mention something else that struck my heart. He said, "Not only did I miss Pastor Dever and his preaching, I also missed the community that was birthed from his preaching."[3]

This has become my prayer recently. I hope that when someone mentions my ministry in the future, that it will not be described as an abstraction of words and sermons, but rather as a humble ministry that has concretely influenced and built you—this gospel community—up.

When I was an academic, I mistakenly believed that my future crown would be centered on my words. It was only after my calling to be a pastor that I understood Paul's heart, which was revealed when he called the Philippian church "my joy and my crown" and said to the Thessalonian church, "because you are my glory, my joy."

Beloved, the thought that I will one day wear you on my head and say, "This community is the joy and glory of my life" is of utmost beauty and something I dare not even dream of. Therefore, let us sing together in the subways and dance together in the landfills.

Let me remind all of you once again that our government is ambitious. Their goal is not only to obtain order in society but to monopolize the meaning of landfills and subway stations. As such, the government is concerned when we dance ballet at landfills. We will find police officers pinning us to the ground

---

[3]Mark Dever and Jamie Dunlap, *The Compelling Community: Where God's Power Makes a Church Attractive* (Wheaton, IL: Crossway, 2015).

when we play the violin in the subway. However, this is part of the meaning of the landfill, for God has allowed them to be ambitious because he wants to magnify the value of faith. In general, the more terrible the performance environment, the greater the "eschatological meaning" of the church's show.

Let us therefore wait in stillness and act in vigor. Out of reverence for God's plan, let us also maintain an honorable respect while we humbly disobey the government's intentions to control the heart and worship of its people, since respecting the opponent that God has placed before you is akin to respecting God.

There are times when we submit through our actions but do not identify with or endorse these actions in our hearts.

Other times, we remain defiant in our actions, but we do not show contempt.

In this way, we pray at dawn and rest at dusk, and the government's power has nothing to do with us.

Yes, the ship is sinking, but we clean our instruments in six days and sing on the Lord's day.

A brother who is willing to "be like sheep among wolves" with you,

Wang Yi

October 21, 2017

13

TWENTY WAYS PERSECUTION IS GOD'S WAY TO SHEPHERD US

WANG YI

In this pastoral letter, Wang Yi lists why Christians ought to see persecution as God's work in their lives. Because of our eschatological destiny, Christians are to remember that this world is fleeting and to prepare for the battle ahead. Wang Yi's twenty points can be summarized into a few key themes. (1) Persecution reveals the Christian's true heart and purifies the church. (2) Persecution demonstrates the kingship and authority of Jesus Christ over the church and progresses the advance of the gospel in this world. (3) Persecution rebukes individualism and fosters Christian fellowship locally and globally. (4) Persecution is manifested because of our union with Christ.

Wang Yi sent this letter to his congregation on November 9, 2017.

To my brothers and sisters who are called to live "self-controlled, upright and godly lives in the present age" (Titus 2:12): may peace be with you.

When Paul talked about marriage, his personal opinion was that it is better to be single than married. However, he was not speaking of the meaning of marriage in regard to creation and redemption. Paul did not deny the value of marriage or having children; instead, he urged believers to "remain as you are," "for this world in its present form is passing away." Those who are married should remain married, not seeking divorce. Those who are single should also remain single, not seeking marriage. This is all for one purpose: so that God's people would not be concerned about themselves, their wives, their children, or the things of the world, but instead would be concerned about the Lord's affairs and how they can please the Lord (1 Corinthians 7:26-32).

When we talk about the conflict between faith and the world, these verses express the belief that everything should be seen from the viewpoint that "the present form of this world is passing away" (1 Corinthians 7:31). Moreover, all things must be discussed with great eagerness to be "anxious about the things of the Lord, how to please the Lord" (1 Corinthians 7:32).

Without this strong eschatological awareness of the fleeting nature of the world and the conflict between the world and faith, anything you think is meaningless. Without this awareness, anything you say is wrong.

Someone shared with me his concern that because the church's posture during this period of church-state tension is that of preparing for war, daily pastoral care will be undermined. I told this believer that it is usually through preparation and drills for war that soldiers accomplish their daily training. The more urgent the situation is, the more effective the training becomes. For the church, there is no daily shepherding without spiritual warfare. On one hand, fighting itself is the Lord's way of shepherding his disciples; on the other hand, the purpose of shepherding is to prepare for the fight.

I have seen many Chinese churches die in spirit as a result of their lack of preparation. During times of persecution, thousands in the Lord's church may be killed by the devil; but after persecution, millions are killed.

So, the following are twenty thoughts I want to share with you on our topic today—what spiritual benefit does the current church-state conflict bring to the church and to Christians? How is this conflict God's way to shepherd us?

1. The possibility of persecution is a test to see if, out of our fear of death, we choose to become slaves. Have our hearts truly been set free by the gospel, and will they remain honorable under any system and in any environment?

2. Our fears show us the deep-rooted servility living in our hearts. The church-state conflict is a test revealing the slavish residue living in our bodies.

3. Persecution shows that the power of the sword has another layer of value for the church. God made the cross to serve as the boundary marker between the church and the world. The cross is the means he uses to show the world the gospel's great power. His intent is that now, through the church, his manifold wisdom can be made known to rulers and authorities in the heavenly realms.

4. The church-state conflict can help us determine whether the obedience we display as we live in Chinese society flows from a slavish submission to authority, or out of a God-loving perseverance; this conflict helps us see whether we are yielding to powerful authority or are showing courage as sheep among wolves. No matter what our reaction, once fear has spread, any reaction based on fear is not one driven by love.

5. This is the difference: obedience flowing from love will enable us to respect a humble government worker who acts legally, leading us to show him great respect as if he were a king. At the same time, when we face the unrighteous deeds of our national leader, we will also be brave enough to regard him as a tyrant.

6. The church-state conflict is also a test to see if we are cowardly and bullying at heart, obeying the powerful but despising the humble. This sort of obedience is not biblical obedience, but it is the mark of the lowly.

7. Only when you are able to obey those who are more humble than you is your obedience to those who are more powerful in line with the Bible. In the same way, it is only when you are able to despise the unrighteousness of the most powerful that your rebuke to the humble flows out of humility.

8. The church-state conflict has vividly revealed this difference in the sharpest manner, a way that cannot be covered or disguised.

9. This conflict also tests if we have experienced dignity and liberty because of Christ. This is what the Bible describes as a faith and obedience that acknowledges "there is no authority except from God, and those that exist have been instituted by God." (Romans 13:1). This type of obedience makes for a temperament of conservatism, knowing both the time to obey and the time to resist. The liberty of Christ leads to an obedience and a resistance which both flow from the same submission to the divine order.

10. Therefore, persecution tests if you are truly gospel-rooted in your theological conservatism. When a God-obeying, theologically conservative individual obeys the government, evil is not fueled but rather restricted. When a God-obeying, theologically conservative individual resists, the moral order of society is not disrupted but consolidated.

11. For this reason, when Christians obey the government, pro-democracy advocates who change society in a positive way might criticize us as loyalists who help the government maintain social stability. But when

Christians choose to obey God over people in church-state conflicts, we are accused again, this time by pragmatists, of inciting subversion against the state.

12. This is also a test to see if we place value on the evaluation of the world or on the praise of Christ. The church-state conflict, as compared to any other type of conflict, more fully reveals the confrontation and distinctions between the church and the world. As a result of this clash, the social relationships of Christians will be exposed and re-evaluated by the world. One of the most significant benefits of church-state conflict is that any Christian who faces it cannot continue as a silent disciple.

13. Therefore, every church-state conflict throughout history is a moment in which God's kingdom moves forward. It requires believers to stop living like they are on vacation and to return to their posts. When Paul says "remain as you are," he is referring to the lifestyle of "readiness" which Christians are to display in the world. Conflict between the church and the state puts an end to any false state of peace and instead reveals the universal truth of continual, ongoing spiritual warfare. In this war, the real hindrance is not the world or the government but the power of sin and fear in a Christian's life.

14. Every church-state conflict is a moment for God to cleanse his church. As the house church forefathers said: "Freedom is for wide distribution; tension is for selection."[1] Through persecution, the Lord expels false believers from the church, exposes false teachers, and preachers who are not called to teach lose their opportunity to take advantage of the church.

15. Test yourself to see if you are crazy for the gospel. When you are threatened with death for the gospel, you find out for whom you really live. When faced with the risk of job loss, you know for whom you really work. When you may lose fortune and position for the sake of the gospel, you find out whether you are crazy for money or crazy for the gospel.

16. Therefore, one great benefit of this church-state conflict is realizing how much we overestimate our spiritual lives. This miscalculation is where almost all problems in our daily lives come from. If Christ had not been

---

[1] This quote comes from the oral testimony of an elderly house church leader, Yang Anxi (杨安溪). Yang Anxi, "The Hand of God in China," *Church China* 16 (2009年03月号), www.churchchina.org /archives/090301.html.

arrested, Peter would not have known he could not make it, and the disciples would not have admitted their disbelief. Believers who live at ease usually misunderstand their piety. Only when the absolute temperature drops do we feel the cold and truly long for light.

17. The news about persecution as well as the persecution itself gives us a real opportunity to share with churches being persecuted, murdered, imprisoned, and humiliated in North Korea, the Middle East, and throughout the world. It keeps us from arrogantly despising missionaries who are martyred for the Lord and prevents us from holding at arm's length those who are zealous for God. The experience of sorrow helps us weep more intensely with those who weep, and the danger of bondage binds us more tightly with those in bondage.

18. The church-state conflict is also the best antidote for individualism or the prosperity gospel. Through conflict, God shows that faith itself is a relationship between two kingdoms, not of a solitary spiritual life. Church-state conflict reveals the power of community. For instance, one hundred Christians together are more dangerous than twenty together; a group of Christians with pastors, elders, by-laws, and elections is more dangerous than a loosely bound group of Christians without any influence. Through this danger, God shows us the value of community. The focus of Christ's kingdom is not ourselves but the community. What earthly political powers fear most is not divided Christians but a holy community governed by God.

19. Therefore, the greatest benefit of the church-state conflict is our union with a Christ who himself was judged. Caesar's focus was not whether you believed in Jesus (as they often said, "We do not care if you believe in Jesus"), but whether you believe Jesus is "the king." Persecution forces us to answer the world the same way we answer the Lord: "Yes. He is the king." In this way, we allow the police to tear their clothes and say, "What else can we say? They are inciting subversion of state power."

20. That is because church-state conflict is determined by the nature of the gospel. Church-state conflict means the cross; and the cross means conflict between the church and the state. In the United States, this may be presented in two extreme ways: mass shootings in churches or the verdicts of the Supreme Court. In China, it is shown through secret police, imprisonment, bans, border control, threatening those landlords who

rent space to churches, as well as controlling thought and speech. The cross is the border between the world and the church. To walk from the world to the church you must pass by the cross; in the same way, that is how you return from the other side.

Brother Wang Yi,
who wishes with you to consider everything a loss and see suffering as trivial.

14

HISTORY IS CHRIST WRITTEN LARGE

WANG YI

This sermon is one of Wang Yi's most important theological reflections. Many of Wang Yi's theological themes and concerns are most clearly distilled in this chapter—the eschatological destiny of history, the cross as the center of Christian identity, the state's desire to replace God's sovereignty, and the spiritual battle over the allegiance of humankind. Not only does he offer a Chinese analysis of Western church-state theology, reflecting on errors made by the Protestant reformers, but he argues that the Chinese house churches are the inheritors of these older debates and the next frontier of church-state theology globally. He implies that the spiritual battle between the house church and the secular authoritarianism of the CCP is the future of Christianity and that Christianity in other cultural contexts will also eventually face similar battles and questions.

In his closing remarks, Wang Yi indicates his explicit desire to be jailed for the glory of God and the increase of Christianity in China. Moving forward, the majority of his writings focus on preparing for suffering personally.

Prevented from leaving Chengdu in November 2017, this sermon was delivered in absentia to the Jakarta 2017 conference, organized by Stephen Tong in commemoration of the five hundredth anniversary of the Protestant Reformation.

Dear Rev. Dr. Stephen Tong, pastors, elders, brothers and sisters,

I will share this great theme with you through Colossians 1:15-20, a great biblical passage on Christology. I am going to summarize the meaning of this Scripture with a famous saying by Eric Voegelin, a twentieth-century political philosopher. He declared that, "History is Christ written large."[1] Since the age

---

[1]Eric Voegelin's statement was delivered in his 1965 Ingersoll Lecture, "Immortality: Experience and Symbol." Wang Yi quotes in Chinese from the English translation.

of Noah, God has allowed human history to continue. God's covenant with Noah means that history is written by God, and God uses history to write about his saving grace. Therefore, history is Christ written large, because all history is from him, through him, and to him. This is not only the case for the five hundred years of the Reformation history but also for the past two hundred years of the Protestant faith in China. It is also true for the history of persecution of the Christian church under the Communist Party in the last sixty-plus years. Furthermore, it will also be true for future history. It is because the cross of Christ is the center of history. The cross did not just stand at Calvary outside of the city of Jerusalem. Revelation 11 tells us that Sodom and Egypt were where Christ was crucified, which means the cross of Christ is also standing at the center of the entire world. In this way, the cross of Christ is also standing at the center of the entire human history.

Paul[2] said that we are to be subject even to the unjust masters, just as we are to the Lord. Over the past sixty years, the church in China has always been subject to an unjust authority. On the one hand, the Three-Self churches have gone too far in their subjection to such an extent that their subjection has become total surrender, and patience has become allegiance. In this manner, the church has lost its supremacy and transcendence. The total surrender of the church to unjust authorities made the church part of the injustice. On the other hand, the house churches have always been subject to this authority. They have never rebelled, rioted, or incited to subvert the rule of the Communist Party. I was once arrested and brought to the police station. The officer there asked me, "Have you ever engaged in activities that try to subvert state power?" I asked whether praying counted as subversion? I often pray to the Lord, saying, "O Lord, we have been oppressed so hard, can you reach out your arm to overthrow this political regime overnight? Or are you going to harden the heart of Pharaoh so that your glory and power will be manifested in the future?" I prayed, "O Lord, you have millions of children in China, and we are all waiting eagerly for this day to come." I asked the police officer whether this prayer counted as subversion of state power? He thought for a moment and replied, "This does not count." Then I said, "Well, then there is nothing else, because prayer is the secret weapon of the church, the atomic bomb of the church. It is because God has given us the power and conduit of prayer that he calls us to be obedient, even to unjust authorities." I continued to recite Colossians 1:16 to the officer:

---

[2]Should be Peter, as found in 1 Peter 2:18.

> For by him all things were created, in heaven and on earth, visible and invisible, whether thrones or dominions or rulers or authorities—all things were created through him and for him. (Colossians 1:16)

Some commentators believe that the phrase "thrones or dominions or rulers or authorities" represented a list of offices of the angels or other spiritual powers in the folk religions at that time. This is also why Paul later reminds us that we are not to worship angels. In ancient times, all pagan societies assumed that the spiritual order in heaven was the same as the political order on earth. Both are hierarchical systems. As senior officials rule over the ones in lower ranks, the greater gods rule over lesser gods. So in the case of Chinese folk religions, the order is from the protector of the horses to the Marshal of the Heavenly Canopy, from the kitchen god to the Jade Emperor, but Christ is above all. All these gods are fake, while Christ is real. These gods are the result of the ultimate imagination of humankind, while Christ is the ultimate revelation of God.

The problem of the Three-Self church is that it does not believe that the history of China is Christ written large. In particular, it does not believe that the history of China after 1949 is also Christ written large. If you believe in the sovereignty of God, believe in the transcendence and supremacy of Christ as Creator, and believe in God's unfailing and omnipotent care of all things great and small in this universe, you will not accept any review by the Religious Affairs Bureau of the church's teaching and pastoral ministry, or allow unbelieving communist cadres to speak during church gatherings, nor will you accept the United Front Work Department's accreditation of pastors,[3] because you cannot accept the love for the Party and country, and the support for socialism as the conditions to be called for ministry by God. God commands us to be obedient in patience, not for us to sing songs and beat drums to support them. If you truly believe that Christ is the Savior, and believe that you are forgiven, cleansed and born again in the blood of Christ on the cross, you will especially find it impossible to accept the government's organization of our pastors to study Xi Jinping's speeches. In China today, if a servant of God truly believes in this Scripture in Colossians 1:15-20, he can never for the life of him accept any of these things.

God has the supreme sovereignty and the supreme plan of salvation. This is exactly the reason enough for us to be obedient and continue to live under the authority of the thrones or dominions or rulers or authorities in heaven or on earth. If an individual is essentially ruled by a king who has resurrected from

---

[3]See the "United Front Work Department."

the dead, then what does it matter if he is temporarily under an unjust government? Just as a godly wife who is essentially the bride of Christ, and has a personal, real and living relationship in life with the Most High, what loss does she have to submit to an unreasonable and unjust husband on earth. Since this light momentary affliction cannot impair our eternal weight of glory beyond all comparison, then the temporal and light government over us in this lifetime is nothing more than a mosquito bite. Just as Mao Zedong himself said that on this tiny globe, a few flies dash themselves against the wall. Ten thousand years are too long, so the world is trying to seize the day and the hour. All the dreams of this world have to be fulfilled before death. But Christ's love for us is more than ten thousand years, and he loved us before the common era. The cross has shattered the curse that all the dreams have to be fulfilled before death. Only those who have been crucified with Christ on the cross may live in humility, yet with honor beyond all comparison, may live in poverty, yet be exceedingly rich. They can even live in death, instead of being dead while living.

Modern biblical scholars discover that this passage is actually written in a form of poetry. Therefore, it is a great Christ hymn just like Philippians 2:6-11 and 2 Timothy 3:16. The Christ hymn in the book of Philippians praises how Christ humbled himself from the highest to the lowest and was then exalted to the Most High. Thus, incarnation and cross are the two astonishing turning points in the gospel. To believe in Jesus is to live in-between these two turning points. The power of the gospel and the filling of the Holy Spirit are dependent on the marks that these two turning points leave upon our lives. Like the land being plowed deep, or a piece of paper being repeatedly folded, or a seal being heavily carved by a knife, it is impossible not to have marks. It is even impossible to be restored to the original state. Therefore, Paul boldly declared to the world, "From now on let no one cause me trouble, for I bear on my body the marks of Jesus" (Galatians 6:17).

However, today the Chinese government, the Chinese culture, and most Chinese intellectuals and people are still troubling us. This is because they have not seen on our bodies the marks of Jesus. They have not seen enough, or the marks are not deep enough, or there long enough, so they do not believe that they are indelible. They think that being Chinese is our innate characteristic, and being Christian is just a lump of mud on our Chinese faces, so with a little more effort, they will be able to wash us clean. Even if they fail to wash us thoroughly, at least they can wash us into a "Christianity that is in

compliance with Socialism," into a Christianity that is Sinicized, Confu-
cianized, or "Partyized."[4]

But this Christ hymn in the book of Colossians follows a different kind of
logic, which first talks about Christ as the Creator then the Savior. Colossians 1:15-17 praises Christ as the Creator who works together with the Father,
who is of the same essence as the Father and of equal power with the Father. All
things were created through him. Augustine specifically pointed out that since
everything was created, clearly time was also created through him and for him.[5]
This proves that Christ is begotten, not made, and he exists outside of time. Just
as the Nicene Creed proclaims, he was begotten from the Father before all ages
and is the Creator from everlasting to everlasting. This is what it means to say
that history is Christ written large.

The mystery of the gospel is that this Christ who is written large became the
Christ written small. If he did not become the Christ written small, we would not
have been saved. But once he became small, the world could not recognize him,
which exposed the blindness of the world. So Colossians 1:18-20 transitions to
praising Christ as the Savior. After Paul's praise of this cosmic Christ, the Christ
written large, he suddenly mentions the death of Christ. He says that his death
became the cause of all who died and rose again, and he became the beginning,
the firstborn from the dead. Death sounds abrupt here, connecting two things
that are impossible to be connected, which is the Creator and the Savior. There
are two "firsts" here. In creation, he is the first. Now in salvation, he is also the
first. There are also two "all things" in this passage. One is the "all things" in
creation. This "all things" did not come into being by themselves but were created.
The other "all things" is mentioned in salvation. This "all things" after the fall of
humanity cannot heal themselves but can only be healed by salvation.

Thus, as in the book of Philippians, at last Paul places the focus of the hymn
on the cross.

> And through him to reconcile to himself all things, whether on earth or in
> heaven, making peace by the blood of his cross. (Colossians 1:20)

Once, I preached the gospel to the police officer who arrested me. I said, "In
1949, you established this regime by shedding blood. Later in 1989, you defended
this regime in the same way.[6] What about the future? In the future, when you

---

[4]See "Sinicization of Christianity."
[5]Wang Yi is likely paraphrasing book 11 of Augustine's *Confessions*.
[6]See "Tiananmen Square Protests of 1989."

lose power, you may still have to shed blood. Isn't that what has been recurring for the past thousands of years? No one has been able to break this cycle of history. However, the Bible says that the blood of Jesus enables us to get out of this cycle. The blood of Jesus on the cross can reconcile all things to himself. Since it refers to 'all things,' it certainly includes China, the millions of Communists and the millions of people in it."

I said to him, "According to this Scripture, I must tell you that the Communist Party will pass away. All of the powerful emperors and the political powers established by them in Chinese history are part of this cycle. But when the Communist Party passes away, the church will still be there. The church will always exist. Why? Because the peace established by the blood of man is short-lived. Only the peace established by the blood of Christ lasts forever. Whether you believe it or not right now, let me ask you: Isn't it better? Isn't it more agreeable to your conscience and doesn't it give you more inner peace?"

I said to him, "I am telling you about a power that will last forever. But this power does not demand lands, swords, or all the authority in this day. On the contrary, it is willing to humble itself and submit to the swords and authorities on earth. If you want to use the earthly power today to oppress the eternal power, this Scripture has already revealed the end result. History is Christ written large, not Xi Jinping written large. If you recognize that the existence of soul, the sin deep in the heart of humanity, the faith of humanity and the eternal destiny of humankind are beyond the jurisdiction of your government, then I earnestly wish to be always subject to you. I would love for you to rule China until our Lord Jesus Christ comes again, for it is very troublesome and dangerous to change the government."

Dear brothers and sisters, now I want to talk about two points, about the relationship between the church and the world based on this Scripture.

First, since the Enlightenment, the rise of "state sovereignty" has become the biggest idol that human societies worship for the past five hundred years.[7] According to the sixteenth-century Italian[8] scholar Jean Bodin's definition, state sovereignty means that the state constitutes an essence that is eternal, supreme, and unrestrained by any other power.[9] Over the past five hundred years, Progressivism of history has caused various revolutions against the sovereignty of Christ in

---

[7]The idea of the sovereignty of the state gained both legal and moral force during the Enlightenment. In particular, the social contract as proposed by Thomas Hobbes in *Leviathan* (1651) was accepted as a mechanism for establishing state sovereignty.

[8]Jean Bodin should be French, instead of Italian.

[9]In his 1576 treatise *Six Books of the Republic* (*Six livres de la République*), Bodin argued that it is inherent in the nature of the state that sovereignty must be absolute (supreme) and perpetual (eternal).

secular politics. In other words, the main change in Western societies after the Reformation is the denial of Colossians 1:15-17. In the words of Eric Voegelin, it is simply humanity's self-deification in the achievement of modernity.[10]

This is an issue that the Reformation did not address. It is because since the Reformation in the sixteenth century, till the time of the Westminster Confession of Faith in 1646, or for Europe until the time of the Treaty of Westphalia in 1648, the political order in Europe was understood to be bound by faith in God and the law of God. Or it was acknowledged and respected that there was a higher spiritual order and spiritual authority. The idea that the nations of the earth have the supreme, eternal, and autonomous authority in human societies is completely a modern and anti-Christian concept and product. Thus, for Westminster theologians, the state itself was never considered the greatest threat to monotheism, or the greatest idol of the future world.

When it is declared in the preamble to the US Constitution that "We the People of the United States in Order to form a more perfect Union" according to the freedom bestowed by our "Creator," America became the last nation in human history that was established on monotheism and voluntarily placed its state power under the higher spiritual order, because the word *Creator* in the US Constitution is in the singular form, indicating that he is the only one.

However, today only Britain and America retained, at least nominally, in the constitutional tradition, the concept of the Reformation time, that the rule of the state is placed in a lower status, under a higher and eternal dominion. This acknowledges that the rule of God is the source of legitimacy of state power. Except these two countries, almost all countries in the world are the products of the modern concept of state, which believes in the supremacy of state sovereignty.

One thing I want to point out in particular is that the greatest impact of this change on the church is that for the past two hundred years, the gospel preached by the church has increasingly ignored Colossians 1:15-17 and only preached Colossians 1:18-20. In other words, we no longer preach a cosmic Christ and his eternal reign but only the salvation of Christ on the cross. The church has even developed a sophisticated theological narrative and communication skills that avoid to preach verses 15 to 17 and focus only on verses 18 to 20. We have altered the gospel of the church into a quasi-gospel under the monstrous sovereign state.

---

[10]This may be a much-condensed summary of Voegelin's views expressed in *The New Science of Politics: An Introduction* (University of Chicago Press, 1952).

This is why we can preach the gospel to individuals, but it is difficult to preach the gospel to the nation. We find it difficult to tell a nation as a whole that you are wrong, you are not the supreme, eternal, or unrestrained sovereign entity in the universe but only an administrator who is temporally allowed to exist by God and under God. Eventually all your actions are subject to God's final judgment. This has led the church today to continually psychologize the gospel and reduce the meaning of salvation to the healing of the heart. It is very difficult for us to preach the gospel of "the one eternal power." On Christmas Eve when we remember the birth of Jesus Christ, we can hardly even proclaim, Behold, "the government shall be upon his shoulder!" (Isaiah 9:6).

The greatest worship battle the church has to face is not what songs we should sing during worship services. Rather, it is an age-old battle between the sovereignty of Christ and the sovereignty of the state in worship. In China, this battle of worship clearly manifests in whether to sing red songs in the church, whether to hang the national flags in our sanctuaries, whether to participate in political studies, whether to remove the crosses from the top of church buildings, whether to join the Communist Party, whether to wear the red scarves, whether we can have a corporate worship of God, whether we can baptize the youth under the age of eighteen, and so on.

The second point I would like to make is that the Chinese rulers' and the Chinese people's understanding of ruling has never been restrained by monotheism since the ancient days to the year of 2017. The worship of state, government, and political leaders has also never been broken by the worship of Christ. I would go as far as to say that even among the Chinese house churches we are still not so convinced by Colossians 1:15-17 that the fear and resentment of the Communist Party as rulers still binds us to this day. It not only binds the Three-Self churches, but it also binds the house churches. For more than half a century, we have obeyed the rulers, but our obedience has been less out of a free conscience in Christ and more out of the same fear and concern for the benefits of the flesh as the rest of the nation. Likewise, the hatred and indifference in us, just like the rest of the nation, stops us from preaching the gospel with a fervent heart. Because we have a crazy ruler, few of us are crazy about the gospel in China. In fact, not enough Christians have been imprisoned in China, not enough people have lost their jobs for believing in Jesus, and too few have been jailed for preaching the gospel. Too few churches have been shut down by the government for meeting and worshiping in public. The number of the martyrs has not been fulfilled yet. The will of the real man is not yet strong enough. The Chinese church has suffered too little. The suffering that the Chinese church is able to bear has not been enough. The Lord has given us too much, but we have given him too little, because the gospel has not completely removed our worship of kings, for you will worship whomever you fear. Well, let us boldly admit that we are afraid of the Communist Party. Believers are afraid of losing their public offices; pastors are afraid of losing their churches; men are afraid of not being able to make money; women are afraid of being fined for having children. Who is most afraid of the church being persecuted? Not the believers, because when the church is persecuted, they can simply switch to another one. It is the pastors and church leaders who fear persecution of the church most, because once the church is persecuted, they could lose their jobs. And to start all over again is difficult. Starting over requires to repent again, to be obedient again, and to be filled with the Holy Spirit again. So sadly, in Chinese church today, it is not the believers but the pastors who are most afraid of the Communist Party.

Back then, Emperor Kang Xi did an inscription for the Catholic church with the words "the true principle of all things."[11] It seemed to be a response to Colossians 1:15-17, which declared that Christ is the Lord of all. But Kang Xi did not recognize that Christ was also the principle of his imperial power and constituted a restraint on his reign. Therefore, starting with him, China banned Christianity for one hundred years.

This passage shows that as Creator, Christ rules over everything. But as the Savior, Christ was humbled to death. Thus, between these two, in his saving love, God provided the world a space where two orders coexist: one is the order of God, the other is of Satan. When these two orders are reflected in the world, one is the order of Christ, the other is of Pharaoh. The cross is the boundary between these two orders, the only way and heavenly ladder that connects the present world and the future time.

Beginning with the exodus, every expansion of God's kingdom in history has corresponded to the most powerful empire on earth at that time. Moses' time corresponded to Egypt. The period before and after the exile corresponded to Assyria, Babylon, and Persia. The time of "silence" corresponded to the Greek Empire and the New Testament period to the Roman Empire. The Pharaoh also has many names. In Babylon he was called king, in Rome Caesar, and in China

---

[11]The original words in Chinese are 万有本原 (wan you ben yuan).

the emperor. In the twentieth century, he was called the head of state; in China the General Secretary. Essentially, they are of the same order of Pharaoh. The core feature of this order is that humankind is god, or the state is god.

In human history, only Europe dissolved this pharaonic order in the thousand years after its Christianization. In Europe, at least in theory, whether thrones or dominions or rulers or authorities, all powers were based on the kingship of Christ. They all acknowledged that they executed power under the higher sovereignty of Christ. In other words, during the medieval times, the order of the monarchy formed part of a greater order of Christ. This is what "Christendom" truly means.

The Reformation began to break the idea and application of this Christendom. When the personal meaning of the gospel was rediscovered, the world revealed its unbelief. After that, through the effort of the Puritans, another new governing order was gradually established in British and American societies, an order between the order of Christ and that of the Pharaoh. This is the Western constitutional and republican system in the British-American sense.

However, the major change in Western societies in the last hundred years has been the resurgence of the pharaonic order in the modern Western states. In fact, since the seventeenth-century English thinker Thomas Hobbes, the so-called Leviathan state monster has gradually freed itself from the restraint of Christianity and grown into an upgraded version of the Pharaonic order with the development of the British-American constitutional and republican tradition. In other words, the pharaonic order is a virus program hidden in the weakest version of the "British-American Christendom" in the West after the Reformation, while the Fascism and Soviet Union were the outbreak of this virus in Western societies so far.

However, in China, this pharaonic order that denies the sovereignty of God has never collapsed, because after the complete disappearance of Egypt, Babylon, and Persia, China is the virus itself in today's world. God spent more than one hundred years and used unprecedented revolutions, disastrous wars, and the rises and falls of several regimes to break this ancient and sinful nation. Today, in the sense of Colossians 1:18-20, millions of Christians in the house churches and a portion of Christians in the Three-Self churches may already constitute the largest evangelical church in the world. But in the sense of verses 15 to 17, the order of Christ has not yet impacted the souls of this large people group overall. The order of Pharaoh is still very powerful and dominates the hearts of the Chinese people with its spirit-controlling power. As a matter of fact, it gravely weakens the ability of the church to preach the gospel.

However, dear brothers and sisters, since God is still patient with us, why cannot we be patient? Since God has scattered the Chinese among the nations over the past hundred years, does this not show that Christians in China, in Malaysia, in United States and Canada, although in our gospel missions we love the souls and communities in the countries we live, ultimately we do not belong to our countries but to the eternal power of God. Yes, we belong to a kingdom that is built on the blood of Christ on the cross, a kingdom that will reconcile all things to God. And the true mark that shows we truly belong to this kingdom of Christ is not our success, our wealth, or our reputation, but the mark of the cross of Jesus on our bodies. This is a mark that cannot be rubbed away, wiped off, or erased.

For this reason, it is good for some to make money for the Lord, and it is better for others to be imprisoned for the Lord. It is good for some to live for the Lord, and it is better for others to die for the Lord.

O Lord, may you grant the future Chinese society to your church, or please allow me to leave the world to be with you. O Lord, may you grant a great revival to your church in China, or let my tongue stick to the roof of my mouth. O Lord, raise up a large number of servants who are faithful to your kingdom and your rule to face a new round of persecution, or make them lose their churches and their high positions in their churches. O Lord, may you choose innumerable missionaries, church planters, and evangelists, who will work in season and out of season, going through all the cities and villages of China until the gospel fills every prison and jail, or take away our properties, degrees, and our middle-class lifestyle, lest one day we come to meet you only with these things. O Lord, enable us to give money when we have money, to give lives when we have lives; let us be passive and non-cooperative in Chinese society but be active in the preaching of the gospel; let us not envy the wicked, nor fear the powerful; let us not sing the songs of Babylon; not worship the image of Nebuchadnezzar; not give high fives to sins. Lord, hear this urgent yet imperfect prayer of your child, in the holy name of our Lord Jesus Christ, Amen.

15

AN OPPORTUNITY FOR CHURCHES TO WALK THE WAY OF THE CROSS

WANG YI

The following is an edited and condensed excerpt of a much longer interview that took place in February 2018 with Wang Yi and another prominent pastor from Beijing. The interviewer anonymously published the transcription shortly before Chinese New Year and it circulated widely online over the holiday. The stated intention of the interviewer was to provide house church pastors with material upon which to reflect and pray as the new year arrived, so that there might be a unified response to the New Regulations going forward in 2018.

The full interview discusses the government's motivations behind the regulations, whether house churches should break into small fellowships, how ecclesiology influences house church responses to the regulations, what testimony the house church presents to Chinese society, and why house churches in big urban centers must take the heat for small rural churches. Both pastors argued that at the heart of the New Regulations is the Chinese Communist Party's unwillingness to recognize two kingdoms—the spiritual kingdom and that of the sword. Instead, the CCP strives for one sphere of authority under the state. Because of this, the pastors argue that the house churches need to be unified rather than isolated, sharing a common identity and willingness to suffer as one body in resistance.

In this excerpt, Wang Yi explains how his theology informs his response to the New Regulations. Arguing against the threat of individualism, he believes that the ultimate purpose of the church is not merely fellowship among believers but rather filling the earth with God's image and glory through his redeemed people. Because of this, any decision that reduces the church's visible presence stands against God's will

for the spread of the gospel in China. Ultimately, Wang Yi asks his readers if they are
willing to pay the price for the church's recent growth in China.

The center of God's creation and redemption is his church. Before the foundation of the world, he chose his people in Christ Jesus. As the first fruits, his people await the day when all things will be united in Christ. We are created for community, and we are redeemed for the kingdom, the body of Christ.

We are kept on earth, rather than being carried directly to heaven after our baptism, because of the Great Commission—to spread the gospel to the ends of the earth, to teach believers to observe everything the Lord has commanded us, to establish worship, and to return to the original purpose of creation, which is to fill the earth with God's image and glory through those whom God has saved. The church is first and foremost God's kingdom.

Under difficult circumstances, this kingdom can exist even in invisible forms. In the 1950s and 1960s there was no visible church in this land. Yet those believers who were scattered and persecuted still made up the kingdom of God. This never ceased. People ask, "If persecution comes, should we still keep the visible form of the church?"

There are two views. One is the modern, individualistic understanding of the gospel, which influences our position on downgrading the church to fellowships. The focus is still on "me"—"I" need help from others. To put it in a worldly way, "We hold together for warmth." Fellowship is good for my personal growth. If one holds an individualistic understanding of the church and the gospel, his response will be about his own salvation and how many people he can lead to Christ. Yet the church is not established from the perspective of individual members; the head of the church is Christ. So on the other hand, the church is the kingdom of God.

Sometimes under difficult circumstances, this kingdom exists in invisible ways. The breakdown of the visible church does not mean the kingdom has disappeared. Under such circumstances, people ask, "Why should we keep the forms of the visible church? What should the church defend in order to grow and develop?" This is complex. Many churches' responses are related to their understanding of the situation, of Chinese society, and of the relationship between church and state.

In the past six months, I surveyed my colleagues and asked how many felt our church was under persecution. I took this survey four or five times. In the beginning half thought we had a 50 percent chance of being persecuted. A week ago, 80–90 percent of them thought we had a 50 percent chance of being persecuted. Those who frequently bypass the firewall think the danger is not that high, while those who don't bypass the firewall think the danger is higher.[1]

Our reactions are tied to our sources of information and our understanding of society, including our fear of the state and politics. Sometimes we want to dress up our decisions as theological responses, but this differentiation is necessary. Some churches' responses are not based on theology but on different sources of information, different understandings of the situation, different personal experiences, and even fear. We try to dress up a lot of worldly stuff as theology, which is extremely dangerous. In situations like these, we tend to be weak.

The emergence of Chinese urban churches over the last decade was brought about by God in a relatively relaxed environment. Our way of the cross, our suffering for the Lord, our grasp of the situation, and our self-evaluation have not yet been seriously tested by God. Therefore, we tend to overlook our corruption and fear in the midst of weakness.

We have been like frightened birds, with deep-seated fear of the state and political powers. Facing the New Regulations with our salvation in mind helps us face our fear, timidity, weakness, and corruption. As the New Regulations challenge our faith, do we have true freedom in Christ?

When believers today face such external challenges, we should focus on whether we have been fearlessly filled with the Holy Spirit in Christ. In the Bible, the byproduct of being filled with the Holy Spirit is speaking the word of God with boldness. Our challenge is ourselves: Can house churches in China today preach the word of God with boldness because we are filled with the Holy Spirit? Do we have true freedom through the gospel of Christ? Our response to the New Regulations should come from the gospel itself more than from our assessment of external factors. Often our assessments are not reliable (depending on our sources of information, life experience, and geographic location). We must ask whether our response is one that centers on the gospel. This says nothing about our view of the church but only our view of salvation. This is the first point—face the challenges of the New Regulations with our salvation in mind.

The second point is the ecclesiological perspective. No matter the government's intention, we must seek God's will. God would never intend to reduce church worship through our response to the New Regulations. Churches in

---

[1]China's firewall is a complex technological system that monitors, regulates, and limits internet information and access, particularly of traffic to foreign websites.

China have indeed gone through periods without large congregations. We have experienced decades with only small groups, family worship, and gatherings of two or three people. In the past ten years, we saw God leading Chinese house churches into a new age. If not for the New Regulations, we would be talking about new buildings, pastoral systems, church planting and evangelism. Should we stop talking about these things?

God's will is to build visible congregations where God's people can gather as a church (size is not important) for public worship and sacraments. Will the churches' responses to the New Regulations diminish our worship? If what we do diminishes our worship, then our response is wrong and contradictory to God's guidance of the Chinese house churches over the past ten years. If the response is more church planting, that is certainly good.

Take the Presbyterian church, for example. To establish a new church there must be qualified elders. First, this requires a certain size: a small group is unlikely to have two to three mature elders. Second, this takes time: it could take even ten years before two or three qualify as elders. If a church's stability is disrupted and it downgrades to small groups, realistically it will have no manpower to plant a church.

Suppose we have a church of two hundred members. Over the past seven to eight years, it has become a congregation with three qualified elders and Christ-centered pastors, teachers, and evangelists. Yet now because of the New Regulations, the church downgrades to eight small groups. There will not even be one qualified elder in each group. The church's teaching, worship, and governance are weakened. This is not proactive church planting but a demolition of what God has built. If however, the church is preparing to split into two congregations, or sending a group to plant a church, that would be great. This would be the right way to grow a church organically. If the church downgrades into small groups, the church is taking a step back and the result is separation of the body of Christ.

Is it worthwhile for us to pay the price for Sunday worship, church government, and the administration of the sacraments? Should we walk the way of the cross and not give up easily? This is the most critical question.

Some churches choose to scatter. I do not criticize them, because they have done so based on their understanding. If today's situation is as bad as it was in the 1950s and 1960s, maybe we will all have to scatter. We have to pay the price; if things become severe enough, it is likely we will not hold public worship with more than fifty people. Even if that happens, we still believe that a visible body of Christ will continue in China.

But the current question is: Would you pay the price for what God has done through the house churches in China over the past decade? For the urban church planting movement, for congregation building, for the formation of Christ's body, for the slow maturing of an ecclesiology that informs our teaching, pulpit building, administration of the sacraments, church officer training, and discipleship? Are these worthy of walking the way of the cross, even to imprisonment, until we cannot take it anymore?

We should respond step by step, rather than overreacting and downgrading in advance. Downgrading in advance is tied to ecclesiology, to courage, and being Spirit-filled as a result of one's soteriology; it is also tied to a faulty judgment of the situation.

Moving forward, we are accelerating church planting. Intentionally planting a church is different from small groups. We launched one new congregation at the end of last year; we plan to do so again in March; we may launch one more this year. This is consistent with the logic of building up the church and letting current events bring new energy to our movement.

According to our ecclesiology, the fundamental issue is the church-state relationship. China's governing philosophy sees politics and religion as one. The state does not accept a spiritual authority in the realm of faith. Therefore, our response carries significant evangelistic and apologetic purpose.

We have an opportunity to demonstrate to society what the church is; why spiritual authority should not be in the hands of those who wield the sword; why we can accept or at least endure external governance but cannot allow our faith, worship, teaching, shepherding, church offices, and members to come under the state's review and control. This is an opportunity for the church in China.

In the 1980s and 1990s there were several rounds of persecution of house churches in China, but over the past twenty years there has not been a nationwide persecution, only individual cases for certain believers and churches in certain areas. This is an opportunity, as the government makes a new attempt.

I believe this is the CCP's last attempt in the hope of complete suppression or strict limits on the development of Christianity in China, even to the point of adopting legislation, mandatory enforcement, and possible criminal cases in the future (though probably not many). The government is sparing no expense to suppress house churches. This may not be successful. It may be abandoned after a few high points.

It is like the Edict of Milan in AD 313. Before Christianity was legalized, it suffered one last severe persecution in AD 311, which seemed violent but did not last long.[2] The church's response to the New Regulations is a large-scale evangelistic and apologetic movement that no individual church, minister, or believer could do in the past. This is God's will and the church has an opportunity to demonstrate with humility, gentleness, and a resolute heart, that the essence of this church-state relationship is the boundary between a spiritual kingdom and a worldly kingdom with swords.

The church's position on the church-state relationship is shaped by our ecclesiology. All other religions are beneficiaries of Christianity's position on this issue, because they do not have a philosophy of separation between church and state. In its response to the New Regulations, the church must hold firm to this position. We must explain why our faith supports this separation and why we firmly reject the sinicization of Christianity, government intervention in churches, and exams for pastoral qualifications.

Today's churches must examine whether we should firmly reject government intervention. If yes, how do we show that we are motivated by faith, not by political goals? We must be willing to take the way of the cross and suffer for our faith. It is not about dodging, but we want to let society and the country know why our faith rejects the government's limitation of and control over what we believe. I am willing to pay this price. I am willing to show you this willingness.

This is the way of evangelism and apologetics. The church has an opportunity to contend, persevere, and pay the price for our faith in front of society and its rulers. If this is the first nationwide persecution of house churches in the last twenty years, it is also the church's first evangelistic and apologetic opportunity in the last twenty years. This way of the cross is consistent with a theology of the cross that God has put in our hearts.

[Our house church movement] advocates for a gospel- and Christ-centered church; we teach that the cross is our center. As we face the New Regulations, unless churches in China, the Reformed churches, and the churches involved in [our movement] demonstrate that we are willing to pay the price for what we teach, we are betraying this teaching. This is an opportunity for the churches in China to have not only a message to preach, but also leaders with testimonies.

As the church responds to the New Regulations, we must consider the testimony the church presents to Chinese society. While the church is not always

---

[2]In the Edict of Milan of 313, Emperors Constantine I and Licinius proclaimed the toleration of Christianity within the Roman Empire. The edict provided all persons under Roman rule with freedom of worship, legal rights as Christians, the right to assemble churches, and the return of confiscated property.

at its best, it still has a good reputation among Chinese people today. In traditional Chinese culture and society, there is only one group of people who, with no practical (economic or political) gain in mind, hold on to their conscience and pursuit of faith to the point that even government persecution cannot force them to give up. They express their goodwill by reacting not in violence but in gentleness. In Chinese society, only the Chinese church has this type of testimony over the past few decades.

Yet the testimonies of the house churches have not been well known by the majority of society. How many people knew of Yuan Xiangchen or Wang Mingdao? I guess no more than ten million Chinese people. Their testimonies were limited to an isolated system. But with tens of millions of believers, today's house churches are more broadly known by Chinese society.

Today, at least 200 to 500 million Chinese people know about the house churches. With the social changes of the past two decades, more and more Chinese, including those who pursue freedom and democracy and care for society, have gradually seen the testimonies of the house churches. These are all brave people who hold onto freedom of conscience. The house churches are different; we do not take to the streets or resist with political campaigns. The church is low-profile and gentle. How the Chinese house churches react to the New Regulations and bear witness for Christ today could have an unimaginably positive influence on the future of the gospel movement in China.

Finally, I would like to add one more perspective. Churches in big cities must stand up for churches in smaller cities and villages.

Biblically, I think it is wrong for any congregation to react to the New Regulations solely on the ground of its own benefit or loss. The decision has to be made from a kingdom perspective—churches in all of China are Christ's body. We are one church.

Urban churches tend to endure more pressure than rural churches. Churches in medium-sized cities tend to endure more pressure than churches in second- and third-tier cities. Over the past ten years urban churches have begun to emerge in cities such as Beijing, Shanghai, Wuhan, and Chengdu, with public gatherings of more than a hundred believers (some climb to three hundred or more). We don't know what the final results of the current persecution will be. Is the goal to crack down on congregations with over a thousand believers and leave those with a hundred alone, or is it to crack down on those with a hundred and leave those with fifty alone? We have no idea.

Churches in Beijing, Shanghai, and Chengdu must stand firm, because this is your responsibility. You stand among brothers and sisters within the body of Christ all over this country; if you are quick to give up, churches in smaller cities will give up even more so. If your congregation of two hundred members gives up without persecution from the sword or political authority, a church of fifty in a smaller city will have to give up to avoid imprisonment. If you can hold on, churches of fifty in smaller cities may be okay.

All churches in this country are part of the body of Christ, one church. In this storm, you must hold on for your brothers. You cannot only think of your own congregation. You have come to your privileged position as a church in an urban center and enjoy so much common grace, but it may be that God will use you to stand up for your brothers, to hold on against the sword and the authorities. This is a crucial burden for the whole body of Christ.

Most churches do not need to follow our example and pursue this path. But at the national level, there is a need for several churches that will pursue legal procedures to voice their opinions publicly. Churches that are not equipped need not do likewise. In fact, I would suggest they don't do this. But it would be beneficial if there are churches that are willing to do this. Among the hundreds and thousands of churches that are persecuted, it would be great if there were ten or even a hundred churches who were willing to do this. The purpose is so that most of the other churches can focus their energy on other things instead of legal matters.

If we are to be persecuted as a representative church, then we are willing to suffer this for the church of our Lord. Our strategy is the following: if our sanctuary gets shut down, we will find other venues. If they come after us once, twice, or three times, we will endure. If we can no longer find a place in Chengdu and are chased out of everywhere we go, we will gather in the open. If they are not willing to handcuff us in public, they will never bring this church down. Either they apprehend us immediately by the law, or they put us under house arrest like Jin Tianming and take away our freedom. If they deal with us illegally, it is a testimony to society that the government is unlawful and reckless. To persevere in this way would serve as a very good testimony.

If a church of several hundred members attracts this kind of heat, they won't be able to carry out a second case. Thus, we will have to wait until the other pastors and I are apprehended, losing our freedom. Not until this final situation do we retreat into small groups. We can have twenty midweek small groups, gathering on Sunday in five to six meeting spaces. Small groups and Sunday worship would be distinct. If a pastor is freed, we will immediately resume gathering. We will await legal proceedings to voice our opinions through due process.

The first and greatest challenge is aimed at pastors and preachers, not at believers. Pastors of this generation face a greater risk. When a church faces these things, believers carry on with their lives, but pastors pay the greatest price. If they apprehend anyone, it will be the pastor. This is a test for this generation of pastors, to test their courage in the gospel. Are pastors willing to pay the price and lead the church? Pastors of the house church: Are you willing to walk the way of the cross by depending on the power of the gospel? This will not only affect you and your family's lives but also the church of our Lord and millions of God's people. If they are timid and weak, how can we help them? We should not rebuke. We should have fellowship with them in the gospel, but we should be courageous.

The second challenge is the unity of the church. Will the house churches of China dissolve? Persecution will certainly bring some unity to the churches, and that is our hope. Can the churches encourage one another, be in harmony, and be united, fostering greater solidarity and networking, as a result of the New Regulations? Divisions on a small scale, but unity on a large scale. That is one of the greatest challenges the New Regulations will bring.

16

"CHRIST IS LORD. GRACE IS KING. BEAR THE CROSS. KEEP THE FAITH."

WANG YI

The following is excerpted from an extended interview conducted by a Chinese writer with Wang Yi and the leadership of Early Rain Covenant Church in October 2018. The interviewer published it online anonymously and it was widely shared on the social media platform WeChat.

In this excerpt, Wang Yi articulates his growing conviction that his church's struggle with the government is not one of rights and constitutionality but rather a moral, spiritual struggle. The problem with persecuting the church is not that believers suffer. Though believers do not desire suffering, they know they are walking the way of the cross with Jesus. Rather, the problem with persecution is that it is detrimental to society. It endangers the souls of persecutors, limits the opportunities for people to hear the gospel, and invites God's judgment on the nation. The church is God's light in this world, and as such it must remain open and bright in order to bless society. The church serves as the world's watchman, and if the church is silenced the city suffers from the inability to hear its voice.

WE NEED A GOSPEL MOVEMENT

Some scholars say by the year 2030, China will have 240 million Christians and become the largest Christian country in the world. That might happen. But it seems to me that since 2017, the number of Christians has dropped, perhaps even by 5 million. The growth of the Chinese house church over the past two or three years may even be declining. There are maybe 80 million Chinese Christians.

Looking back, we see that 1927 to 1937, all the way to the revival of the 1940s, formed the spiritual strength of the Chinese house church after 1949. The growth of the Chinese house church from the 1980s until now is due to the blood of the martyrs and a few revival preachers. The New Religious Regulations are a turning point. Today's house church is no longer the church of the second half of the 1970s and 1980s, which grew out of suffering.

The main bulk of the house church is very weak, even afraid. If the purpose is to avoid sacrifice and spare one's own life, then the army will inevitably become very weak. This is similar to the recent state of the Chinese house church. The churches where crosses have been torn down are completely different from those of the 1980s and 1990s. The more churches during that time were oppressed, the more courageous they became. Wherever persecution went, the gospel spread. If it does not engage with mainstream culture, if it does not impact Chinese society, if it does not come in sharp conflict with emperor worship, the church can grow to 80 million, but it cannot naturally grow any further.

What circumstances caused the Chinese house church to grow to 80 million? It has peaked in civil society through the private sector (it cannot preach openly and is not legally recognized). We have been engaging in guerrilla warfare in society, politics, economics, and culture. We have not been fighting a positional war. Under these circumstances, 80 million is the peak. If we want to reach new heights (150 million is an entirely different magnitude), then we need a new round of persecution. Current growth may already be at a standstill. Persecution and the New Religious Regulations force the church to react.

We must come before God to pray for the church and for ourselves. If a new gospel movement does not arise within China in the next ten to twenty years, it will be difficult for the church to reach a greater scale of magnitude in the future.

Let us look at the five main Chinese house church networks during the 1980s and 1990s.[1] As Chinese church ecclesiology has developed over the past dozen or so years, believers have all been in the same place. During this time, new local churches were formed, visible bodies of Christ were established, shepherding and teaching were emphasized, and residential pastors arose. This has been an important movement. It has led to a transition to local churches and church planting.

The recent religious regulations attack this kind of church, not individual Christians. You can practice your religion freely, but you cannot practice it

---

[1] The "Five Main Groups" of Chinese house church networks in the 1980s and 1990s were the Fangcheng Group and Tanghe Group in Henan Province; the Yingshang Group and Lixin Group in Anhui Province; and the Wenzhou Group in Zhejiang Province.

openly with others. You cannot practice on the streets, and so on. The visibility and expansion of the church throughout society is the target of their attacks.

In the past, we treated the formation of presbyteries and gospel movements as the same thing, but, though related, they are not the same. In church history, no movement has ever been started through the overtures of a general assembly. They come out of movements and cultures created by individual churches or people, who then influence more people and churches, eventually forming a gospel movement.

A MISSIONAL COMMUNITY

My hope is that Early Rain Covenant Church will be a missional church that promotes a gospel movement. In January of this year, the church decided to express our mission with the phrase "Christ is Lord. Grace is King." We then decided that the path to carry out this mission is "Bear the cross. Keep the faith."

For the past few years we have consistently discussed the vision of the three "hua."[2] One aspect [of this vision] is the nurturing and formation of God's children by the local church. In this regard, we emphasize the same things as the traditional house church: the preaching of the Word, the ministry of worship (the sacraments as the means of grace are very important), and the formation of fellowship. This is the Word-centered church structure of the Reformed tradition.

The other aspect is gospel movement, which is split into two parts. The first is preaching and church planting. Brothers and sisters are clear that the church must establish churches that plant churches. (Our church is starting one or two at the moment and now has seven total.) Brothers and sisters know that starting church plants is the direction this gospel movement needs to go. The second can be generally referred to as the cultural mandate. Brothers and sisters clearly see that the church has a great burden for preaching, for church planting, for education, and for culture.

We feel deeply that more and more people in Chinese society today are hopeless. They long to find a way out through religion. The church's voice is clear and distinct. When it is attacked by social and political powers and does not retreat and is not afraid, this attracts all classes of people. They don't come because they want to do the same things we're doing but because they want to obtain whatever it is that is driving these people to do them, which is the gospel itself.

[2]See "Jonathan Chao."

First, the pulpit must address society's needs, emphasizing Christ-centered preaching. The church's teaching focuses on humanity's fallenness (connecting with people's hopelessness about their jobs, marriages, society, and country). When this general despair is vividly portrayed, your hopeless heart can then find satisfaction in the gospel.

Second, we emphasize ecclesiology. In our membership class, we ask everyone to share their experiences with communal life. Their general response is either that they have none (never having participated in community life prior to the church) or that they have lost hope in it. We emphasize evangelism through the church. Brothers and sisters in our church have formed the opinion that the best method of evangelism is to bring people to church. One sister brought her father to church. After church ended, a brother came up and hugged him. She said, "My father has not been hugged like this by anyone for many decades."

Third, as we confront this general despair within society, we emphasize mercy ministries. Even though very few people participate in these, they are necessary. Many people who feel hopeless about Chinese society are encouraged by the church's mercy ministries and are deeply moved. Our church often attracts liberal intellectuals, young Nationalists, human rights activists, and people from civic circles. When they see the church doing small, practical things, they are very moved.

For example, one brother was originally engaged in human rights activism. His first time coming to our church was when he attended our June Fourth prayer meeting last year.[3] He was shocked. He had never been to a place like this where so many people were openly commemorating June Fourth, singing hymns, and praying. He cried listening to the worship music. Later, he moved to Chengdu to begin catechesis. He was baptized this year and decided to serve the church full time. Many people who are hopeless about society come to know their Savior Jesus Christ through justice and mercy ministries in the church.

WE ARE NOT TRYING TO PROTECT OUR RIGHTS

The church is not speaking in order to defend itself. God has given the church the role of a watchman. The church has a mission to let the world know who the church is. Through the existence of the church and the gospel it preaches, the world must come to understand itself. This is related to apologetics and missions.

---

[3]See "Tiananmen Square Protests of 1989."

Looking at the historical church experience, we see that as the early church faced persecution by the Roman Empire, there arose a large number of martyrs. There were also many apologists who defended the faith, telling the persecuting world, including the emperors, what we believe, why we believe it, why we do what we do, and why we hold to these positions. There has always been an apologetic tradition throughout church history. This was also the case during the Reformation. Luther and Calvin both wrote apologetic documents defending the faith. In Chinese history, Wang Mingdao wrote "We—For the Sake of Faith" in 1955, which is also an apologetic work.

When the government persecutes the church, we do not think it is harmful only to the church. It is also harmful to the government. Even unbelievers are harmed, because their opportunity to hear the gospel is diminished. It is not just believers who are being suppressed. All people are harmed. God's blessing might be removed, and he may discipline them because this is something God is displeased with. The church has the responsibility to proclaim these things to society and to the authorities.

We are not fighting the persecution of the church within the public square using the language of the public square. This is not "fighting for rights." The church explicitly refuses to appeal to worldly authority. We do not say that it is wrong for the government to do this because it violates the constitution, and we do not say that it is wrong for the government to do this because it violates its own laws. We only mention our faith. It is wrong for the government to act in this way because the Bible says it is wrong. We believe the Bible, we believe God, and therefore we believe this is wrong.

We are not the only ones who will suffer loss. You will also suffer; the whole country will suffer. If we do not proclaim this, we have not fulfilled our responsibility as watchmen. This sin will then come upon us. But if we tell the world, and the world still keeps doing what it wants, this sin has nothing to do with us. This is a gospel act. It is an apologetic and missional act, not a human rights movement.

This persecution is directed against an ecclesiology. The goal is not to make every person renounce his or her faith but to prevent believers from gathering. Why is the government tearing down crosses? Because you have publicly influenced society. How should the church respond? By continuing to uphold our ecclesiology.

Therefore, we are asking pastors to reveal their identity as pastors. If pastors do not speak out, the church will not know what to do and many believers will not know which course to follow. Pastors are not only responsible for their own congregations, they also have a shared responsibility for the Lord's flock. Churches in many places are small and weak. Some may not even have pastors. They need to be comforted. We can encourage them and help them affirm and hold onto their faith. We can let them know what the basic attitude of Christians should be as they face these situations.

In this sense, the joint statement [we issued] instructs and pastors the Lord's flock in China.[4] Pastors who sign the statement may face increased danger. The decision of whether or not to sign is not made out of consideration of the benefits for one's church but consideration of how it will influence the kingdom. This is a shared burden. As more pastors sign the joint statement, they divide the pressure among themselves. This allows churches under a lot of pressure to reduce that pressure and churches that are not under pressure to take some of that pressure. The body works together.

Liberals see individual rights as foundational. This is contrary to Christianity and the conservative gospel. The beliefs I held before I believed in God I now criticize. Liberal ideology is continually fermenting in the minds of young people. Many in the younger generation use individual rights and their individual selves as the standard to make sense of the church.

The church holds to the opposite of liberalism. The church does not eliminate the individual, but it values community. Individual significance is made clear and fulfilled in the context of community. The church values responsibility over individual rights. The Bible teaches self-denial and responsibility, not individual rights.

AN OPEN CHURCH

A dozen years ago, the church wanted to become a part of public society. That openness meant being recognized in society, which was symbolized by legalization, maybe even having a gospel position—the church being given space to do more things (even advocating for universal values within civil society). For pastors, this was a kind of linguistic strategy. "Doing this is good for society." They used this rhetoric because they were speaking to the government. But this strategy has weak ecclesial ontology.

When I speak of openness, I am not talking about obtaining a position in mainstream society. I am saying that the house church has a tendency to

---

[4]See Chapter 16 "A Joint Statement by Pastors: A Declaration for the Sake of the Christian Faith."

privatize itself and may not be conscious of the church's place in the universe and in world history.

In the past, we hid underground. It appeared as though we didn't have any relationship to politics. In reality, this resulted in a high degree of politicization. You are viewing yourself through their framework. You think of yourselves as Christians meeting together. "We don't need to establish a church. We're just meeting together." In reality, this is the Chinese house church's privatization of self-knowledge. It reflects a low view of eschatology. In reality, you are understanding yourself according to the rationale of this world, not a spiritual understanding.

The church is shining, open, and bright. The church must openly manifest itself in the world. God wants to show his church to the world: "This is my church, my children, the body of Christ on earth."

Ephesians 3:10 says, "so that through the church the manifold wisdom of God might now be made known to the rulers and authorities in the heavenly places." God has placed the church in the most open places throughout the whole world so that everyone will see it, in order to display his wisdom in salvation. We need to correct the church's understanding of itself. The openness I talk about has nothing to do with legal status. The church is already open. Openness means the church does not need to be recognized by the government in order to exist openly. The church has existed openly from the beginning.

We want to strengthen our ecclesiology. It is not easy to find a form of expression aimed at the current situation in China. Our ecclesiology is weak, and not just church formation—no one is being appointed to holy office and confessions of faith are not clear—but also our understanding of ourselves. Who am I? What relationship do I have with world history? If God is sovereign over all the kingdoms of men, then what relationship do I have with the kingdoms of men?

When I was taken in for the first time on May 12, they said I was being charged with "picking quarrels and provoking trouble." They used a few articles I wrote about the religious regulations as evidence. They were most offended, not by the point I made about the constitution—that according to Chinese law these regulations are wrong—but rather that I said they are evil from a religious perspective, that they are hostile to Christ's church and to God. This was intolerable because I used an entirely different language. He said, "How can you use the word 'evil'?" I said, "Evil is a moral and religious term. If you believe in God, then there is righteousness and evil in relation to him. If you don't believe in God, then saying you are evil is just like saying you are ugly. There would be nothing for you to be embarrassed about. Why then are you so anxious?" It was difficult for him to talk about this in political terms, because I was using religious terminology. He and I were talking in different realms.

According to the Bible, this law is wrong. They will say, "This is what the law says," and we will say, "We are Christians. The Bible is our highest authority." We [church workers] don't discuss questions of the law. Those are for lawyers to discuss. Our team of lawyers will file lawsuits. They will use legal terminology, and of course they will also emphasize our faith. But the church directly speaks the language of the Bible. Our highest authority is the Bible. The way we expressed this in the past was, "The Religious Regulations are wrong because they violate the constitution." But since May 12 and June 4, we have given up this way of speaking. The church has switched to using ecclesial language.

THE MEANING OF THE "WAY OF THE CROSS"

Because of sin, the present world is an inversion of the world that God created. The cross flips this world back around. The gospel has a strong eschatological nature. The gospel is not good news about how this present life is transformed. Even though this life is part of it, the focus of the gospel extends to eternal life. In this present life that is flipped upside-down by sin, the good news of eternal life is manifested through inversive means—the means by which Jesus saves us. The cross is what we believe, and it is also the means by which we believe. The cross is not only the content but the form, and this form tells us the world is not yet complete—God's creation is not yet finished. My life is also not complete when I leave the world at eighty years old.

How then do I manifest an invisible world? How do I show my true wealth in this life? I show it through poverty. How do I display resurrection power? Through suffering. I have the ability to suffer. I can give because I have. What I give testifies to what I have.

In the movie *Hacksaw Ridge*, Desmond Doss would not use a weapon because of his faith. How did people know that what he said was true? They beat him and saw how he reacted. If, after being hit, he got angry and hit back, what he was talking about wasn't real. But if, after being bullied continuously, he still kept saying the same things, then what he said was true, or at least he believed it was true.

So Christians witness for Christ in this world through the subversive means of the cross. My life, God's creation, and the entirety of world history are all unfinished. The cross means you build your hope on the future instead of realizing it in the present.

PART III

ARREST AND THE WAY OF THE CROSS

As 2018 progressed, it became increasingly clear that arrest and detention were imminent for Wang Yi. In order to preserve his beliefs and true commitments should he come under duress or be prohibited from speaking, and to encourage his congregation's perseverance, Wang Yi wrote a series of essays outlining his intended response to persecution, included in part three.

In the full interview titled "An Opportunity for Churches to Walk the Way of the Cross" from part two, Wang Yi said, "I've shared with church colleagues and brothers and sisters that if someone wants to discuss something with you, the simplest method is to first show your cards. If you do this, you will be at ease. After you have thought clearly about what you want to undertake and what you're willing to undertake through the grace of God, you can place that thing to the side. You don't need to think about it anymore. This has also helped me to make my own resolutions. After I communicate this resolution, in reality I also hope that relevant government departments will see it. This reduces the cost of communication. Some things become easier if I already know what I'm going to do. This is also a kind of psychological preparation for me, for my family, and for the church. Because when you aren't quite sure what cards you've got, you are continually thinking about them. But when you've decided for sure, there is nothing more to think about. You are free."

Though Wang Yi and the leadership of Early Rain anticipated government interference, the intensity and extent of the government's eventual attack was surprising. On December 9, 2018, the police began systematically arresting and detaining not only Wang Yi and the elders and deacons of Early Rain, but also their wives, hundreds of laypeople, and the teachers of Early Rain's primary school, middle school, college, an affiliated seminary, as well as numerous children. The entirety of the church's sizable property was seized, and in many cases, destroyed. More than one hundred Early Rain members were forced to leave Chengdu and return to their hometowns, often facing rejection by their families. The events were highly organized administratively, involving hundreds of police and government personnel and meticulous planning.

The interference with Early Rain Covenant Church did not end after the arrests and raids on December 8 and 9. Over the course of the following four months, members of the church continued to be threatened and harassed. The church estimates that more than three hundred individuals were taken to police stations between December 2018 and April 2019. According to reports from Early Rain, the list of abuses church members experienced includes homelessness due to repeated eviction under government pressure; electricity, internet, and phone service being cut off; families being threatened with the removal of their children; confiscation of passports and restriction of travel; constant monitoring, surveillance, and photographing of individuals; interrogation, including of children without parents present; separation of nursing mothers from their babies for extended periods of time; discharge from places of employment under government pressure; confiscation of personal property and seizure of bank accounts; vandalism of personal homes; and the prevention of mothers from taking their children outside to play. In a few more severe cases, ERCC has claimed individuals went missing for days and even weeks; at-risk children were removed from ERCC foster families; and various beatings, including of a mother while her child was in her arms. One of the most severe cases of detention involved a lay leader of the church being held in solitary confinement in a room without natural light for seven months.[1]

Wang Yi's teenage son was kept under strict house arrest with his grandmother; he was not permitted to leave his home, nor to receive guests. Wang Yi's elderly mother claims to have been verbally abused and physically beaten by a police officer. Jiang Rong, Wang Yi's wife, was held in criminal detention for seven months. On June 14, 2019, Jiang Rong was permitted to reunite with her son and reside in a government-arranged apartment; in 2020, they were returned to their home. Apart from close relatives, no one has been able to speak with her.

On December 26, 2019, Wang Yi was sentenced to nine years' incarceration and Qin Defu (覃德富), an elder of Early Rain who was responsible for publishing hymnbooks and Christian literature, was sentenced to four years of incarceration. Both men were

---

[1]English translations of Early Rain's public updates can be read at China Partnership, "LIVE POST— Early Rain Covenant Church Urgent Updates," December 14, 2018, www.chinapartnership.org /blog/2018/12/live-post-early-rain-covenant-church-urgent-prayer-updates.

denied their chosen lawyers throughout the proceedings and were instead supplied with lawyers appointed by the government.

Early Rain has not yet been able to meet again in person. All attempts at corporate worship, even outside, have been stopped by authorities. Some small groups have been able to meet in person, while others remain online. The various churches of Western China Presbytery welcomed the members of ERCC to periodically participate in the Lord's Supper as long as they remained. Most of the churches in the presbytery began to be prevented from entering their public meeting spaces in 2020.

17

A JOINT STATEMENT BY PASTORS

A DECLARATION FOR THE SAKE OF THE CHRISTIAN FAITH

THE LEADERSHIP OF EARLY RAIN COVENANT CHURCH

In early September 2018, Wang Yi and the leadership of Early Rain Covenant Church posted a joint statement in response to the New Religious Regulations, which came into effect at the beginning of the year. The statement was published on Early Rain's church website and on Wang Yi's personal blog and signatures were collected by email. The latest update on Wang Yi's blog included 446 signatures from house church pastors and elders across China, many of whom have since faced repercussions for signing. Many signatories were well-known figures in the house church, including Jin Mingri, however, they were not representative of the house churches at large and some pastors were critical of the statement, including some among Wang Yi's associates.

We are a group of Chinese Christians, chosen by the Most High God to be his humble servants, serving as pastors for Christian churches throughout various towns and cities.

We believe and are obligated to teach the world that the one true and living triune God is the creator of the universe, of the world, and of all people. All humans should worship God and not any individual or thing. We believe and are obligated to teach the world that all people, from national leaders to beggars and prisoners, have sinned. They will die once and then be judged in righteousness. Apart from the grace and redemption of God, all men would eternally perish. We believe and are obligated to teach the world that the crucified and risen Jesus is the only head of the global church, the sole savior of all humankind, and the everlasting ruler and supreme judge of the universe. To all who repent and believe in him, God will give eternal life and an eternal kingdom.

In September 2017, the State Council issued the new "Regulations on the Administration of Religious Affairs" and began implementing these regulations in February 2018. Ever since then, Christian churches across China have suffered varying degrees of persecution, contempt, and misunderstanding from government departments during public worship and religious practices, including various administrative measures that attempt to alter and distort the Christian faith. Some of these violent actions are unprecedented since the end of the Cultural Revolution. These include demolishing crosses on church buildings, violently removing expressions of faith like crosses and couplets hanging on Christians' homes, forcing and threatening churches to join religious organizations controlled by the government, forcing churches to hang the national flag or to sing secular songs praising the state and political parties, banning the children of Christians from entering churches and receiving religious education, and depriving churches and believers of the right to gather freely.

We believe that these unjust actions are an abuse of government power and have led to serious conflicts between political and religious parties in Chinese society. These actions infringe on the human freedoms of religion and conscience and violate the universal rule of law. We are obligated to announce bad news to the authorities and to all of society: God hates all attempts to suppress human souls and all acts of persecution against the Christian church, and he will condemn and judge them with righteous judgment.

But we are even more obligated to proclaim good news to the authorities and to all of society: Jesus, the only begotten Son of God, the Savior and king of humankind, in order to save us sinners was killed, was buried, and rose from the dead by the power of God, destroying the power of sin and death. In his love and compassion, God has prepared forgiveness and salvation for all who are willing to believe in Jesus, including Chinese people. At any time, anyone can repent from any sin, turn to Christ, fear God, obtain eternal life, and bring great blessing from God upon his family and country.

For the sake of faith and conscience, for the spiritual benefit of the authorities in China and of society as a whole, and ultimately for the glory, holiness, and righteousness of God, we make the following declaration to the Chinese government and to all of society:

1. Christian churches in China believe unconditionally that the Bible is the Word and revelation of God. It is the source and final authority of all righteousness, ethics, and salvation. If the will of any political party, the laws of any government, or the commands of any individual directly violate the teachings of the Bible, harming men's souls and opposing the gospel proclaimed by the church, we are obligated to obey God rather than men, and we are obligated to teach all members of the church to do the same.

2. Christian churches in China are eager and determined to walk the path of the cross of Christ and are more than willing to imitate the older generation of saints who suffered and were martyred for their faith. We are willing and obligated under any circumstance to face all government persecution, misunderstanding, and violence with peace, patience, and compassion. For when churches refuse to obey evil laws, it does not stem from any political agenda, it does not stem from resentment or hostility, it stems only from the demands of the gospel and from a love for Chinese society.

3. Christian churches in China are willing to obey authorities in China whom God has appointed and to respect the government's authority to govern society and human conduct. We believe and are obligated to teach all believers in the church that the authority of the government is from God and that as long as the government does not overstep the boundaries of secular power laid out in the Bible and does not interfere with or violate anything related to faith or the soul, Christians are obligated to respect the authorities, to pray fervently for their benefit, and to pray earnestly for Chinese society. For the sake of the gospel, we are willing to suffer all external losses brought about by unfair law enforcement. Out of a love for our fellow citizens, we are willing to give up all of our earthly rights.

4. For this reason, we believe and are obligated to teach all believers that all true churches in China that belong to Christ must hold to the principle of the separation of church and state and must proclaim Christ as the sole head of the church. We declare that in matters of external conduct, churches are willing to accept lawful oversight by civil administration or other government departments as other social organizations do. But under no circumstances will we lead our churches to join a religious organization controlled by the government, to register with the religious

administration department, or to accept any kind of affiliation. We also will not accept any "ban" or "fine" imposed on our churches due to our faith. For the sake of the gospel, we are prepared to bear all losses—even the loss of our freedom and our lives.

All pastors, elders, and ministers of Chinese churches are welcomed to cosign the joint statement.

18

IN THE FACE OF PERSECUTION, WHAT WILL I DO?

WANG YI

This straightforward list of resolutions was first published on Wang Yi's blog on October 14, 2018, two months before his arrest. It is important to note Wang Yi's personal history as a human rights lawyer and his knowledge of the Chinese system for understanding his expectations and precautions.

I prayed before Christ and after careful consideration, I have determined to resist by peaceful means when the government oversteps the boundary of the secular power God has given it—attacking and usurping the spiritual affairs that belong to God and his church.

Below are the details of my plan. As a house church pastor and Presbyterian minister, all of these are based on my conservative evangelical position and Calvinist theology. This does not mean that every faithful, Reformed pastor or believer must do so in like manner. Due to each of our unique contexts and responsibilities, God will grant his faithful children particular duties and practices in this spiritual battle. This does not mean that my confidence has been strengthened to the point where I can fully adhere to these positions and practices in the face of threats, false charges, and violence.

I pray that the death of Christ will always be on me so that the power of Christ's resurrection will cover me at all times. I know fully and acknowledge that I am an unworthy sinner, but I hope that Christ's sovereignty and grace will not forsake me in persecution. Let the Lord's Spirit always accompany me, so that even in forced isolation I can hold onto these positions with great perseverance and hope until I see the glory of the Lord or return to the pulpit by the Lord's victory.

My positions and resolutions have been recognized by my fellow ministry partners—the elders of Early Rain Covenant Church. This could also be provided as a case for reference and adoption for the members of the body who share my positions and responsibilities.

1. DO NOT STOP GATHERING TOGETHER

Under no circumstances will we stop or give up on gathering publicly, especially the corporate worship of believers on Sunday. God's sovereignty is higher than any secular authority, and the church's mission and the Bible's teaching regarding not neglecting to gather is higher than any secular law. Regardless of whether the Religious Affairs Bureau and the police take administrative and forceful measures against Sunday worship, whether or not their enforcement follows due process, I will resist by peaceful means. I will not cooperate with the police banning, shutting down, dissolving, or sealing up the church and its gathering. I will not stop convening, hosting, and participating in the church's public worship until the police restrict my personal freedom by force.

2. NO COOPERATION

Even if the police resort to violence, I will continue to resist in a peaceful manner. I will not use the slightest power God has given me to cooperate with the police's attack on the church and worship. On days other than Sundays, when the police administer its duties with due process, I will physically submit and cooperate in honor of their God-given authority. When the police do not follow due process and illegally enforce the law, I will still resist physically in a nonviolent manner until the police restrict my personal freedom by force. I will not use the slightest strength God has given me to cooperate with the police in their illegal behavior.

3. DISOBEDIENCE

I will not accept or obey a government agency's decision to ban, seal up, and dissolve the church and its gatherings. I will not obey any of the police's commands when it comes to persecuting and banning the church, as God has not granted the government the authority to do so. In places where the church or family retain their property rights, I will tear off the government's seals and break its chains. Unless the police restrict my personal freedom by force, I will not stop calling for, hosting, and participating in the church's corporate worship by peaceful means.

4. NOT SIGNING

I will not sign any document of administrative decision sent by the Religious Affairs Bureau, nor will I sign any documents by any other government agencies partnering to persecute the church. Similarly, I will not sign any police transcripts or any other document when I am interrogated on matters related to faith and church.

5. NO CONFESSION

With the exception of sharing the gospel, I will not accept or answer any question related to the church and faith from an administrative investigation by the Religious Affairs Bureau.

Except for providing my personal information and sharing the gospel, I will not answer any questions the police ask or interrogate me with regarding my faith and the church, and I will not provide any documentary evidence that the administration and law enforcement could use to convict my faith and the church, unless the police torture me brutally to the point of crushing my health and spirit.

6. REQUEST TO READ THE BIBLE

Beginning on the day coercive measures are taken, I will request the freedom to obtain and read the Bible during my breaks from inquiry and interrogation. If I cannot acquire or am forbidden to read the Bible, I will disobey in a peaceful manner and will not cooperate with the police's inquiry and questioning, either until I acquire the Bible or until the police torture me brutally to the point of crushing my health and spirit.

7. NOT PLEAD GUILTY

Whether in interrogation, questioning, or court trial, I will not admit to any crimes imposed against me on matters of faith and church, whether it is the accusation of inciting subversion of state power, creating disturbances, illegal business operations, disturbing social order, or sabotaging law enforcement by cult organizations, and such common charges to persecute and frame the church, or any other charges. I will not plead guilty, will not repent, and will not seek or agree to any form of release based on my admission of guilt, such as immunity from prosecution, probation, service of sentences outside prison, release on parole, release on bail, or residential surveillance at a designated location. If I am under criminal detention, either I will be sentenced and serve out my prison term or I will be acquitted, with no room for compromise or negotiation for a third option, unless the police torture me brutally to the point of crushing my health and spirit.

8. DISOBEYING IDEOLOGICAL REFORM

The so-called reform through labor is a form of ideological reform for prisoners through forced labor and political education that was adopted in communist countries, such as the Soviet Union, North Korea, and China. As a Christian, I will physically obey any unjust sentences and submit to the prison's discipline. But even though I serve this term, I will not be reformed ideologically. I will neither plead guilty nor repent; my conscience forbids me from submitting to any reform measures based on my admission of guilt, such as compulsory political education or watching related TV programs, compulsory participation in flag ceremonies, compulsory writing of ideological reports, and compulsory singing of red songs or shouting of slogans. I will disobey such reform measures by peaceful means and will be ready to bear any cost for my response, unless the prison authority tortures me brutally to the point of crushing my health and spirit.

9. REFUSAL TO PAY PENALTIES OR FINES

Whether I am under administrative penalty or by judicial measures, I will not, for the sake of faith and the church, pay one penny of penalty, fine, or bail, as the government has no authority to impose a fine on the church for the sake of faith.[1]

10. REFUSAL TO ACCEPT THE ADDITIONAL PENALTY OF DEPRIVATION OF POLITICAL RIGHTS

The so-called political rights mainly consist of voting rights, the right to be elected, and the right to hold public office.[2] As a Chinese citizen, I have no such fake rights; as a servant of God, neither do I care about my ownership of them.

---

[1] An "administrative penalty" enables the government to impose sanctions on a Chinese citizen who violates administrative regulations but has not committed a criminal offense. The various forms of administrative penalties include warnings, fines, confiscation of income or property, suspension or revocation of licenses, suspension of business, and detention.

[2] The Constitution of the People's Republic of China states that the government ensures the political rights and freedoms of its citizens, including the right to vote and to be elected; the right of free speech and a free press; and the right to free assembly.

However, the so-called political rights also include freedom of speech, assembly, and publishing which involves faith, conscience, and the church, just as the Westminster Confession of Faith, chapter 20, section 2 says, "God alone is Lord of the conscience." The government has no right to deprive the God-given human conscience and the freedom to express faith; therefore, I will not accept the additional penalty of the so-called deprivation of political rights; as soon as my personal freedom is restored, I will do my utmost to preach the gospel, shepherd or plant churches, write and publish articles, and live out the Great Commission given by the Lord Jesus Christ, until I lose my freedom again.

11. PERSIST IN SHARING THE GOSPEL

Whether in the police station, detention center, prison, or any other detention facility, I will share the gospel once I am in contact with any person. Secular government and laws have no right to deprive anyone of the opportunity to listen to the gospel, nor do they have the right to deprive a pastor the freedom to preach the gospel to others. Only the gospel of Christ can truly reform a sinner. I will do my utmost in my detention to practice the gospel commission, unless the police torture me brutally to the point of crushing my health and spirit.

12. REFUSAL TO ACCEPT GOVERNMENT-DESIGNATED DEFENSE LAWYERS

Only the lawyer appointed by me or my wife can represent me in my administrative or criminal case. Under no circumstances will I accept a defense lawyer designated by the government.[3]

13. REFUSAL TO APPEAR ON TV OR CONTACT OFFICIAL MEDIA

As long as my personal freedom is not restored and I have not met my family and my brothers and sisters, I will not accept interviews and filming arranged by the prison authorities, official media, or any other domestic media. I will not record any video either under police control or anywhere outside the interrogation room to avoid being distorted and edited as a guilty plea on TV, unless the police torture me brutally to the point of crushing my health and spirit.[4]

---

[3] The Chinese government may designate legal representation for a defendant who has no appointed lawyer (due to financial duress or other reasons), however, the defendant's designated lawyer is often removed from the case and replaced by a government-appointed lawyer in political cases.
[4] Many defendants accused of political crimes have made confessions on TV and national media, which are later used as evidence against the defendant.

14. DEMAND PUBLIC TRIAL

If I am prosecuted for matters of faith and the church, I will demand a public trial of my case from the court. If the court does not follow due process and does not hold a public hearing, and does not allow my wife, my family, brothers and sisters, friends, and the media to be present and observe the trial, I will physically disobey such a court hearing, because a court that has a secret trial is no longer one that the Bible commands me to obey. I will refuse to appear in court and to submit to any command of the judge. I will respond with no speech and no defense to all unlawful trials of the church and faith except for when I share the gospel.

May the Lord bless me with so much reverent fear for him to the point I am not afraid of any power that does not fear him.

May the Lord grant me peaceful resistance, positive perseverance, and joyful disobedience in all matters of conscience, faith, and the church, and in everything that relates to the flesh and damage to external rights, may he grant me the power of patience and silence.

May the Lord remove the potential in this process to lash out in hate and resentment.

May he have mercy on me and support me in my weakness when I am in isolation.

May the Lord help me so that from the day of my detention I will pray every day for all those in power related to my case, as well as officials in the police force, national security, the prosecutor's office, the court and other government agencies.

May the Lord choose among them repentant and believing children and have mercy on their lowly souls.

May the Lord lead at least one of them to faith through this process, and give my heart great joy and comfort.

I also ask the Lord Jesus to remove the burden and concerns for my wife, family, the church, and everything else during my detention, so that I will entrust everything to the Lord, be faithful only to the Lord, and focus on practicing these fourteen resolutions as my longings for and service to my family, as shepherding and teaching my congregation, and as fulfilling my responsibility to the kingdom of God.

19

MY DECLARATION OF FAITHFUL DISOBEDIENCE

WANG YI

Wang Yi wrote "My Declaration of Faithful Disobedience" in September and October 2018 and commended it to the leadership of Early Rain for public distribution should he be detained for more than forty-eight hours, the longest duration of his previous detentions.

In his declaration, Wang Yi makes a sophisticated argument for disobedience, not as a matter of civil withdrawal or disengagement, but rather as a matter of the church's allegiance to an alternative kingdom. The kingdom to which Wang Yi gives allegiance is not a distant reality; it exists as truly and concretely here and now as it will in eternity.

As such, Wang Yi maintains that political change is not the goal of his pastoral calling. Governments are instituted by God for the curtailing of evil and the Christian need not fear them, though they may seek to harm the church. Invoking a prophetic voice, he calls the actions and laws of the Chinese government against the church sinful and evil, freely rebuking that which stands against the gospel. Yet, the goal of his rebuke is not political overturn; rather, he desires to testify to Christ, his cross and kingdom, and the reality of eternal life. The greatest evil persecution of the church enacts is not the revocation of personal rights, but rather the prevention of unbelievers from hearing the gospel. For Wang Yi, the individual Christian and the collective church are indeed called to civil disobedience but only in order to testify to the kingdom of heaven which has already entered this reality and permeates society until Christ's return.

Translation of Wang Yi's language of "faithful disobedience" requires nuance. Is he talking about disobedience of a civil or spiritual nature? His concepts intermingle. In

the end, Wang Yi defines "faithful disobedience" as peaceful, meek, actively forbear-
ing, joyful, and inevitable for the progress of the gospel. It must not do damage to the
soul of the Christian engaged in such disobedience or produce hatred or bitterness; it
must also be nonviolent. Wang Yi believes that the world is fundamentally opposed
to Christ, his gospel, and kingdom, and it will demand of the Christian an allegiance
the believer may not give it. As such, the posture of the Christian will inevitably be one
of disobedience to the powers of this world.

Forty-eight hours after Wang Yi's arrest, "My Declaration of Faithful Disobedience"
was shared publicly by Early Rain. It was immediately translated into English and
read by hundreds of thousands around the world. Global Christians should consider
several things from this document. (1) Contemporary stories of the persecution of
Christians ought to spark conversations, and even debate, among nonpersecuted
Christians about the role of suffering in our union with Christ. (2) Wang Yi's theology
of "faithful disobedience" contributes to the long lineage of thought on nonviolent
engagement of the state by the church. His perspective is neither Anabaptist in its
abandonment of civil engagement, nor does it promote nonviolent protest as with
the teaching of Martin Luther King Jr. Wang Yi's understanding of the kingdom of
heaven, his belief that all Christians are called to bear the cross, as well as his cultural
context of engagement with a hostile, secular government, position him to offer new
insight upon which to reflect.

On the basis of the teachings of the Bible and the mission of the gospel, I respect the authorities God has established in China. For God deposes kings and raises up kings. That is why I submit to the historical and institutional arrangements of God in China.

As a pastor of a Christian church, I have my own understanding and views, based on the Bible, about what righteous order and good government are. At the same time, I am filled with anger and disgust at the persecution of the church by this Communist regime, at the wickedness of their depriving people of the freedoms of religion and of conscience. But changing social and political institutions is not the mission I have been called to, and it is not the goal for which God has given his people the gospel.

For all hideous realities, unrighteous politics, and arbitrary laws manifest the cross of Jesus Christ, the only means by which every Chinese person must be saved. They also manifest the fact that true hope and a perfect society will never be found in the transformation of any earthly institution or culture but only in our sins being freely forgiven by Christ and in the hope of eternal life.

As a pastor, my firm belief in the gospel, my teaching, and my rebuking of all evil proceeds from Christ's command in the gospel and from the unfathomable love of that glorious king. Every individual's life is extremely short, and God fervently commands the church to lead and call any anyone to repentance who is willing to repent. Christ is eager and willing to forgive all who turn from their sins. This is the goal of all the efforts of the church in China—to testify to the world about our Christ, to testify to the Middle Kingdom about the kingdom of heaven, to testify to earthly, momentary lives about heavenly, eternal life.[1] This is also the pastoral calling that I have received.

For this reason, I accept and respect the fact that this communist regime has been allowed by God to rule temporarily. As the Lord's servant John Calvin said, wicked rulers are the judgment of God on a wicked people, the goal being to urge God's people to repent and turn again toward him.[2] For this reason, I am joyfully willing to submit myself to their enforcement of the law as though submitting to the discipline and training of the Lord.

At the same time, I believe that this communist regime's persecution of the church is a greatly wicked, unlawful action. As a pastor of a Christian church, I must denounce this wickedness openly and severely. The calling that I have received requires me to use nonviolent methods to disobey those human laws that disobey the Bible and God. My Savior Jesus Christ also requires me to joyfully bear all costs for disobeying wicked laws.

But this does not mean that my personal disobedience and the disobedience of the church is in any sense "fighting for rights" or political activism in the form of civil disobedience, because I do not have the intention of changing any institutions or laws of China. As a pastor, the only thing I care about is the disruption of humanity's sinful nature by this faithful disobedience and the testimony it bears for the cross of Christ.

As a pastor, my disobedience is one part of the gospel commission. Christ's Great Commission requires of us great disobedience. The goal of disobedience is not to change the world but to testify about another world.

---

[1] Translated literally, China (中国, *zhong guo*) means "Central Nation" or "Middle Kingdom" (with other countries being traditionally termed "peripheral" and "barbaric").

[2] Wang is not directly quoting Calvin, but rather paraphrasing his words. In book 4, chapter 20, section 25 of his *Institutes of the Christian Religion*, Calvin says, "They who rule unjustly and incompetently have been raised up by him to punish the wickedness of the people," and, "A wicked king is the Lord's wrath upon the earth." In Calvin's commentary on the book of Romans, he says of Romans 13:3-4 that "a wicked prince is the Lord's scourge to punish the sins of the people." John Calvin, *Institutes of the Christian Religion*, ed. John T. McNeill and trans. Ford Lewis Battles, vol. 2 (Louisville, KY: Westminster John Knox Press, 2006), 1512.

For the mission of the church is only to be the church and not to become a part of any secular institution. From a negative perspective, the church must separate itself from the world and keep itself from being institutionalized by the world. From a positive perspective, all acts of the church are attempts to prove to the world the real existence of another world. The Bible teaches us that, in all matters relating to the gospel and human conscience, we must obey God and not men. For this reason, spiritual disobedience and bodily suffering are both ways we testify to another eternal world and to another glorious king.

This is why I am not interested in changing any political or legal institutions in China. I'm not even interested in the question of when the communist regime's policies persecuting the church will change. Regardless of which regime I live under now or in the future, as long as the secular government continues to persecute the church, violating human consciences that belong to God alone, I will continue my faithful disobedience. For the entire commission God has given me is to let more Chinese people know through my actions that the hope of humanity and society is only in the redemption of Christ, in the supernatural, gracious sovereignty of God.

If God decides to use the persecution of this communist regime against the church to help more Chinese people to despair of their futures, to lead them through a wilderness of spiritual disillusionment and through this to make them know Jesus, if through persecution he continues disciplining and building up his church, then I am joyfully willing to submit to God's plans, for his plans are always benevolent and good.

Precisely because none of my words and actions are directed toward seeking and hoping for societal and political transformation, I have no fear of any social or political power. For the Bible teaches us that God establishes governmental authorities in order to terrorize evildoers, not to terrorize doers of good. If believers in Jesus do no wrong then they should not be afraid of dark powers. Even though I am often weak, I firmly believe this is the promise of the gospel. It is what I've devoted all of my energy to. It is the good news that I am spreading throughout Chinese society.

I also understand that this happens to be the very reason why the communist regime is filled with fear at a church that is no longer afraid of it.

If I am imprisoned for a long or short period of time, if I can help reduce the authorities' fear of my faith and of my Savior, I am very joyfully willing to help them in this way. But I know that only when I renounce all the wickedness of this persecution against the church and use peaceful means to disobey, will I truly be able to help the souls of the authorities and law enforcement. I hope God uses me, by means of first losing my personal freedom, to tell those who have deprived me of my personal freedom that there is an authority higher than their authority, and that there is a freedom that they cannot restrain, a freedom that fills the church of the crucified and risen Jesus Christ.

Regardless of what crime the government charges me with, whatever filth they fling at me, as long as this charge is related to my faith, my writings, my comments, and my teachings, it is merely a lie and temptation of demons. I categorically deny it. I will serve my sentence, but I will not serve the law. I will be executed, but I will not plead guilty.

Moreover, I must point out that persecution against the Lord's church and against all Chinese people who believe in Jesus Christ is the most wicked and the most horrendous evil of Chinese society. This is not only a sin against Christians. It is also a sin against all non-Christians. For the government is brutally and ruthlessly threatening them and hindering them from coming to Jesus. There is no greater wickedness in the world than this.

If this regime is one day overthrown by God, it will be for no other reason than God's righteous punishment and revenge for this evil. For on earth, there has only ever been a thousand-year church. There has never been a thousand-year government. There is only eternal faith. There is no eternal power.

Those who lock me up will one day be locked up by angels. Those who interrogate me will finally be questioned and judged by Christ. When I think of this, the Lord fills me with a natural compassion and grief toward those who are attempting to and actively imprisoning me. Pray that the Lord would use me, that he would grant me patience and wisdom, that I might take the gospel to them.

Separate me from my wife and children, ruin my reputation, destroy my life and my family—the authorities are capable of doing all of these things. However, no one in this world can force me to renounce my faith; no one can make me change my life; and no one can raise me from the dead.

And so, respectable officers, stop committing evil. This is not for my benefit but rather for yours and your children's. I plead earnestly with you to stay your hands, for why should you be willing to pay the price of eternal damnation in hell for the sake of a lowly sinner such as I?

Jesus is the Christ, son of the eternal, living God. He died for sinners and rose to life for us. He is my king and the king of the whole earth yesterday, today, and forever. I am his servant, and I am imprisoned because of this. I will resist in meekness those who resist God, and I will joyfully violate all laws that violate God's laws.

First draft on September 21, 2018; revised on October 4. To be published by the church after forty-eight hours of detention.

APPENDIX: WHAT CONSTITUTES FAITHFUL DISOBEDIENCE

I firmly believe that the Bible has not given any branch of any government the authority to run the church or to interfere with the faith of Christians. Therefore, the Bible demands that I, through peaceable means, in meek resistance and active forbearance, filled with joy, resist all administrative policies and legal measures that oppress the church and interfere with the faith of Christians.

I firmly believe this is a spiritual act of disobedience. In modern authoritarian regimes that persecute the church and oppose the gospel, spiritual disobedience is an inevitable part of the gospel movement.

I firmly believe that spiritual disobedience is an act of the last times; it is a witness to God's eternal kingdom in the temporal kingdom of sin and evil. Disobedient Christians follow the example of the crucified Christ by walking the path of the cross. Peaceful disobedience is the way in which we love the world as well as the way in which we avoid becoming part of the world.

I firmly believe that in carrying out spiritual disobedience, the Bible demands me to rely on the grace and resurrection power of Christ, that I must respect and not overstep two boundaries.

The first boundary is that of the heart. Love toward the soul, and not hatred toward the body, is the motivation of spiritual disobedience. Transformation of the soul, and not the changing of circumstances, is the aim of spiritual disobedience. At any time, if external oppression and violence rob me of inner peace and endurance, so that my heart begins to breed hatred and bitterness toward those who persecute the church and abuse Christians, then spiritual disobedience fails at that point.

The second boundary is that of behavior. The gospel demands that disobedience of faith must be nonviolent. The mystery of the gospel lies in actively suffering, even being willing to endure unrighteous punishment, as a substitute for physical resistance. Peaceful disobedience is the result of love and forgiveness. The cross means being willing to suffer when one does not have to suffer. For Christ had limitless ability to fight back, yet he endured all of the humility and hurt. The way that Christ resisted the world that resisted him was by extending an olive branch of peace on the cross to the world that crucified him.

I firmly believe that Christ has called me to carry out this faithful disobedience through a life of service, under this regime that opposes the gospel and persecutes the church. This is the means by which I preach the gospel, and it is the mystery of the gospel that I preach.

The Lord's servant,

Wang Yi

First draft on September 21, 2018; revised on October 4. To be circulated by the church after forty-eight hours of detention.

20

HOW SHOULD THE CHURCH FACE PERSECUTION?

LI YINGQIANG

The following is a letter to the members of Early Rain from Li Yingqiang, the last elder to be arrested. Li Yingqiang wrote this letter in hiding just a few hours before being discovered. In an attempt to avoid detection through his cellphone, he wrote with pen and paper. The letter was discovered by other members who then circulated photographs of the letter online. Li Yingqiang describes the church's plan for the coming days, including where to attempt to continue to worship.

Beloved brothers, sisters, and fellow workers:

Thank the Lord! Just as the year 2018 is about to end, God has given us a reward in the form of this large-scale persecution that arrived on December 9.

Since yesterday evening until noon today, over one hundred pastors, elders, staff, and brothers and sisters have been taken away. As of now we still do not know where they all are, and even if we did know it would be difficult for us to help them. But, thankfully, we know for certain that the Lord's loving face is shining upon them. They are within the gracious, sovereign providence of the Lord. He will be with them in the midst of their chains and trials.

The apostle Peter says, "Beloved, do not be surprised at the fiery trial when it comes upon you to test you, as though something strange were happening to you. But rejoice insofar as you share Christ's sufferings, that you may also rejoice and be glad when his glory is revealed. If you are insulted for the name of Christ, you are blessed, because the Spirit of glory and of God rests upon you" (1 Peter 4:12-14).

Beloved brothers and sisters, do you have joy? Are you rejoicing in the fact that you are suffering with Christ because of this church? Do you know that we are blessed? The Lord is bestowing on us poor people today treasures of glory from heaven! The Lord himself is bestowing on us weak people comfort from heaven! The Lord Jesus is shining on us blind people his great light. Those of us brothers and sisters standing on the front lines of the gospel war will earn great spiritual riches!

Thank the Lord for being with us in this trial. Thank the Lord for cultivating us according to his true Word! Thank the Lord for training us through these days of hardship! Thank the Lord for sculpting us through today's persecution! May the Lord give us great joy and true hope and make us strong through reliance on him.

What these next two days or next few weeks hold we do not know. These days are in the hands of the Lord. Just as he turns the dew into frost and the rain into snow, just as he makes the fragrance of the plum blossom waft across the bitter cold, we are in the hands of the Lord. How wonderful it would be if, because of this suffering, we might be able to give off the sweet fragrance of the gospel!

Beloved brothers and sisters, I'm afraid this "great persecution" will become the status quo for us in the future. I don't know if you know this, but three years ago on December 9, persecution was officially unleashed against Living Stone Church in Guiyang.[1] Police also went to the homes of those brothers and sisters one at a time. They would use multiple police officers and community workers to control just one person. Their small groups were also broken up one by one. How should we respond to these things in the days to come? According to the contingency plan prepared by our session of elders, there are a few things we must do.

1. Those elders who are still free must take up the responsibility of pastoring the whole church, waiting for the pastor and elders to be released. If Pastor Wang Yi is not released within forty-eight hours, those elders who are still free must lead the church down the next stretch according to the order decided on previously.

2. Regardless, Early Rain Covenant Church must not alter the statement of faith and the path of openness that it has proclaimed publicly in the past.

---

[1]On December 9, 2015, more than one hundred policemen and government officials blocked congregants of Living Stone Church (活石教会, *huo shi jiaohui*) in Guiyang, Guizhou Province, from entering the building for a prayer meeting. Pastor Yang Hua (仰华) and his wife were stopped by police and forcibly removed from the premises. The police then broke into the church and confiscated all computers and other equipment. One year later in December 2016, Yang was tried in court and sentenced to two and half years in prison. In January 2018, a Guiyang district court ordered the sequestering of Living Stone's property and fined the church seven million RMB (around one million USD). Yang was released from prison after serving his full sentence in June 2018.

And we will not alter our previous stance on the relationship between church and state or our beautiful spiritual inheritance from the Chinese house church of walking the way of the cross. We will not register with the Religious Affairs Bureau; much less will we join the Three-Self church.

3. We will not easily relinquish our church building and retreat to our small groups. Regardless of who is leading the church, they must try to return to the church building that God has given us.[2] Neither paper seals nor arrests should hinder our determination to worship in our church sanctuary.[3] Unless all elders, preachers, and seminary students able to lead public worship and the preaching of God's Word lose their freedom, we will not retreat to small groups. If we cannot enter the church building, we will rent another place. If there is no place indoors where we can worship, we will begin worshiping outdoors.

4. Meeting in small groups is our last resort. If there is even a very small possibility of worshiping together as a whole church, we will not retreat to small groups. But if we must meet in small groups and encounter opposition while doing so, we are willing to pay an even greater price to bear witness to the great work of the gospel in our lives. We are willing to have two hundred, three hundred, or five hundred people arrested and imprisoned. May the whole world know that we are joyfully willing to receive this persecution for the sake of our faith.

Beloved brothers and sisters, I am writing this letter in "hiding." May you all be filled with joy in the gospel of Christ. May you welcome, filled with hope, the even heavier cross and more difficult lives that lie ahead of you.

"Christ is Lord. Grace is king. Bear the cross. Keep the faith."[4] This is the vision Early Rain Covenant Church received from the Lord. May we all obtain it, cherish it, put it into practice, and live it out!

Loving you all,

Elder Yingqiang

December 10, 2018

---

[2] ERCC also met at two additional locations—ERCC Baihua and ERCC Grace. The three locations were relatively independent of each other, but all belonged to the same presbytery.

[3] When police officers and representatives of the Religious Affairs Bureau ban a church from meeting, they post the official decree on the entrance to the church and plaster paper seals across the doors. Breaking the seals means breaking the decree and violating the law.

[4] This is an official motto of ERCC.

21

THIS IS ALSO WHERE I STAND!

JIN TIANMING

The following is a statement of solidarity with Wang Yi from Jin Tianming, pastor of Shouwang Church in Beijing. It was first published on ChinaAid's website on December 13, 2018, a few days after Wang Yi's arrest.

On the night of December 9, I learned that Pastor Wang Yi is out of contact and over a hundred members of Early Rain Covenant Church, including elders, deacons, ministry staff, and brothers and sisters were taken away by Chengdu police. Many of them are still in custody, and others remain out of contact. Chengdu police continue to suppress and persecute Early Rain Covenant Church; even until today it has not stopped. According to Early Rain Covenant Church's urgent prayer request issued on the evening of December 12, Pastor Wang Yi has been placed in criminal detention under the charge of "inciting to subvert state power."

Early Rain Covenant Church released Pastor Wang Yi's "Declaration of Faithful Disobedience," which he wrote prior to being arrested, and instructed the church to publish should he be detained for more than forty-eight hours. As I was reading this declaration of faith, my heart was deeply moved. Honestly, before the Lord, what Pastor Wang Yi declared as his stance on the relationship between the church and the state is also where I stand. As for our obedience to God that expresses itself in faithful disobedience, each pastor and church will respond differently according to the guidance of the Holy Spirit, particularly in the approach, the extent, and the areas of involvement. Each Christian may have different expressions because of their freedom of conscience. But the one thing to which we must all share and hold fast to is to obey God and witness to Christ.

Pastor Wang Yi is our dear brother, a servant whom God has been using for his special purpose within the Chinese church for the last ten years. During his current criminal detention under the charge of "inciting to subvert state power," many dear brothers and sisters of Early Rain Covenant Church are being persecuted. As a pastor who has received the same call of the Lord and called to serve in the same land, I declare, what Pastor Wang Yi declared as his stance on the relationship between the church and the state is also where I stand!

> On the basis of the teachings of the Bible and the mission of the gospel, I respect the authorities God has established in China. For God deposes kings and raises up kings. This is why I submit to the historical and institutional arrangements of God in China.
>
> Changing social and political institutions is not the mission I have been called to, and it is not the goal for which God has given his people the gospel.
>
> At the same time, I believe that this Communist regime's persecution against the church is a greatly wicked, unlawful action. As a pastor of a Christian church, I must denounce this wickedness openly and severely.
>
> But this does not mean that my personal disobedience and the disobedience of the church is in any sense "fighting for rights" or political activism in the form of civil disobedience.

Let us all raise our hands for Pastor Wang Yi, in remembrance of Early Rain Covenant Church.

Pastor Tianming

December 13, 2018, from Beijing

22

LETTER FOR ALL CHRISTIAN CHURCHES TO PRAY

WESTERN CHINA PRESBYTERY

The following is a call to the global church to prayer for Early Rain written and published by the Western China Presbytery, of which Early Rain was a founding member. It was sent directly to members of the presbytery on December 12, 2018, and later distributed online.

Dear brothers and sisters in Christ, who are also called as children of God and disciples of Christ,

Peace be with you!

We trust that you have heard the news that since December 9, 2018, Early Rain Covenant Church, a church that belongs to our Lord Jesus Christ, has been attacked and persecuted by the secular authorities. God's children are being persecuted unconstitutionally and illegally and are experiencing great suffering.

After losing contact with Pastor Wang Yi and his wife for over forty-eight hours, his family was told that Pastor Wang Yi was in criminal detention on suspicion of "inciting subversion of the state"; Elder Tan Defu has been lost to contact for over seventy-two hours; Elder Li Yingqiang is under criminal detention on suspicion of "internet provocation"; and Deacon Ge Yingfeng is under criminal detention on suspicion of "illegal business operations."

Forty-seven brothers and sisters are being detained at Xinjin County Legal Learning Center and two sisters were strip-searched.

One sister is now at the hospital delivering a baby while her husband has been out of contact for almost seventy-two hours.

Additionally, the police took away some elders, deacons, staff members, and brothers and sisters by force, to the point where some even suffered violence, receiving scars and wounds on their bodies. While they are gradually being released, they are still under surveillance.

Up until now, ministry staff members are still being dragged to the police stations and the government is still putting pressure in various ways on church members, demanding them to sign a pledge agreeing not to attend Early Rain Covenant Church. Many are being monitored at home and some brothers have been deported back to their hometowns. The authorities have used landlords to force some brothers and sisters to relocate, and the total number of congregants directly subjected to illegal persecution is well over a hundred.

The government has also seized the church's sanctuary and all other facilities, closed down the seminary, the college, the academy, and issued penalties banning several church plants.

Its purpose is to destroy the Lord's church, which is obviously severe religious persecution.

Yet we are deeply aware that this is not only a persecution from the secular government but also Satan's scheme to attack God's church; it is a spiritual battle against God's people, and no child of God is left out.

As the Western China Presbytery of the Reformed Presbyterian Church, we are bound to stand with them. We share with Early Rain Covenant Church the same catholic, orthodox faith, and therefore identify with the persecution they are under because we are part of the body of Christ. The persecution they suffer for the sake of Christ is the persecution we are going to suffer. "All who desire to live a godly life in Christ Jesus will be persecuted" (2 Timothy 3:12). They are experiencing suffering and we are willing to suffer with them. "If one member suffers, all suffer together; if one member is honored, all rejoice together" (1 Corinthians 12:26).

Since this is a spiritual battle, we are not wrestling against flesh and blood, but against the spiritual forces of evil in the heavenly places. "For we do not wrestle against flesh and blood, but against the rulers, against the authorities, against the cosmic powers over this present darkness, against the spiritual forces of evil in the heavenly places" (Ephesians 6:12). For the weapons of our warfare are not of the flesh but of the divine power of the Holy Spirit. "For the weapons of our warfare are not of the flesh but have divine power to destroy strongholds" (2 Corinthians 10:4).

Therefore, what we need most is to go before the presence of God through prayer, so we may receive spiritual power to bear witness to the Lord and to identify with the members who are in spiritual warfare.

Meanwhile, we appeal to the churches of God to join in this spiritual battle through your prayers, your encouragement, your comfort, and your support, to hold with love the members in distress, and to crush Satan's neck with your knees and tears. If possible, please make efforts to provide for their practical needs, such as visiting their families, taking care of their children, cooking, or opening up your home for those who are in need of refuge.

Please pray for the members behind bars. May the Lord grant them confidence and strength so that they would be as bold as Paul and Peter to preach to the kings and prisoners about Christ who died and was raised.

Please pray for the members who are frightened and for those who have been released but are still being monitored. May the Lord keep them, whether free or bound, from losing heart, so that they may testify to the true, trustworthy, and glorious gospel before their family, neighbors, and law enforcement.

Please pray for the members who are facing pressure to sign the pledge not to attend the church. May the Lord guide them through the Holy Spirit in all circumstances, so that whether they turn left or right they will hear the voice that says "that is the right way," so that they may walk in it.

Please pray for the ministry team of Early Rain Covenant Church. May the Lord fill them with his unifying Spirit, his Spirit of wisdom and discernment, and grant them strength, courage, love, and self-control so that even in distress they will not be restricted by hardship. May the Word of the Lord increase and multiply through them.

Please pray for every church member of Early Rain Covenant Church. May the Lord turn all of them into warriors of the gospel, and grant them confidence so that in the midst of the storm they will be rooted even more deeply and made more resilient.

Please also pray for the police officers and local community leaders who have been involved in the attack. May the Lord have mercy on them as most of them do not know the truth but are only doing what they were ordered to do. May the Lord reveal the mystery of the gospel truth to them through the sufferings of brothers and sisters. May the Lord call some among them, so that they will come to know the true ruler—Jesus Christ.

Through this storm, may the Lord's church be a city set on a hill that is built firmly on the rock, a lamp on a stand that shines light into darkness.

Oh, the depth of the riches and wisdom and knowledge of God! How unsearchable are his judgments and how inscrutable his ways!

> "For who has known the mind of the Lord,
>> or who has been his counselor?"
> "Or who has given a gift to him
>> that he might be repaid?"

For from him and through him and to him are all things. To him be glory forever. Amen. (Romans 11:33-36)

May all members in the Lord pray together in one voice, saying,

Our Father in heaven,
Hallowed be your name.
Your kingdom come.
Your will be done, on earth as it is in heaven.
Give us this day our daily bread.
And forgive us our sins as we forgive those who sin against us.
And lead us not into temptation, but deliver us from evil.
For the kingdom, the power, and the glory are yours, now and forever. Amen.

Sharing these with the members of the Lord's body,
May God bless you and use you,
Western China Presbytery of the Reformed Presbyterian Church
December 12, 2018

CONCLUSION

HANNAH NATION

FEBRUARY 2022

The writings that have recently begun to emerge from certain urban branches of the Chinese house church are interesting to consider. Where do Wang Yi and many of his contemporaries best fit in the landscape of theology?

The first obvious marker is that they are Reformed in their posture toward the city. Wang Yi, and others in his various networks, frequently reference Calvin and Luther, along with a substantial number of more contemporary theologically conservative Presbyterian and Reformed Baptist writers. For example, Timothy Keller and Mark Dever have had a significant impact on many urban Chinese house church writers. Yet, though these American pastors are perhaps some of the closest theological partners to many urban house church writers, the Reformed evangelical church in the United States has not had the publishing or reading habits in place to see the Chinese house churches as theologically relevant. Much of American evangelical writing on cultural and social engagement assumes a triumphant status for the church, and where the assumption of status isn't made, the concern is how to regain it, through either the culture wars or polite winsomeness. Reformed evangelicalism in America has yet to seriously turn its ear to counterparts seeking to engage a Reformed understanding of the city from positions of powerlessness.

A second marker of the writings coming from many urban house churches is the hint of liberation and neo-Anabaptist theology with regard to the state. Wang Yi's boldness in rebuking the powers that govern Chinese life and renouncing any complicity of the church in sustaining, supporting, or submitting to those powers may remind the reader of work coming from outside the Reformed tradition. However, there is an important difference of context that separates this particular stream of Chinese thought from the liberationists. Whereas the liberation theologians have written against powers not their own, that is, the European and American colonial powers, Wang Yi and his counterparts write against powers with whom they share a cultural identity. It would be odd to include Wang Yi's theology among the postcolonialists. The Chinese theologians that came from the Three-Self Patriotic Movement in the twentieth century are most rightly identified with postcolonial theology. Perhaps the writings of the twenty-first-century urban Chinese house church are examples of what comes after post-colonialism in theology—a post-postcolonial engagement with political theology. For the state they rebuke is not foreign but rather, their own. Their fight is not international but internal. This immediately links Wang Yi and his contemporaries to certain neo-Anabaptist thinkers, such as John Howard Yoder and Stanley Hauerwas, but simply due to the fact that Wang Yi and his contemporaries write outside the stream of Western theological tradition makes that connection tenuous. One cannot underestimate the difference in perspective between an American or European neo-Anabaptist writing against the vestiges of democratic Christendom and a Chinese Calvinist writing against an atheistic totalitarian state.

A third mark of the theology coming out of the urban house churches is their situational nature, and perhaps this harkens to the writings of the early church under the Roman Empire. Context always matters, but it really matters for those without the privileges of academic institutional theology. There are some who would say the Chinese house churches are not engaged in writing theology. To say this would be to suggest that the first hundred years of Christianity were likewise untheological. Theology can mean the laborious work of academics and the great tomes such as Calvin's *Institutes* or Barth's *Dogmatics*. But theology can also mean Clement's Letter to the Romans, Polycarp's apologetic, and the Didache. For the Chinese house churches, theology most often looks like the careful and faithful preparation of weekly sermons and what they communicate to people about God. We have not yet seen the house church's Martin Luther; we are still in "House Church Theology 1.0." But the theological writing taking place today is laying the groundwork for the more robust and extensive thought that *will* come.

Even since Wang Yi's arrest in 2018, the most important theological topics within the Chinese house church have shifted. Wang Yi's engagement with political theology remains acutely relevant. However, one of the most pressing questions in the years following his incarceration is one churches around the world ought to be familiar with: How ought Christians to think about the church meeting digitally? Like most churches around the world, the house churches in China faced significant restrictions on their ability to meet in person with the breakout of the Covid-19 pandemic at the beginning of 2020. For Early Rain, however, the issues surrounding digital church were not new. It became a significant topic of discussion immediately following the attack on their church in 2018. With the prevention of their meeting in person in any form, Early Rain turned to meeting online with each other. For many years, their interim pastor in the face of Wang Yi's absence did not even reside within China. Their situation and the situation of house churches across China invite another stream of dialogue regarding the pressing issue of digital ecclesiology. Ought we to think differently about digital church when it is a necessity due to active persecution rather than an accommodation due to temporary disruption? To answer the question is beyond the scope of this closing essay. But my hope is that the relevance of a persecuted, sacramental, Reformed, Chinese house church's decision on the matter would not be lost to those debating the issue in America and beyond. We would do well to solicit the Chinese house church's theological opinion on this topic, and others, more often.

Wang Yi remains incarcerated. There is no access to him to know how he is doing. Some reports have stated that he remains in good physical health. But no reports give us an answer regarding the state of his soul. Our response ought not to be to heroize him, for the church does not benefit from making heroes of mere men. Rather, our response ought to be prayer for Wang Yi, his family, and Early Rain Covenant Church.

Persecution does not automatically make a person a more sanctified Christian. Nor does it necessarily clarify one's thoughts and beliefs. As Jesus' disciples' responses to his crucifixion remind us, fear can cause people to do and say many things they severely regret. It was not the social and political pressure on the early church alone which empowered the apostles to preach the gospel to the nations, but rather, it was the arrival of the Holy Spirit indwelling the church and guiding its response to marginalization and persecution. Pray for the same Spirit to guide and equip not only Wang Yi, but all Christians in China.

We know there are two things Wang Yi deeply desired to have access to, should he ever be jailed: a Bible and paper and pen. Pray for his continued access to both so that he might grow in his discernment of the Holy Spirit's work in this world and order and communicate his theology in response.

GLOSSARY

The **Anti-Christian Movement** of 1922–1927 was an intellectual and political movement to purge China of Christianity's influence. It was launched when two books, *Christian Education in China* and *The Christian Occupation of China*, were published to demonstrate the growth of Christianity in China, providing both Communists and Nationalists with examples for their arguments about Christianity's imperialistic motives. When the World Student Christian Federation announced its plans to hold a large conference at Tsinghua University in Beijing in 1922, dozens of student groups formed into anti-Christian federations across China and organized protests, petitions, and rallies among China's intellectuals. In 1925, eleven Chinese protestors participating in an anti-Christian demonstration were killed by International Settlement police (a joint police force created by the various Western colonial powers), igniting the May Thirtieth Movement. Protests increased and many churches and Christian schools were damaged or occupied. At the end of 1926, the government declared that all foreign schools and educational institutions must submit to the supervision of government administration, that Chinese nationals must be installed as directors of all private schools, and that religious education was no longer permitted to be a compulsory component of a school's curriculum. In 1927, six Christian missionaries were killed in Nanking, resulting in many missionaries withdrawing from China's interior and over three thousand leaving China altogether. The Anti-Christian Movement came to an end with Chiang Kai-shek's conversion to Christianity and the rise of the Nationalists to power in 1927, who needed to court Western powers for military assistance with the Japanese invasion of Manchuria in 1931.

The **Anti-Rightist Campaign** of 1957 was a movement to weed out those disloyal to the Chinese Communist Party (CCP). Under the direction of Mao Zedong, the CCP ferreted out intellectuals and Party members by encouraging them to openly criticize Party policies in order to help it improve during the Hundred Flowers Campaign; after speaking up, they were harshly denounced, attacked, and punished. Scholars estimate that 550,000 Chinese intellectuals, many of whom were the top professionals in their respective fields, as well as thousands of Christians, were politically persecuted in this movement.

The Boxer Rebellion was a violent peasant uprising at the turn of the twentieth century aimed at removing the foreign colonial powers and missionaries from Chinese soil. "Boxer" was a foreign term used for the Yi He Quan (义和拳, Righteous and harmonious fists) or Yi He Tuan (义和团, Righteous and harmonious militia), a mystical secret society that believed its martial arts made them impervious to harm, including bullets. At the end of the nineteenth century, the Boxers influence in China's northern provinces increased, and the local government courted their assistance against encroaching foreign powers. Eventually, the Boxers began attacking Western missionaries and Chinese Christians. When bands of Boxers approached Beijing in 1900, the various European powers who had established colonial footholds in China dispatched a joint militia to intervene; however, the Empress Dowager Cixi ordered her imperial troops to turn away the international forces, giving the Boxers open access to the capitol. The Boxers took control of the city and began destroying churches and the homes of foreigners, as well as killing large numbers of Chinese Christians. As conflict escalated, Cixi herself ordered all foreigners in Beijing to be killed. In response, the European powers mustered an army, which captured Beijing and looted the city, forcing Cixi to flee. An estimated hundred thousand people were killed, including several hundred Christian missionaries.

Cardinal Gong Pinmei (龚品梅枢机, Ignatius Kung, 1901–2000) was a Catholic priest who opposed the Chinese Catholic Patriotic Association and the Communist Party's control of the Chinese Catholic church. Gong was born in Shanghai to a Catholic family, ordained as a priest in 1930, and appointed as Shanghai's bishop shortly after the birth of the People's Republic of China in 1949. Gong was sentenced to life in prison in 1955. In 1985, he was released to house arrest and two years later relocated to the United States. Unbeknownst to him, he was secretly made a cardinal by the pope during his imprisonment, a fact he did not discover until he had fled from China.

The **Chinese Civil War** was fought from 1945 to 1949. Beginning in the late 1930s, China was divided into three areas of competing government control under

Nationalists, Communists, and the Japanese. Overlapping with WWII, the Communists and Nationalists united to combat the Japanese in the Second Sino-Japanese War, whom they defeated in 1945. The Communists and Nationalists then turned their armies on each other, eventually leading to a Communist victory in 1949.

Chinese Catholic Patriotic Association (CCPA). Unlike Protestant churches, which interact with the government independently, the state of Catholicism in China is dependent on the relationship between the Vatican and the Chinese government. Similar to the Protestant churches' submission to the Three-Self Patriotic Movement (TSPM), all Catholic churches in China are required to submit to the CCPA, which maintains the right to appoint bishops, since its founding in 1957. In response, many Catholic churches have chosen to exist underground. The Vatican has had no official relations with China since 1951, but there has been a mutual effort to reestablish diplomatic channels in recent years. Pope Francis has been particularly active in expressing his desire to visit China and improve relations, and in 2018 a historic deal was negotiated in which the Chinese government recognized the pope as the head of China's Catholic communicants and the Vatican recognized those bishops appointed by the CCPA, thereby delegitimizing any bishops anointed underground.

The **China Christian Council (CCC)** is an organization formed in 1980 to come alongside the Three-Self Patriotic Movement (TSPM) to oversee all Protestant religious activity in China, including church order, theological education, religious publishing, international exchange, academic research, and social services. The CCC participates in the World Council of Churches.

The **Chinese Communist Party (CCP)** is the ruling political party of the People's Republic of China (PRC). It was founded in 1921 by Chen Duxiu and Li Dazhao and came to power in 1949 when Mao Zedong defeated Chiang Kai-shek's Nationalist government in the Chinese Civil War. The highest ruling body of the CCP is the National Congress, which convenes every five years to determine matters of state. The preeminent leader of the CCP is the general secretary, currently Xi Jinping.

"The Christian Manifesto" (基督教宣言, *jidujiao xuanyan*) is a document drafted by Wu Yaozong and promoted by various Christian leaders calling for support of the new Communist government. The document was published in the *People's Daily* (人民日报, *renmin ribao*) and *Tian Feng* (天风) in 1950 with forty original signatories. The document expresses support for the Chinese Communist Party (CCP), the Common Agenda (the temporary constitution of the new People's Republic of China), and for severing the church's ties with all Western missionary activity. The Christian Manifesto is widely recognized as the founding document of the Three-Self Patriotic Movement (TSPM) and was used as a litmus test for the patriotic submission of Christians to the CCP. By 1954, the manifesto had received 417,389 signatories, about one half of all Protestant Christians in China.

The Civil Affairs Bureau (CAB) is the local branch of the Ministry of Civil Affairs (MCA) found in each Chinese city. The MCA was founded in 1978 to oversee social and administrative affairs (e.g., marriage registrations, funerals, social welfare, nonprofit organizations). Some religious affairs also fall under the administration of the MCA, particularly registration of places of religious activity. For a house church to register with the CAB requires its legal representative to fill out an application with the MCA and consent to the relevant regulations, thereby incorporating into the Three-Self system.

The **Cultural Revolution** was a movement led by Mao Zedong from 1966 to 1976 in an effort to reignite revolutionary fervor among Chinese citizens and solidify his own historic legacy. In the early 1960s, Mao grew increasingly fearful that the Communist revolution would diminish in the light of increased economic depression, his diminished political role, and the social stratification he perceived to be taking place in urban China. Mao's goals during the Cultural Revolution were to purify the CCP and ensure loyalty to Mao-thought among its leaders, to reduce the elitism of China's cultural, educational, and healthcare institutions, and to organize the urban youth into the Red Guards in order for the younger generations to experience revolution. China was thrown into social and economic chaos as the Red Guards were encouraged and permitted to denounce and attack any signs of "bourgeois" infiltration and influence. Schools were closed and many among the older generation of intellectuals and professionals were attacked, abused, and even killed. The Red Guards split into rival factions in competition over who most loyally adhered to the cult of Mao. The Red Guards grew in power, to the point of enacting the political overthrow of various provincial governments. In 1968, Mao dispatched the army to retake the institutions from the Red Guards, who were then sent to China's rural areas for reeducation. Mao, his closest political allies, and the various leaders of the CCP descended into a protracted struggle for power during the final years of the revolution in the 1970s. Eventually, after Mao suffered a severe stroke and died in 1976, Deng Xiaoping was identified as the next leader of the CCP and China began to economically recover.

Ding Guangxun (丁光训, **K. H. Ting, 1915–2012**) served as chairman of the Three-Self Patriotic Movement (TSPM) and president of the China Christian Council (CCC) and held many high-level political posts. Ding served the YMCA in China and the Canadian Student Christian Movement before moving to New York City to study at Columbia University and Union Theological Seminary. After time in Europe serving the World's Student Christian Federation, Ding returned to China in the early 1950s and served in leadership of Nanjing Theological Seminary. When the TSPM was launched in 1954, Ding was elected to the movement's standing committee. Ding was consecrated as an Anglican bishop of the Anglican-Episcopal Province of China (AEPOC) in 1955. During the Cultural Revolution, Ding lost his positions, despite his strong pro-CCP stance. He returned to prominence in the 1970s, serving as vice president of the University of Nanjing and later as president of the CCC and chairman of the TSPM. In 1985, Ding helped found the Amity Foundation, which is the sole legal Bible publisher and printer in China. In 1988, Ding proclaimed that the Protestant church should be brought into alignment with socialism and began to focus on a reconstructed theology. Ding dismissed justification by faith alone and his soteriology was popularized as "justification by love" (因爱称义, *yin ai cheng yi*).

Ji Zhiwen (计志文, **Andrew Gih, 1901–1985**) was a Protestant evangelist in China in the 1930s-1940s. Ji's father was a Confucian scholar and his mother was a devout Buddhist; however, he began high school at a missionary school at the age of 18, where he heard the gospel and was converted. After committing to a life of ministry, Ji began to work with Shi Meiyu (史美玉, "Mary Stone") and the Bethel Mission, preaching across southeastern China itinerantly. Ji joined the Bethel Worldwide Evangelistic Band in 1931 with John Sung and several other coworkers. Between 1931 and 1935, their band reportedly traveled over 50,000 miles, visited 133 cities, held nearly 3,400 revival meetings throughout China, and preached to an estimated 500,000 listeners. In 1947, Ji founded the Evangelize China Fellowship (ECF) in Shanghai and Hangzhou. After the communist revolution, Ji and his wife moved to Hong Kong.

Jia Yuming (贾玉铭, 1880-1964) was an influential Protestant theologian. He graduated from a Presbyterian seminary in 1904 and was ordained as a pastor in Yizhou, Shandong. He pastored several churches over twelve years and baptized hundreds of believers. In 1915, Jia was employed by Nanjing Jinling Seminary to teach theology. In 1919, he became vice president of North China Theological Seminary, a newly formed fundamentalist school, and then became principal of Jinling Girls' Theological Seminary in 1930. In 1936, Jia founded the Chinese Christian Bible Institute and served as its principal. Jia served as vice chairman of the 1948 World Gospel Conference in the Netherlands. When the Three-Self Patriotic Movement (TSPM) was established in 1954, Jia was assigned the position of vice chairman. Jia was conflicted about joining the TSPM, but did so in order to protect his seminary, a decision he reportedly regretted until his death. When the Anti-Rightist Campaign started in 1957, Jia was persecuted, despite his affiliation with the TSPM.

Jing Dianying (敬奠瀛, 1890–1957) was the founder of the Jesus Family, a large, independent charismatic network of Christian communes that began in northern China in the 1920s. Jing was greatly influenced by Pentecostalism and his communes emphasized a simple, collective life and fervent prayer. Hundreds joined the movement and during the 1930s and 1940s, Jing and his wife itinerated to help start new communes. By 1948, 127 communes existed in the northern Chinese countryside. When the Three-Self Patriotic Movement (TSPM) was created, Jing openly supported it and brought the entire Jesus Family network under its oversight. Despite his compliance, Jing was accused of "antirevolution activities" and sentenced to ten years in prison in 1952. He received parole four years later due to liver failure and died in 1957.

Jonathan Chao (赵天恩, Zhao Tianen, 1938–2004) was an expert on Chinese church history and a pioneer of theological education for the house church movement. He was also an advocate and spokesperson for China's house churches internationally. Zhao grew up in the Chinese diaspora and decided to dedicate his life to evangelism in China as a teenager. He was educated at Geneva College, Westminster Theological Seminary, and the University of Pennsylvania. While in seminary, Zhao became convinced of the need to aid China's house churches with theological education. Zhao's vision was threefold: (1) evangelization of the Chinese nation; (2) "kingdomization" of the Chinese church; (3) and Christianization of the Chinese culture. Zhao established China Evangelical Seminary in the United States (1960s), Taiwan (1970s), and Hong Kong

(1980s). He also established the Chinese Church Research Center in Hong Kong in 1978, the Research Center of Christianity and Chinese Culture in Taiwan in 1986, and China Ministries International in Taiwan and the United States in the mid-1980s. Zhao traveled to China more than one hundred times to train and encourage pastors and was eventually blacklisted from entering the country. Zhao wrote many books for the Chinese church, including *A History of Christianity in Socialist China, 1949–1997* and *Wise as Serpents, Innocent as Doves: Christians Tell Their Story.*

Lin Xiangao (林献羔, **Samuel Lamb, 1924–2013**) was a prominent house church pastor in Guangzhou. Due to his refusal to join the Three-Self Patriotic Movement (TSPM), Lin was condemned to spend twenty-two years in various labor camps. He continued to preach throughout his confinement. Upon his release in 1978, Lin restarted his church in Guangzhou. Rongguili Church (荣桂里教会), as Lin's church came to be known, grew exponentially, with multiple services per week and thousands of attendees. Authorities shut down the church in 2018.

The **Nationalist Party, or Kuomintang (KMT)** was established in 1912 under the leadership of Sun Yat-sen. In the 1920s, leadership passed to Chiang Kai-shek, who defeated the regional warlords governing China and reunited the country. The Nationalist government was established in 1928, with the Nationalists as the sole ruling political party. The Nationalists allied with the Communists during WWII; however, when Japan was pushed out of China in 1945, the two parties turned to fight each, igniting the Chinese Civil War. The Communists defeated the Nationalists in 1949.

Ni Tuosheng (倪柝声, **Watchman Nee, 1903-1972**) was a teacher, writer, and church leader who founded the Local Churches (地方召会), a widespread independent network of house churches in mainland China, as well as Taiwan and North America. Many controversies surrounded his life, ministry, and theology; nevertheless, he is regarded as a martyr by many in the house church. Ni was raised as a third-generation Christian and deeply influenced by Methodist evangelist Yu Cidu (余慈度, Dora Yu) and Margaret E. Barber, a former Anglican turned independent missionary. Through Yu and Barber, Ni was introduced to Brethren theology, which focused on plural eldership, the illegitimacy of denominations, and the centrality of the Lord's Supper. Ni believed there should only be one church in one location, i.e., one Local Church. He began the first

"Local Church" in Shanghai with a handful of women and China Inland Mission's Charles Judd. In the 1930s, many Local Churches were set up in the provinces and major cities across eastern China. Ni was established as the highest authority in the Local Churches, with apostolic authority given to his deputies. In the 1940s, Ni launched a massive evangelism effort in China's unreached areas resulting in the Local Church growing to 700 churches with 70,000 members by 1949. Ni was given the opportunity to flee mainland China in 1950, but he chose to remain with his fellow churches. Under government pressure in 1951, Ni urged the Local Churches to support and join the Three-Self Patriotic Movement (TSPM). In 1952, Ni was arrested and charged with tax evasion and corrupt business practices related to both church and business dealings. The TSPM organized "accusation conferences" and demanded denouncements of Ni by Local Church members. Ni was sentenced to fifteen years in prison, after which he was transferred to various forced labor farms. He died in Anhui in 1972. After his death, guards found a piece of paper under his pillow that stated a commitment to die for his belief in Christ of the Son of God.

The **People's Republic of China (PRC)** was established with the defeat of the Kuomingtang Nationalist government by the Chinese Communist Party (CCP) in 1949. Chairman Mao Zedong declared its establishment in a speech delivered on September 21, 1949. The PRC is a socialist republic ruled by a single political party. The general secretary of the CCP acts as the president of the PRC. Aside from a brief period of strife after Mao's death, the PRC has primarily been under the control of five successive leaders: Mao Zedong (1949–1976), Deng Xiaoping (1978–1989), Jiang Zemin (1989–2004), Hu Jintao (2004–2012), and Xi Jinping (2012–today).

The **National Public Complaints and Proposals Administration** is a state agency whose duty it is to receive complaints and civilian petitions. Municipal administration offices are subordinate to a national administration, which is subordinate to the General Office of the State Council of the PRC.

The **Religious Affairs Regulations** were first announced by the State Administration for Religious Affairs (SARA) in 2004; the second and most recent version of the regulations were released in 2017 and took effect in 2018. The New Regulations oversee all religious institutions and organizations in China regarding assets, religious education, activity venues, religious professionalization, and legal responsibilities. Their stated purpose is to protect the religious freedoms of China's citizens; however, they presuppose oversight of all religious activity within China by the CCP and they have served as the legal basis for disbanding churches who do not submit to the TSPM.

The **State Administration for Religious Affairs (SARA)**, originally the Religious Affairs Department, was established in 1951 to control religious affairs and to oversee the submission of all religious organizations to the CCP's policies. In early 2018, SARA was incorporated into the United Front Work Department. The TSPM, CCC, and CCPA fall under the oversight of SARA.

The **Sichuan Earthquake of 2008** killed almost ninety thousand people on May 12, 2008. The earthquake measured a magnitude of 8.0 at its center in Wenchuan County, northwest of the provincial capital of Chengdu. The majority of buildings in the affected area collapsed, and the Chinese government faced a major scandal in the quake's aftermath as mass corruption was revealed in the construction of the area's schools. Almost seven thousand schools collapsed in the quake, and the government admitted that as many as one thousand of them suffered from shoddy construction. Many Chinese activists who have sought to investigate corruption in school construction in Sichuan have been arrested and jailed.

"Sinicization of Christianity" is a policy that aims to further bring Chinese Christianity into conformity with Chinese Communist Party (CCP) ideology. It is part of the larger agenda to bring all religions within China under CCP oversight, as unsanctioned religious activity is viewed as a threat to national stability. Sinicization, which literally means "becoming Chinese," should not be confused with contextualization; rather, it is political direction and control of religious theology and praxis. Xi Jinping inaugurated the most recent campaign in a speech delivered at the National Religious Work Conference in 2016. In 2018, a five-year plan for developing a "Christianity that is consistent with socialism" was released by the Three-Self Patriotic Movement (TSPM) and the China Christian Council (CCC). The key principles outlined in the document include (1) the sinicization of Christianity will be led by the CCP and guided by socialism; (2) the sinicization of Christianity means the adaptation of Christian theological thought to socialist society; (3) the sinicization of Christianity will be implemented by personnel who are trained to promote patriotism and socialism in China's government-sanctioned colleges on theology; (4) scholars-in-training will be indoctrinated with hermeneutics, text books, and Bible translations that promote the core values of socialism.

Song Shangjie (宋尚节, John Sung, 1901–1944) was an important Chinese evangelist during the revivals among both mainland Chinese and the Chinese diaspora during the 1920s and 1930s. Song went to the United States in 1920, under the urging of his family and church to study the Bible. Instead, Song studied chemistry for six years, earning his PhD in 1926. Song described his time in the States as a period of lost faith, and when in 1926 he entered Union Theological Seminary the liberal teaching of his professors confirmed his skepticism. However, in 1927 he experienced a dramatic spiritual rebirth. Afterward, Song came into conflict with his professors and classmates due to his frequent exhortations to abandon liberal theology and turn instead to fundamentalism. Soon after, Song experienced a mental health crisis and was committed to a psychiatric hospital. After his release, Song returned to China, where he was appointed as a preacher and evangelist by the Methodist church. After a few years, he joined an itinerant evangelistic team in Fujian for three years. He joined the Bethel Worldwide Evangelistic Band (伯特利环球布道团) in 1931, preaching widely across China with several other famous evangelists. Song was asked to leave the preaching band in 1933. Song's experiences at Union and with the preaching band disillusioned Song to working with foreign missionaries, whom he often saw as dismissive of Chinese coworkers and extravagant in the midst of China's poverty. He spent the next eight years as an independent itinerant preacher, traveling across mainland China and most of Southeast Asia at the expense of his own health: he suffered from various serious ailments and severe pain. Song's most significant theological legacy in the Chinese church is his emphasis on "the way of the cross" and the Christian's call to suffer with Christ. He died shortly before his forty-third birthday.

The **"Three Fixed Policy"** requires that all Three-Self Patriotic Movement (TSPM) churches only evangelize at "fixed locations" within "fixed areas" approved by the government, by "fixed personnel" who have received preaching permits from the State Administration for Religious Affairs. The policy forbids individuals to preach in other towns, cities, and provinces than their permitted location.

Three-Self Patriotic Movement (TSPM, 三自爱国运动) is the official name of the government-sanctioned Protestant church in China. The three principles of self-governance, self-support (versus financial dependence on the West), and self-propagation (indigenous evangelism) were originally articulated as guidelines for establishing local churches by Western missionaries and missiologists in the nineteenth century, most notably Henry Venn. These Three-Self principles formed the foundation for Wu's "The Christian Manifesto" (基督教宣言). The "three selves" were used to express churches' separation from all foreign institutions and structures and to declare their submission to the CCP under the new People's Republic of China. Over four hundred thousand Christians signed the manifesto in the following decade, while those who did not do so were persecuted. The TSPM was established in 1954 to structure Christianity under communist authority, lending the term *Three-Self* overt political implications in China. During the Cultural Revolution the TSPM itself was banned along with the house churches. The government finally reinstated the TSPM in 1979 once the Cultural Revolution was over and formed the China Christian Council (CCC). The TSPM and the CCC are known as the *liang hui* (两会) or "the Two Organizations" that relate to Protestant Christianity in China. The TSPM submits to the United Front Work Department of the CCP.

The **Tiananmen Square Protests of 1989**, commonly known in Chinese as the June Fourth Incident (六四事件, liusi shijian), were pro-democracy protests in 1989 led by students and workers that ended in a massacre of civilians by the People's Liberation Army (PLA). As post-Mao China began to reform economically, many students began agitating for further political and educational reforms, as well as for freedom of speech, freedom of the press, and anticorruption measures. Protests led by students from Peking and Tsinghua universities formed on Tiananmen Square, Beijing's most prominent and historic public space, with their numbers growing to an estimated hundred thousand people. The protests spread to most of China's major cities and escalated over the following weeks to include hunger strikes. Initial attempts to send in troops in May were thwarted by throngs of residents blocking the streets, but in the first few days of June the government decided to quell the protests by whatever means necessary. The first shots were fired late on June 3 as army tanks cleared blockades along the roads to Tiananmen. Estimates of the death toll vary, but there is general scholarly and journalistic consensus that the death toll was around three thousand civilians, mainly local Beijing workers. After clearing the roads in the early morning hours of June 4, the army surrounded the student protestors on the square. Several prominent older academics who were sympathetic to the movement were able to negotiate a safe retreat from the square, and the students were escorted away by the army. After the protests were disbanded, the government conducted mass arrests and many student leaders fled the country.

Tian Feng (天风) is the official magazine of the Three-Self Patriotic Movement (TSPM). It was initially founded in 1945 by Wu Yaozong as a YMCA publication and was later brought under the TSPM. In the early 1950s, the magazine published many articles denouncing foreign missionaries, criticizing churches and pastors who refused to join the TSPM, and promoting the new Chinese government. The magazine was discontinued in 1964 and later relaunched in 1980 after the restoration of the TSPM post-Cultural Revolution.

United Front Work Department (UFWD) reports directly to the Central Committee of the Chinese Communist Party (CCP) and works to neutralize opposition to the Party's policies and authority and to ensure influential Chinese individuals and groups are in line with the Party and its agenda. Its work is focused on both managing opposition within China and on targeting overseas Chinese communities as particularly important for supporting CCP agendas and foreign policy.

Wang Mingdao (王明道, **1900–1991**) was a pastor, evangelist, and initial leader of the Chinese house church. Wang founded the Christian Tabernacle in Beijing in 1937, which grew to be one of the largest evangelical churches in Beijing with 570 members when the CCP gained control of China in 1949. Wang refused to join the newly formed Three-Self Patriotic Movement (TSPM) because he believed its leaders were theologically liberal and the true church ought to remain separate from the government. Wang had demonstrated independence from political intrusion under Japanese rule, enabling him to argue that his church already exhibited the threefold principles of self-governance, self-support, and self-propagation. Wang began to openly criticize the TSPM and wrote numerous articles calling China's Christians to refuse to submit to CCP oversight. One of his most important articles was "We—For the Sake of Faith." In 1954, Wang was heavily criticized during a public accusation meeting; however, his support grew and he remained free. Authorities arrested him in 1955, along with his wife and eighteen church members. They also closed the Christian Tabernacle and shut down his popular *Spiritual Food Quarterly* (灵食季刊, ling shi jikan). After Wang was sentenced to fifteen years in prison, he signed a confession and announced his support of the TSPM. However, upon his release he revoked his statement to the authorities and was promptly rearrested and resentenced, along with his wife. In 1979, due to political pressure from the United States, the Chinese government told Wang he was free to return home; however, he refused to leave without his name being cleared. Eventually, the prison tricked Wang into leaving in order to alleviate international political pressure on China. Wang was nearly blind and deaf upon his release and had lost all of his teeth. He and his wife lived in Shanghai with their son until their deaths. Wang left a legacy of fundamentalism, piety, and suffering in the Chinese house churches that remains a widespread distinction of Chinese Christianity today.

"We—For the Sake of Faith" was an essay by Wang Mingdao written in 1955 and published in the *Spiritual Food Quarterly*. The essay is a defense of Wang's decision not to join the Three-Self Patriotic Movement (TSPM) and argues that all true Christians should follow suit. Wang makes his argument theologically, arguing that the fundamental reason Christians should not join the TSPM is because it is run by liberal theologians who deny the fundamentals of the faith such as the virgin birth, the resurrection, future judgment, and individual salvation from sin. Wang claims that he has debated China's liberal theologians such a Wu Yaozong and Ding Guangxun for decades and it should not be surprising that he would refuse to unite with them, stating that though Christians should be charitable and peaceful with those of other religious practices, it is impossible for true Christians to countenance false Christians. "We—For the Sake of the Faith" moves point by point through the fundamentals Wang believes are essential to Christian faith and includes several lengthy excerpts from prominent Chinese liberal theologians to demonstrate the theology Wang criticizes. The essay does not contain any direct critiques or mention of the Chinese Communist Party (CCP) or of the government or communism generally.

Wei Wenxiang (魏文祥, 以撒, Isaac, 1900–?) was a leader of the True Jesus Church (TJC). TJC is an independent Christian sect founded in 1917 by Wei's father, Wei Enbo. The TJC was influenced by various Pentecostal practices and by a belief in the seventh-day Sabbath. By 1949, the TJC had over one hundred thousand members and seven hundred churches. Wei was against Chinese churches receiving foreign financial support and the involvement of foreign missionaries. He was arrested and disappeared in 1951. Nothing is known about his whereabouts and presumed death.

Wenzhou (温州) is a city in Zhejiang Province that has a special significance in the history of Protestant Christianity in China. Before the Communists came to power, Wenzhou had the largest Christian population in China. In 1958, Pingyang County in Wenzhou was designated as an experimental area for the Chinese Communist Party (CCP)'s elimination of religion, including Christianity. The project involved serious and widespread religious persecution. During the Cultural Revolution, Wenzhou's churches went underground. Beginning in the 1980s, Wenzhou saw a great revival of Christianity, leading the church in Wenzhou to be considered one of the exemplary cases of Christianity surviving and even growing during the Cultural Revolution. Official government numbers determine 10 percent of Wenzhou's population to be Christian and it is commonly called China's Jerusalem or Antioch. Several of its networks have evangelized and grown across the country, constituting the so-called Wenzhou model. Wenzhou was targeted by the CCP for testing of the "Sinicization of Christianity." Between 2014 and 2015, local authorities removed and demolished one thousand publicly visible crosses from church buildings, the majority of which were Three-Self Patriotic Movement (TSPM) churches. All churches were required to install national flags and video cameras in their sanctuaries and church members working as civil servants were required to report and document their religious activities to their work units.

Wu Weizun (吴维僔, 1926–2002) is widely known as "China's Epaphras." Wu refused to join the Three-Self Patriotic Movement (TSPM); instead he began conducting prayer meetings in his home and wrote a series of mailed correspondence with other house church Christians across China called *Communications in the Lord* (主内交通, *zhu nei jiaotong*). In 1957, Wu was sent to the countryside for reeducation. He was then arrested in 1964 and sentenced to life in prison, and eventually he was sent to labor camp. In 1981 the remainder of his sentence was lifted, but Wu refused to admit to any crime and rejected his reduced sentence. In 1987, he was declared to have repented due to good behavior and forced to leave the prison. He immediately wrote to the court, declaring that he had in fact not repented and would never recant his beliefs. He moved to a small hut adjacent to the prison wall and remained living there for fifteen years, where he continued his letter writing and received Christian visitors. Wu's letters were widely disseminated among house church Christians in the 1990s.

Wu Yaozong (吴耀宗, Y. T. Wu, 1893–1979) was the architect and chief leader of the Three-Self Patriotic Movement (TSPM) in the 1950s and 1960s. Wu was baptized and joined a Congregational church in Beijing in 1918. During the 1920s, Wu joined the YMCA staff and traveled abroad to study at Union Theological Seminary in New York City. Wu was a strong proponent of the social gospel and was critical of the gospel of individual salvation. After completing his studies, Wu worked for the China National YMCA during the 1940s and founded *Tian Feng*, the preeminent Chinese Protestant magazine. With the Chinese Communist Party's (CCP) victory in 1949, Wu was invited to participate in United Front Work Department activities. As a pacifist he was initially critical of the use of force by the CCP, but he slowly grew sympathetic to the cause. Wu served as the head Protestant delegate to the first Chinese People's Political Consultative Conference (CPPCC) and announced his full support for the CCP. Wu was the chief drafter of "The Christian Manifesto," a document which declared loyalty and submission to the new People's Republic of China and the CCP. Wu chaired the creation of the TSPM. Despite heading the TSPM and serving as a member of the Standing Committee of the National People's Congress, Wu fell victim to the Cultural Revolution and was sent to forced labor until shortly before his death in Beijing in 1979. Wu's theology is the official teaching of the TSPM in accordance with the "Sinicization of Christianity."

Xi Jinping (习近平, **b. 1953**) is the General Secretary of the Chinese Communist Party (CCP) and president of the People's Republic of China (PRC). Due to increased centralization of political power during his tenure and the removal of presidential two-term limits in 2018, he is widely regarded as the most powerful Chinese leader since Mao Zedong. Xi has effectively built a personal cult around himself and has been able to place his key supporters in strategic positions throughout China's central government. One of his close associates, Xia Baolong (夏宝龙), was the secretary of the Zhejiang Provincial Party Committee 2012–2017. During this period, Xia ordered the removal and demolition of thousands of crosses from Zhejiang's church buildings, most prominently in Wenzhou, as part of the CCP's plans for the "Sinicization of Christianity."

Xie Moshan (谢模善, **Moses, 1918–2011**) was a well-known house church leader, pastor, and editor of several Christian magazines and books. In 1956, Xie was arrested and imprisoned for refusing to join the Three-Self Patriotic Movement (TSPM). He spent twenty-three years in prison and forced labor camps. After his release in 1979, Xie turned down the opportunity to relocate to the United States, choosing instead to live in poverty in Beijing and serve the house church. Xie was imprisoned two more times, first in 1985 and then in 1994. In his later years, Xie helped mentor the next generation of house church leaders. He wrote, taught, and trained house church pastors, and served as president of China Holy Anointment Theology Seminary.

Yuan Xiangchen (袁相忱, Allen, 1914–2005) was a well-known house church pastor. Yuan was converted in 1932 after hearing the preaching of Wang Mingdao. He began theological studies at Far East College of Theology in 1934 and began to write and publish in 1937. After graduation, Yuan felt called to preach the gospel in rural China and began itinerating along with his wife, young son, and a foreign missionary. He returned to Beijing in 1945 and established a prayer room from which to preach the following year. Yuan refused to join the TSPM in 1950, arguing that his church was already self-sustaining. Yuan was arrested in 1958 and sentenced to life in prison; he then spent twenty-one years in labor camps. Yuan was released in 1979. He subsequently started a house church that grew to be one of Beijing's most prominent congregations. Yuan was invited to the Presidential Prayer Breakfast by President Bill Clinton in the 1990s; however, he declined the invitation in order to avoid any political affiliation for his church and to avoid fellowship with TSPM delegates who were simultaneously invited.

FURTHER READING

Baugus, Bruce P. *China's Reforming Churches: Mission, Polity, and Ministry in the Next Christendom.* Grand Rapids, MI: Reformation Heritage, 2014.

Bays, Daniel H. *A New History of Christianity in China.* Malden, MA: Wiley-Blackwell, 2012.

Chow, Alexander. *Chinese Public Theology: Generational Shifts and Confucian Imagination in Chinese Christianity.* Oxford: Oxford University Press, 2018.

Fulton, Brent. *China's Urban Christians: A Light That Cannot Be Hidden.* Eugene, OR: Pickwick, 2015.

Hamrin, Carol Lee, and Stacey Bieler. *Salt and Light, Volume 1: Lives of Faith That Shaped Modern China.* Eugene, OR: Pickwick, 2009.

Hamrin, Carol Lee, and Stacey Bieler. *Salt and Light, Volume 2: More Lives of Faith That Shaped Modern China.* Eugene, OR: Pickwick, 2010.

Harvey, Thomas Alan. *Acquainted with Grief: Wang Mingdao's Stand for the Persecuted Church in China.* Grand Rapids, MI: Brazos, 2002.

Johnson, Ian. *The Souls of China: The Return of Religion After Mao.* New York: Vintage, 2017.

Li Ma. *The Chinese Exodus: Migration, Urbanism, and Alienation in Contemporary China.* Eugene, OR: Pickwick, 2018.

Li Ma and Jin Li. *Surviving the State, Remaking the Church: A Sociological Portrait of Christians in Mainland China.* Eugene, OR: Pickwick, 2018.

Lian Xi. *Redeemed by Fire: The Rise of Popular Christianity in Modern China.* New Haven, CT: Yale University Press, 2010.

Nation, Hannah, and Simon Liu. *Faith in the Wilderness: Words of Exhortation from the Chinese Church.* Bellingham, WA: Kirkdale, 2022.

Starr, Chloë. *Chinese Theology: Text and Context.* New Haven, CT: Yale University Press, 2016.

Vala, Carsten T. *The Politics of Protestant Churches and the Party-State in China: God Above Party?* New York: Routledge, 2018.

Wang, S. E., and Hannah Nation. *Grace to the City: Studies in the Gospel from China.* Metuchen, NJ: China Partnership, 2021.

Yang Fenggang. *Religion in China: Survival & Revival Under Communist Rule.* New York: Oxford University Press, 2012.

Yao, Kevin Xiyi. *The Fundamentalist Movement Among Protestant Missionaries in China, 1920–1937.* Lanham, MD: University Press of America, 2003.

GENERAL INDEX

SCRIPTURE INDEX

The Center for
House Church
Theology

Discover what it means to be the church from the fastest growing church in the world.

The Center for House Church Theology (CHCT) desires to foster and further the international publishing of pastors, church leaders, and teachers committed to the historic gospel of grace in China's urban house churches.

Find out more at **housechurchtheology.com.**